Dictionary

of

LATIN LITERATURE

MIDCENTURY
REFERENCE LIBRARY

DAGOBERT D. RUNES, Ph.D., General Editor

AVAILABLE

Beethoven Encyclopedia
Dictionary of American Grammar
and Usage
Dictionary of the American Language
Dictionary of American Literature
Dictionary of American Maxims
Dictionary of American Proverbs
Dictionary of American Synonyms
Dictionary of Ancient History
Dictionary of Anthropology
Dictionary of Arts and Crafts
Dictionary of the Arts
Dictionary of Civics and Government
Dictionary of Dietetics
Dictionary of Early English
Dictionary of Etiquette
Dictionary of European History
Dictionary of Foreign Words
and Phrases
Dictionary of Last Words
Dictionary of Latin Literature
Dictionary of Linguistics
Dictionary of Magic
Dictionary of Mysticism
Dictionary of Mythology
Dictionary of New Words
Dictionary of Pastoral Psychology
Dictionary of Philosophy

Dictionary of Psychoanalysis
Dictionary of Russian Literature
Dictionary of Science and Technology
Dictionary of Sociology
Dictionary of Spanish Literature
Dictionary of Word Origins
Dictionary of World Literature
Encyclopedia of Aberrations
Encyclopedia of the Arts
Encyclopedia of Atomic Energy
Encyclopedia of Criminology
Encyclopedia of Literature
Encyclopedia of Psychology
Encyclopedia of Religion
Encyclopedia of Substitutes and
Synthetics
Encyclopedia of Vocational Guidance
Illustrated Technical Dictionary
Labor Dictionary
Liberal Arts Dictionary
Military and Naval Dictionary
New Dictionary of American History
New Dictionary of Psychology
Protestant Dictionary
Slavonic Encyclopedia
Theatre Dictionary
Tobacco Dictionary
Yoga Dictionary

FORTHCOMING

Buddhist Dictionary
Dictionary of American Folklore
Dictionary of the American Indian
Dictionary of American Men and Places
Dictionary of American Names
Dictionary of American Superstitions
Dictionary of Astronomy
Dictionary of Discoveries and Inventions
Dictionary of Earth Sciences
Dictionary of Explorations
Dictionary of French Literature
Dictionary of Geography

Dictionary of German Literature
Dictionary of Hebrew Literature
Dictionary of Law
Dictionary of Mechanics
Dictionary of Poetics
Dictionary of the Renaissance
Dictionary of Science
Dictionary of Social Science
Encyclopedia of Morals
Personnel Dictionary
Teachers' Dictionary
Writers' Dictionary

PHILOSOPHICAL LIBRARY, INC.
Publishers

15 E. 40th Street   New York 16, N. Y.

Dictionary

of

LATIN LITERATURE

JAMES H. MANTINBAND

PHILOSOPHICAL LIBRARY
New York

Printed in the United States of America

PREFACE

The chief value of this dictionary is that here for the first time, in one convenient volume, the whole span of classical and medieval Latin literature is treated, from the earliest authors of the Republic (e.g., Ennius and Naevius) to the so-called Neo-Latin authors of the Renaissance (e.g., Erasmus and More).

It is only natural that in a work of this scope there should be a certain degree of selectivity. There is no effort to include all the obscure grammarians, annalists, jurists, patristic and theological authors, Popes and Schoolmen. It is to be hoped, however, that enough of a representative selection will be found to make this volume of some value for the teacher as well as for the student.

Entries will be found under the main authors, works, types of literature, periods or trends, characters of literature and mythology, technical terms, and a number of related fields, such as religion, education, classical scholarship, etc. Wherever practicable, brief bibliographical references are appended. Main authors are dealt with under the following headings: life, works (also listed separately) and a general estimate of importance and influence. Dates are A.D. unless B.C. is specified.

As for nomenclature, names of the classical period and late antiquity will usually be found under the *nomen gentilicium,* except for cases where the *cognomen* is the accepted English form. Thus, it would be the most fatuous sort of pedantry to list Cicero and Plautus under Tullius and Maccius. Medieval authors are generally found under their Christian names, as *Thomas* Aquinas and *Peter* Lombard, but in any cases of possible doubt or ambiguity, cross-references will be found.

Thus Sidonius Apollinaris will be found under both names, and John Scotus Eriugena under all three. Consistency has been sacrificed on the altar of intelligibility for, as Augustine says, "melius est reprehendant nos grammatici quam non intellegant populi."

In general, the *terminus ad quem* is the Renaissance. At that time, Latin ceased to be an organic growth and, if it did not die, at least it began to atrophy, except as it continues to be used for scholarly works, and as the official language of the Roman Catholic Church. The composition of works in Latin after the Renaissance nearly always takes on the aspect of an erudite *tour de force*, whether it be the learned Latin of a Jebb, Bury or Munro, or the translation of works into Latin (as an ultimate *reductio ad absurdum*, the author remembers having seen a version of Through the Looking-Glass done into Latin, complete with Jabberwocky!).

In spite of the efforts of author, publisher and proofreader, errors will undoubtedly creep into this dictionary. For these the reader's indulgence is asked.

J. M.

ABBREVIATIONS

OCD: Oxford Classical Dictionary
CLP: Christian-Latin Poetry (Raby)
SLP: Secular Latin Poetry (Raby)
q.v.: quod vide (which see)
qq.v.: quae vide (for several references)
fl.: floruit. The date when a man flourished.
ca.: circa (approximately)
s.v.: sub voce (under the word)
b.: born
d.: died
cos.: consul

Dictionary

of

LATIN LITERATURE

ab (a): For titles beginning with this, see under next word.

Abbo of Fleury: b. ca. 950. Scholar of great versatility. Wrote numerous works dealing with church law (*Collectio Canonum*), grammar (*Quaestiones Grammaticae*), logic (*De Dialecticis Syllogismis*), weights and measures (*De Numero Mensura et Pondere*), history, poetry, astronomy, belles-lettres, chronology, etc. (Manitius)

Abbo of St. Germain: d. 923. Author of an historical epic, *Bella Parisiacae Urbis*, in two books, to which he added a totally irrelevant third book, presumably to symbolize the Holy Trinity. (Curtius, Raby)

Abelard, Peter: 1079-1142. The details of his life, his tragic love for Heloise, etc. are well known. A great teacher, scholar and critic, of the University of Paris. He made many enemies because of his bitter attacks on the Schoolmen of his day. In philosophy, he was a nominalist (q.v.). Held a famous debate on Universals with his teacher, William of Champeaux. Accused of heresy by Bernard of Clairvaux (q.v.) he became a monk at Cluny. One of the leading spirits of 12th Century Humanism, he wrote letters, hymns, and numerous works of prose and poetry. *Sic et Non,* his most important work, is an effort to solve discrepancies in Christian theology, by use of dialectics. (Curtius, Waddell, Raby)

Abraham, de: Allegorical work by St. Ambrose (q.v.).

Academicism: Introduced into Rome by Carneades (q.v.) of the New Academy, this school of philosophy became very popular and influenced many Roman authors, notably Cicero. A philosophy of Platonism and scepticism.

Academics: Partially lost work by Cicero, which treats of the theory of knowledge (epistemology). Earlier edition: *Prior* (Lucullus and Catulus) *Academics.* Later edition: *Posterior Ac.* We have the Lucullus from the *Prior Academics* and Book I, for the most part, of the *Posterior.* Extremely valuable work for the doctrines of the Academy. (Duff, Golden Age)

Accent: In oldest Latin verse (see Saturnian meter) the accent was probably a stress-accent, as it is in English. In most of the Classical period, however, the accent was quantitative.

At the end of the classical period, the trend seems to be toward a stress-accent again. The *Pervigilium Veneris* (q.v.) and the Christian hymns demonstrate this trend. (OCD)

Accentibus, de: Lost work on accents by Censorinus (q.v.).

Accius: (Attius) 170-86 B.C. An early Roman tragedian, his work survives only in fragments. An Umbrian by birth. Cicero knew him. We have 45 titles and about 700 lines of fragments. Among the titles are the tragedies *Andromeda, Atreus, Meleager, Philoctetes, Armorum Iudicium,* the historical plays (praetextae) *Brutus* and *Decius,* a work called *Didascalica,* on Greek and Roman poetry, one on agriculture (*Praxidica*), and others. Accius took a great interest in the reform of language, doubling vowels to indicate length, etc. Noted for his lofty language, he was imitated by Virgil. The famous "oderint dum metuant" is from his *Atreus.* (Duff, Golden Age, OCD)

Acerbus Morena: See Otto Morena.

Achilleid: Unfinished epic by Statius (q.v.). We possess about 1100 lines. Cut short by his death. It is impossible to tell how he meant to continue it, what incidents would have been included, etc. It has Virgilian echoes, Silver-Latin erudition. Probably would have covered more of the story of Achilles than did Homer. (Duff, Silver Age)

Achilles: Title of a lost play by Livius Andronicus (q.v.).

Acilius, Gaius: Early Roman historian, who wrote in Greek. He was interpreter for the Senate when the three Greek philosophers (Critolaus, Diogenes and Carneades) came to Rome as spokesmen for the major schools of Greek philosophy. (Duff, Golden Age, OCD)

Acosta, Jose de: 1539-1600. Spanish Jesuit. Author of *De Natura Novi Orbis.*

Acron: (Acro) 2nd Cent. A.D. grammarian, wrote commentaries on Terence and Horace, and perhaps Persius. (OCD)

Acrostics: Poems in which the initial letters of the lines, read from top to bottom, spell one or more words, frequently, the title or author's name. They occur in Ennius, in the prologues of the Plautine plays, and are very popular in late antiquity. See Optatianus, Homerus Latinus, mesostich, telestich. (OCD, Curtius)

Acta Diurna: Daily Gazette of the doings at the Roman court, containing the social and political news of the day, beginning in 59 B.C. Used by Tacitus and Suetonius (qq.v.).

Acta Martyrorum: Stories of the trials and martyrdom of the early Christian martyrs. See *Golden Legend,* Jacopo da Voragine.

Acta Sanctorum: Records of trials of the early Christian martyrs, published in 69 volumes by Jesuit fathers beginning in the 17th Cent.

Acta Senatus: Official record of the transactions of the Roman Senate; cf. our Congressional Record.

actio: "Delivery." One of the five branches of the study of rhetoric (q.v.).

Acts of the Apostles: Long poem dealing with the events of the Gospels, by Arator (q.v.). It is replete with allegory and mysticism.

Adalbero: 10-11th cents. Bishop of Laon, perhaps pupil of Gerbert (q.v.). Wrote poetry on the Trinity, etc.

Adalbert: Teacher of rhetoric in Bologna in the 12th century. Author of a short work, *Precepta Dictaminis,* and a longer one, *De Dictamine.*

Adalbold of Utrecht: 10th century. Wrote a commentary on Boethius, a biography of Henry II, letters, and possibly two works on music.

Adalger: 10th century cleric, author of *Admonitio ad Nonsvindam,* an exhortation to virtue. Adalger may have been bishop of Augsburg. (Manitius)

Adalhard, Life and Miracles of: Erroneously ascribed to one Gerald. A re-editing of Radbert's biography, with an appendix on the miracles.

Adam: Author of a poem *Contra Feminas* (against women), probably a clergyman of the late 11th century. (Manitius)

Adam of Bremen: German canon, teacher and author. Born in Thüringen (?), came to Bremen in 1066, and became head of the school under the archbishop Adalbert. He wrote the history of the archbishopric of Hamburg-Bremen from its inception to his own day, adding a poetical epilogue. His style is lively and straightforward, and his purpose seems to be to support the Church against the incursions of the temporal powers. He makes good use of source material, and the chronological accuracy leaves little to be desired. Especially interesting is the emphasis on geography, and the descriptions of Scandinavia, the Baltic, Thule (Iceland), and Winland. His style is modeled on that of Sallust. The work is entitled *Gesta Hammaburgensis Ecclesiae Pontificum*. (Manitius)

Adam of Dryburgh: ca. 1200. Author of *De Quadripartito Exercicio Cellae*, and other theological works.

Adam of La Bassée: Canon of Lille, d. 1286, wrote a *Ludus super Anticlaudianum*, a poetical fantasy based on the *Anticlaudianus* of Alan of Lille (q.v.).

Adam du Petit-Pont: (Parvipontanus) Logician of the 12th Century.

Adam of St. Victor: 1130-1192. Great poet and lyricist of the 12th cent. Wrote many hymns, and is an important figure in the development of the Sequence (q.v.). (Raby, CLP)

Adam of Usk: ca. 1352-1430. English chronicler of the 14-15th centuries.

Adamnan: Irish monk of the seventh cent. Wrote a life of St. Columba. Possibly author of a learned commentary included with that of Servius (q.v.).

Addictus: Title of a lost play by Plautus, mentioned by Aulus Gellius. See also *Saturio*.

Adelard of Bath: fl. 1109-1142. One of the great humanists of the 12th cent. Wrote a book on natural philosophy, dedicated to the Bishop of Syracuse. Its title is the same as Seneca's: *Quaestiones Naturales*. Traveled extensively in Italy, Sicily, Greece, Spain, taught in Paris and Laon. His learning covered not only philosophy but also theology, science, astronomy, mathematics, and psychology. Used Aristotle's argument from motion to prove the existence of God. (Waddell, Curtius, Ferm, Enc. of Religion)

Adelmann of Liége: ca. 1062. Pupil of Fulbert of Chartres (q.v.); writer of many letters. In a famous one, he describes the conversations with the "venerable Socrates" (i.e. Fulbert). Also wrote poetry celebrating fame and virtue of his master. (Waddell, Raby, CLP)

Adelphi: Extant comedy by Terence (q.v.). It deals with the rival theories of education held by two elderly brothers, one stern, the other, "permissive," and the effect on two young brothers. One of Terence's best plays, it depends for its humor on characterization rather than on plot situations. The climax of the play occurs when Demea, the stern brother, does a complete aboutface and outdoes his brother in laxity and geniality: he frees slaves, arranges marriages, in short, brings about a reductio ad absurdum of his brother Micio's permissiveness. (Duff, Golden Age)

Adhémar of Chavannes: ca. 988-post 1028. Scholar of Aquitaine who wrote a report of the famous council of bishops in 1028; *Chronicles, Commemoratio Abbatum Lemovicensium,* and also poetry. (Waddell)

Adonis: Probable title of one of the lost plays of Livius Andronicus (q.v.).

Adrian IV, pope: See Breakspear, Nicholas.

Adso of Montier-en-Der: b. ca. 920. Wrote *De Ortu et Tempore Antichristi,* biographies of Frodobert, Waldebert, Bercharius, Basolus; hymns, commentaries on the Ambrosian hymns; a versification of Book II of the *Dialogues* of Gregory the Great; and other works. (Manitius)

Adversus Astrologos: Lost work by Columella (q.v.) attacking fortune-tellers and superstition.

Adversus Nationes: Work in seven books by Arnobius (1) q.v., refuting the concept that Christianity is the cause of the evils of the world. Harsh in its Latinity, the work is full of Lucretian echoes. (Labriolle, Rand)

Aedilicia: Title of a lost comedy by Atta (q.v.).

Aegritudo Perdicae: An epyllion or short epic, ascribed to Dracontius (q.v.) but probably without good reason. It tells of the love of Perdica for his mother Castalia, and the diagnosis by Hippocrates of the youth's illness. Not without merit, it contains, nevertheless, much of the over-fondness for rhetoric that mars most of the poetry of late antiquity. (Raby, SLP)

Aelfric: 11th century. Wrote a grammar, a glossary, a Life of Aethelwold, works on chronology, natural science, hagiography, biblical commentaries, and other works.

Aelius Lampridius: One of the six authors of the *Historia Augusta* (q.v.).

Aelius Paetus Catus: Roman jurist of the Republic (cos. 198 B.C.). Wrote the *Tripertita*, a famous work containing the text of the Laws of the Twelve Tables (q.v.) together with commentaries thereon. This work was called in antiquity "the cradle of the Law."

Aelius Spartianus: One of the authors of the *Historia Augusta* (q.v.).

Aelius Stilo, L.: The first great scholar of Rome, fl. ca. 100 B.C. Stoic in his philosophy, varied in his scholarly interests, embracing the fields of grammar, etymology, literary criticism. Made editions of the old poets and Salian hymns, comments on the laws of the Twelve Tables, wrote on grammar and laid the foundations of Latin philology. Wrote a treatise on sentences (*de Proloquiis*). Cicero and Varro (qq.v.) were among his pupils. (Duff, Golden Age)

Aelred of Rievaux: English monk. b. 1110. Wrote *Speculum Caritatis, De Spirituali Amicitia, Genealogia Regum Anglorum,* and other biographical, historical and philosophical works. (Manitius)

Aeneas: Mythological figure. Son of Venus and Anchises. Hero of Virgil's *Aeneid* (q.v.). In Homer's Iliad, Aeneas is one of the Trojan heroes. Known for his *virtus* and *pietas,* two of the cardinal Roman virtues (qq.v.). Son of Venus and the mortal Anchises. Aeneas appears in Roman literature before Virgil, in the *Bellum Punicum* of Naevius (q.v.) and in the *Annales* of Ennius (q.v.). The love-story of Dido and Aeneas in the fourth book of the Aeneid is one of the great romances of all literature. (Duff, Golden Age)

Aeneas: Title of a praetexta (historical drama) by Pomponius Secundus (q.v.).

Aeneid: The greatest of the Roman epic poems. Written by Virgil (q.v.) at the suggestion of the emperor Augustus, it took its author eleven years to write. Virgil was not satisfied with the poem and left instructions in his will for it to be destroyed. These instructions, needless to say, were not carried out. The first six books of the *Aeneid*, relating the wanderings of Aeneas, the fall of Troy (told in flashback fashion), the love story of Dido and Aeneas, and the hero's descent into the underworld, are broadly modeled on Homer's *Odyssey*. The last six, telling of the settling in Italy, the wars, and the epic struggle between Aeneas and Turnus, imitate the *Iliad*.

Despite these for the most part obvious imitations of Homer, as well as other Greek influences (notably that of Euripides), the work remains an original work of great genius, and the national Roman poem. Aeneas is the "ideal Roman and Stoic." The style is lofty and dignified. Virgil brought the Latin hexameter to a perfection it had never attained before and never reached again. He well merits Tennyson's "wielder of the stateliest measure ever moulded by the lips of man." He has none of the primitive "battle-glee" of Homer, but is filled with profound sadness for human suffering ("sunt lacrimae rerum"). The *Aeneid* ranks with the poems of Dante and Milton for depth of concept and loftiness of expression. Virgil never permits the reader to lose sight of his imperial mission—the glorification of Rome and of Augustus. A fine characterization is that of Dido, the queen of Carthage. The work is full of romance and even mysticism. Among the most memorable scenes are the storm at sea (Book I), the Fall of Troy (Book II), the great love-romance (Book IV), the descent of Aeneas to the underworld, with its vision of the future glories of Rome (Book VI), and the final battle with Turnus (Book XII). Almost immediately after its composition, the *Aeneid* became *the* Roman epic, which it has remained to this day. Its influence on Dante is proverbial. (Duff, Golden Age)

Aesculapius: Latinized form of Asklepios, god of medicine. Brought to Rome in the third century B.C.

Aeserninus: The grandson of Asinius Pollio (q.v.), a noted orator in the time of Tiberius.

Aesiona: (Hesione) Lost play by Naevius (q.v.).

Aesop: A prose collection of beast-fables from the fourth or fifth century, going back to the "Aesop" collection in part. See under Fable, *Romulus.*

Aesopus: Great tragic actor of Cicero's day. Helped revive tragedy as did Roscius (q.v.) for comedy.

Aetatibus Mundi et Hominis, de: A work in 14 books and 23 "periods," dealing with the Bible and world history, by Fulgentius (1). (OCD)

Aethelwald: ca. 700. Disciple of Aldhelm (q.v.), Anglo-Saxon poet, author of religious and secular rhythmical verses previously attributed to Aldhelm himself. Aethelwald became king of Mercia. (Raby, CLP, SLP)

Aethelwulf: Anglo-Saxon monk of Lindisfarne (early 9th cent.). Author of a poem called "the Abbots and miracles of his Church," telling the history of his monastery, the virtues of the monks, etc. (Raby, CLP)

Aetheria: Author of *Peregrinatio Aetheriae* probably in the fourth century; a collection of letters from an abbess to the nuns under her. Tells in colloquial Latin the story of her pilgrimage to the Holy Land. (OCD)

Aethicus Cosmographus: Author of what purports to be an early translation from a Greek original; a geographical chronicle from the Creation of the World to the author's time. Sources are Isidore and Solinus.

Aetia: Lost work by Varro (q.v.); an investigation into the origins of various Roman customs. Modeled on the Greek work of the same name by Callimachus of Alexandria.

Aetiological myth: (also, etiological) One invented to explain some physical fact or natural phenomenon. Examples are the Midas story, which explains the presence of gold in the Pactolus river; the Phaethon story, explaining the Sahara desert, etc. Kipling's "Just So Stories" are modern examples. See under Curtius.

Aetna: A didactic poem in 644 hexameters. Attributed to Virgil and placed among his works (see *Appendix Virgiliana*). The problem of its date and authorship remains unsolved. Its conjectural dates vary from 55 B.C. to 79 A.D. (see "argumentum ex silentio"). After an invocation to Apollo in a solemn, Lucretian vein, the author goes on to dismiss mythological explanations of the volcano, and give "natural" reasons for its activity. In spite of difficulties of style and allusion, the work is not without merit. (OCD, Duff)

Afer: See Domitius Afer, Terence, etc.

Afranius, L.: b. ca. 150 B.C. Author of *fabulae togatae,* of which only titles and fragments survive. His plays had great popular appeal, as they represented domestic Italian life, and were popular even in Imperial times. Most famous titles are *Divortium, Epistula, Fratriae.* Borrowed freely from Terence. Horace compares him with Menander.

Africa: Home of many Latin authors from Terence to Apuleius and Fronto. Especially important for the development of the Church, producing such authors as Tertullian, Cyprian, Arnobius (1), Lactantius, Minucius Felix, and St. Augustine (qq.v.).

Africa: Latin poem by Petrarch (q.v.).

African Anthology: Collection by an unknown author of late African poems, riddles, centos, epigrams, etc. Dating from the 5th or 6th cent., it includes works by Luxorius, Corippus, the *Medea* of Hosidius Geta, riddles by *Symphosius.*

Agamemnon: Extant tragedy by Seneca (2). Falls far short of the lofty drama of Aeschylus. It is very short, and full of the most frigid sort of mythology. Seems intended for reading, rather than stage performance. Shows influence of Livius and Accius, rather than that of Aeschylus.

Agave: Lost pantomime by Statius (q.v.), dealing with the tragic story of Pentheus.

Agellius: See Gellius, Aulus. The name Agellius arose through an incorrect reading of A.Gellius.

Aggenius Urbicus: 5th (?) century author of a commentary on Frontinus (q.v.).

Agius of Corvey: 9th century author of a poem on numbers and a long elegiac poem on the death of the abbess Hathumod of Gandersheim. The latter is in dialogue form, with Agius speaking, and a *Responsio* of grieving nuns (see *Consolatio*).

Agobard of Lyons: Prolific writer of theological works; works against superstition, etc. and author of an acrostic Rhythmus to Bishop Leidrat. (Manitius)

Agri Cultura, de: See Cato (1).

Agricola: Biography by Tacitus (q.v.) of his famous father-in-law. Tells of the general's life, consulship, his British campaigns and victories. Agricola is described as a great general and able administrator. The end of the work is especially fine, containing an apostrophe to the deceased general and an epilogue on the subject of immortality. (Duff, Silver Age)

Agricola, Rudolph: 1444-85. German humanist of the 15th century. Called the "German Petrarch." Had a great love for the classics. Wrote a work entitled *De Inventione Dialectica,* which replaced Aristotle's *Rhetoric* as a textbook at the University of Paris; and a *De Formando Studio* on the reform of the curriculum.

Agrippa, M. Vipsanius: Augustan statesman and general. Wrote memoirs (now lost) and a geographical work used by Pliny (1).

Agrippa of Nettesheim: 1486-1535. German philosopher. wks: *De Occulta Philosophia, De Incertitudine et Vanitate Scientarum.*

Agrippina: Mother of the emperor Nero, by whose order she was murdered. Wrote memoirs (now lost) quoted by Pliny and Tacitus.

Aiax Mastigophorus: Title of a (lost) play by Livius Andronicus.

Ailly, Pierre, d': 1350-1420. French ecclesiastical writer, author of *Libellus de Emendatione Ecclesiae.*

Ailred: Twelfth century English monk, author of *Speculum Caritatis.*

Aimeric: French grammarian of the 11th century. Author of an *Ars Lectoria* (1086), containing a classification of authors into four groups, the gold (autentica), silver (hagiographa), tin (communia) and lead (apocrifa). Christian and pagan authors are separately classified but Aimeric admits that "item apud gentiles sunt libri autentici." (Curtius)

Aimoin of Fleury: 970-1004. Author of a History of the Franks (*Historia Francorum*), Miracles of St. Benedict, *Gesta abbatum Floriacensium,* and other works.

Ajax: Title of a tragedy by the emperor Augustus, destroyed by him as a failure.

Alan of Lille: ca. 1128-1202. One of the greatest of the philosophical poets of the Middle Ages. Belongs to the first period of Scholasticism. Essentially a Platonist. Wrote, besides hymns and sequences for the Church, a long philosophical poem *Anticlaudianus* and a "satire" *De Planctu Naturae,* a mixture of prose and verse in the manner of Boethius and Martianus Capella. See under *Anticlaudianus, Planctu Naturae, de.* Other works: *Parabolae, de Regulis S. Theologiae, Contra Haereticos, Distinctiones,* etc. (Raby, Curtius)

Alberic of Monte Cassino: (Albericus Casinensis) Compiled the first *Ars Dictaminis* (q.v.), which was called *Flores Rhetorici.*

Albericus Casinensis: See Alberic of Monte Cassino.

Albert of Stade: A writer of the 13th century, noted for his extreme brevity. In his *Troilus* he describes a twelve-day battle in fourteen lines. (Curtius)

Albertus Aquensis: (Albert of Aix) Wrote a *Historia Hierosolymitanae Expeditionis,* on the First Crusade. Nothing is known of his life.

Albertus Magnus: (Albert the Great) 1206-80. German Dominican friar, theologian and philosopher. Taught at Paris and Cologne. An eclectic, he is most famous as the teacher of Thomas Aquinas (q.v.). Wrote a *Liber de Causis,* and commentaries on Aristotle and the Bible. Became Bishop of Ratisbon in 1260. Was extremely interested in the experimental sciences. One of the greatest minds of the Thirteenth Century, he was eclipsed by his even greater pupil.

Albinovanus Pedo: Poet of the Augustan Age, friend of Ovid (q.v.). Author of a *Theseid* (now lost) and a poem on the North Sea expedition of Germanicus, from which a fragment of about 20 lines has been preserved by Seneca (1).

Albinus (1), Postumius: Early Roman historian who wrote in Greek.

Albinus (2): Teacher of Galen, ca. 150 A.D. Wrote a Prologue to Plato, and a textbook on Plato's philosophy—a mixture of Platonic, Stoic and peripatetic elements.

Albinus (3): 4th century scholar and grammarian; wrote on music and meters. None of his works have survived.

Albucius, T. (1): 2nd century B.C. orator and Epicurean, referred to, in mockery, by Lucilius.

Albucius Silus, C. (2): Augustan rhetor, he was highly praised by Seneca (1) for his great versatility.

Alcaeus: One of the greatest of the Greek lyric poets, ca. 600 B.C. Horace imitated both his meter and his subject matter (e.g., the famous "Ship of State" ode).

Alcestis: Either the title of a separate work by Laevius (q.v.) or part of his *Erotopaegnia*. The whole subject of Laevius is still shrouded in obscurity.

Alciati, Andrea: 1492-1550. Italian humanist. Wrote *Emblemata, De Verborum Significatione*.

Alcibiades: Brilliant but unscrupulous Athenian general during the Peloponnesian War. A *Life* by Cornelius Nepos survives.

Alcithoë: Lost play by Paccius (q.v.).

Alcuin of York: d. 804. One of the most important figures of the Carolingian Renaissance (q.v.). A man of wide erudition and a great teacher, he wrote letters, school syllabi, treatises on theology, and worked on an improved text of the Vulgate Bible. Taught and wrote on nearly all known branches of learning and science. Also a capable poet, writer of epigrams, hexameters, etc. Charlemagne brought him from England to be Master of the Court School. Retired to monastery of Tours, where he died. Taught the monks to copy manuscripts, and is an extremely important figure in the transmission of texts.

Alcyone: Lost epyllion (q.v.) by Cicero.

Alda: Versified tale or "comoedia" by William of Blois (q.v.), a French poet of the twelfth century. It seems to be based on a second or third-hand version of a play by Menander.

Aldhelm, St.: d. 709, Bishop of Sherborne. Great teacher, writer, and poet of the seventh century. Said to have been the first exponent of Latin-Anglo-Saxon culture. Tried to make Latin the literary language of the Anglo-Saxons. Wrote a poem, *de Virginitate;* a famous letter on metrics; 101 riddles in hexameters; and a poem *de Octo Principalibus Vitiis.*

Aldine: The first printed editions (editio princeps) of classical texts, by Aldus of Venice in the 16th century. (See Editions)

Alea, de: An anonymous cento (q.v.) of uncertain date.

Alethia: Poem by Claudius Marius Victor, a poetical paraphrase of Genesis up to the destruction of Sodom.

Alexander: Lost tragedy by Ennius (q.v.), referring, presumably, to the Trojan prince Paris, who is also called Alexander.

Alexander of Hales: d. 1245. Thirteenth-century theologian and scholastic. Author of a *Summa Universae Theologicae* (incomplete). One of the first to apply Aristotelian categories to church dogma.

Alexander Neckham: See *Neckham, Alexander.*

Alexander of Villedieu: Latter half of the twelfth century. Wrote a grammatical work, *Doctrinale* (1199) which did away with Homer and Virgil and drew all its illustrative material from Christian authors. The Doctrinale supplanted Priscian (q.v.) as a grammatical authority in the later Middle Ages. Also wrote an *Ecclesiale, Compotus, Algorismus,* and other works.

Alexandreis: Epic on Alexander by Walter (Gautier) of Châtillon (q.v.). Among the best of the twelfth century epics, it is largely based on the work of Curtius Rufus (q.v.). (Raby, SLP)

Alexandri Magni Historiae: See Curtius Rufus.

Alexandrian influence: The influence of the Alexandrian school, including such authors as Callimachus, Theocritus, etc., was a profound force in the Latin poetry of the late Republic. Cosmopolitan in its character, stressing romantic love, full of gallantry, prettification, at times shallow and affected, always self-conscious, the Alexandrian school first influenced Laevius (q.v.), author of the *Erotopaegnia,* then Catullus and the rest of the Cantores Euphoriones (qq.v.), and finally Virgil, Ovid and the other Augustan poets. The form of the *epyllion* or toy epic is a typically Alexandrian one, with its bookishness and self-conscious mythology.

Alfenus Varus, P (?): Roman jurist, pupil of S. Sulpicius Rufus (q.v.). Possibly identical with the Suffenus ridiculed by Catullus.

Alfius Avitus: A neoteric (q.v.) of the time of Hadrian. Wrote dimeters on historical subjects.

Alfred the Great: Performed a great service to Anglo-Saxon scholarship by his translations of Orosius, Bede, Boethius, Augustine, the *Dialogues* of Gregory the Great, etc., into Anglo-Saxon.

Alger of Liége: b. 1070. Wrote a History of the Bishopric of Liége. This work is lost. Two works have survived: *De Misericordia et Iustitia* (on mercy and justice), and *De Sacramento Corporis et Sanguinis Domini* (on the body and blood of Christ).

Alimonium Remi et Romuli: Lost praetexta (historical drama) by Naevius (q.v.).

Allegory: Occasionally found in the classical period, as in Horace's ode on the "Ship of State" and Silius Italicus on the "Choice of Hercules." In late antiquity, allegory became one of the favorite forms. Cf. Martianus Capella's *Wedding of Mercury and Philology,* and the works of Fulgentius, Prudentius, Ambrose, etc. (qq.v.). Virgil was interpreted allegorically in the Middle Ages. Christian allegory is well represented by the *Psychomachia* of Prudentius (q.v.), which was very popular and much imitated in medieval times. Alan of Lille (q.v.) is one of the later exponents of allegory. See also Avitus, Nivard's *Ysengrimus, Abraham,* Arator, *Architrenius, Hawk and the Peacock.*

Alleluia: See Sequence.

Alliteration: See Assonance, Ennius.

Alpert of Metz: ca. 1000. Monk at the monastery of St. Symphorian at Metz. Wrote a book on the bishops of Metz (*Libellus de Episcopis Mettensibus*), and one on the changing times (*De Diversitate Temporum Libri ii*).

Alphabetical poems: Poems in which each line begins with a different and successive letter of the alphabet. Typical of the mannered artificiality which became the style in late antiquity.

Alphanus: One of the great figures of the humanistic revival in 11th century Italy. Archbishop of Salerno. Made a pilgrimage to the Holy Land. Wrote odes in honor of St. Matthew. Renowned for his skill in sacred and profane letters, and also as a doctor of medicine. Most famous poem: *Apostolorum Nobili Victoria.* (Raby, CLP)

Altahenses, Annales: Chronicles of the monastery of Altaich, continued at various times by various hands, covers the period from 708 to 1032. The Latinity is clear, if not good. (Manitius)

Altar of Victory, affair of the: The Altar to the Goddess Victory, removed by Constantius, restored by Julian, ordered removed by Gratian. Symmachus (q.v.), leader of the pagan aristocracy in Rome, made a famous and eloquent appeal for its restoration, which was answered by St. Ambrose in an even more famous and more eloquent speech. The *Contra Symmachum* of Prudentius (qq.v.) also deals with the Altar of Victory, which became a cause célèbre in the battle between Christianity and Paganism.

Altercatio Phyllidis et Florae: A poetical debate of the twelfth century. See under *Streitgedicht.*

Altercatio Yemis et Estatis: Poetical debate between Summer and Winter, from a 13th century manuscript. Typical of the medieval *Streitgedicht* (q.v.).

Altus Prosator: A religious poem by St. Columbia (q.v.).

Alulf of Tournai: d. 1141. Wrote a work *Gregorialis* in sixteen books, consisting of restatements, comments, abbreviations, and paraphrases of Gregory the Great's Biblical explanations. Important because it reveals the significance, even at that date, of Gregory's allegorical, moral, and historical explanations. Prologue a verbatim copy of that of Paterius on Genesis. (Manitius)

Amafinius: Author of a (lost) treatise on Epicureanism, mentioned by Cicero. May have influenced Lucretius (q.v.).

Amalar: Pupil of Alcuin (q.v.), sent as ambassador to Constantinople by Charlemagne. Wrote a poem on the voyage, depicting all its horrors and his joy upon returning. Not a very distinguished poet. (Manitius, Raby)

Amalric: Early 13th century theologian, teacher of pantheism (i.e. the doctrine that God is present in all things).

Amarcius: German monk of the 11th century. Wrote four books of *Sermones* or satires.

Amaseo, Romolo: 1498-1552. Italian humanist; champion of Ciceronian Latin.

Amatus of Monte Cassino: b. 1030 in Salerno. Wrote (a) *Liber in Honore Beati Petri Apostoli;* (b) *Historia Normannorum.*

Amazonis: Lost epic by the minor Augustan poet Domitius Marsus (q.v.), or possibly by another Marsus.

Ambiguitatibus, de: See Salvius Julianus.

Ambivius Turpio, L: Actor-director, contemporary of Terence. Played in the comedies of Terence and Caecilius Statius (qq.v.).

Ambrose of Milan, St.: 337-397. Bishop of Milan, at first unwillingly ("nolo episcopari"). A man of great learning, equally capable as orator, teacher, administrator, and man of letters. In early life he was an eloquent lawyer. Famous for Affair of Altar of Victory, when he delivered one of his most important speeches (v. sub Altar of Victory). Rand calls him a mystic. Works: *De Spiritu Sancto* (exegetical), *De Officiis Ministrorum,* a monument of Christian humanism, based on Cicero's *De Officiis* (q.v.), but incorporating Ciceronian Stoicism into Christian thought; *De Abraham, De Arca Noë* (allegory), the *Hexaemeron* (a series of sermons on the six days of creation); *De Helia et Ieiunio, de Nabuthe, De Tobia, Enarrationes in XII Psalmos Davidicos, Expositio in Psalmum 118, Expositio Evangelii sec. Lucam, De Fide, De Mysteriis, De Sacramentis, De Excessu Fratris Satyri.* In addition to the above works he wrote hymns (see Ambrosian Hymnary) and 91 letters, which reveal his stature as a bishop. Altogether a man of great versatility and ability, as a scholar, preacher, orator, administrator, and pedagogue; and one of the greatest of the Church Fathers. (Rand, Labriolle, OCD)

Ambrosian Hymnary: Collection of hymns of the Church of Milan, by St. Ambrose (q.v.) and others. Raby (CLP) says that the real history of hymns in the West begins with Ambrose. It is not always possible to ascertain which of these hymns are by Ambrose, but Augustine himself vouches for the authenticity of some of the greatest: *Deus creator omnium, Aeterne rerum conditor, Iam surgit hora tertia,* and *Veni redemptor gentium.* The Ambrosian Hymnary is a landmark in the development of Christian Latin poetry. Their structure follows the new *rhythmical* poetry, although the verses are quantitative. (Raby, CLP)

Ambrosian Palimpsest: A famous palimpsest (q.v.) of Plautus, discovered by Cardinal Mai (q.v.).

Amicitia, de: (Laelius) One of the most famous of Cicero's philosophical dialogues, and justly so. Duff says of it "for pure beauty it is unsurpassed in Cicero. Its noble calm, its melodious sentences, and its hold upon pellucid brevity give it a rank in literature beside Montaigne's inimitable portrayal of the fervency in affection and community of will which must ally friends." (Duff, Golden Age)

Ammianus Marcellinus: 330-400. The last of the great Roman historians. Born at Antioch, he turned to the writing of history after an honorable military career. His history is a continuation of Tacitus, and covers the period from Nerva to Valens (378). The first 13 books have not survived. Although his Latin is not pure, and the work is marred by a superabundance of declamation, his style is vivid and some of his writing really splendid. Ammianus was not a Christian. Gibbon says he was "without the prejudices and passions which usually affect the mind of a contemporary." (OCD)

Amoebean Verse: A common device of pastoral or bucolic poetry (q.v.). Consists of alternately sung couplets (e.g., a singing contest). Occurs in Virgil and widely thereafter.

Amores: Ovid's (q.v.) earliest work. Immediately secured his fame as a writer of elegy. Deals with the varying moods of love. "Corinna" is the subject. Though the poems lack the passion of Catullus, and the profundity of Tibullus and Propertius (qq.v.), they are graceful and reveal a mastery of the elegiac meter. The best parallel in English is the work of the Cavalier poets. (Duff, OCD)

Ampelius, Lucius: 2nd or 3rd century. Author of a *Liber Memorialis,* or handbook of general knowledge, giving information on geography, cosmography, mythology, history, etc.

Amphitruo: Comedy by Plautus (q.v.). One of the best-known and most often treated of all comic plots. Called by its author a tragi-comedy, it deals with Jupiter's masquerading as Amphitryon, husband of Alcmena, aided by Mercury, who impersonates the slave Sosia. The humor abounds in trickery, mistaken identity, and slapstick. The character of Alcmena is particularly finely drawn.

Amphitryo: Medieval "comoedia" by Vitalis of Blois (q.v.). Also known as *Geta,* after the servant. Tells the story of the Plautine comedy, with considerable variations (e.g. Amphitryon has become a student of logic at the University, instead of a soldier!). The protagonist is the servant Geta.

Analogia, de: Lost grammatical work by Caesar (q.v.), written by him during a journey across the Alps, and dedicated to Cicero. For the subject, see under *Analogy and Anomaly*.

Analogy and Anomaly: The great battle between opposing schools of grammarians at Rome. Most authors who dealt with grammar were drawn into it (e.g. Varro, Cicero, Caesar, Pliny, Quintilian, et al.). The Analogists held that nouns and verbs could be classified into orderly declensions and conjugations on the basis of similarity of form, while the Anomalists dwelt on the irregularities of form. Although neither was very fruitful, both stimulated grammatical studies. Basic to the whole discussion was the question whether language is an organic growth or a purely arbitrary convention. Varro and Caesar favor the analogists, Cicero, Horace, and Quintilian favor the opposing school, and the weight of "consuetudo" or usage. (OCD)

Anastasius Bibliothecarius: Second half of the 9th century. Wrote Lives of Saints, Passions; translated Pseudo-Dionysius; wrote a *Chronica Tripartita; Collectanea;* letters, etc.

Anchises: In mythology, the father of Aeneas and husband of the goddess Venus. In Virgil's *Aeneid,* he is carried from burning Troy on his son's shoulders, shares the latter's wanderings, and, after his death, is consulted in the Underworld. (See *Aeneid*)

Andreae, Johann Valentin: 1586-1654. German theologian, poet. Wrote a work, *Christianopolis,* depicting the ideal state; and numerous other works of prose, poetry and satire.

Andreas Capellanus: Author of a work *De Amore* (On Love) in three books. The first deals with the attainment of love, the second with its maintenance, and the third with its rejection, especially from the Christian viewpoint. (Manitius)

Andreas of Fleury: 11th century. Wrote the Life of Gauzlin, Abbot of Fleury, Archbishop of Bourges, and the Miracles of St. Benedict. His works show a good Latinity, and are much better than most biographies of the time. (Manitius)

Andreas Ratisbonensis: 1380-1438. Bavarian writer of history, partly compiled from earlier sources, partly based on his own observations.

Andria: (the girl of Andros) Play by Terence (q.v.). As in "Waiting for Lefty," the person with the title-role does not appear at all. Play revolves around the love of the youth Pamphilus for the Andrian girl, his father's insistence that he marry a girl he does not love, and the tactics of a wily slave. He discovers that the Andrian is really the daughter of the neighbor whose other daughter his father wants him to marry.

Andromache: (Lat. Andromacha) Wife of Hector, popular subject for tragedy from Euripides to Racine. Ennius and Naevius (qq.v.) wrote plays on this subject.

Andromeda: Heroine of Greek mythology, in the Perseus story. Subject of tragedies by Livius Andronicus, Ennius, and Accius (qq.v.).

Andronicus, Livius: See Livius Andronicus.

Angelic Doctor: See Thomas Aquinas.

Angelram of St. Riquier: d. 1045. Pupil of Fulbert of Chartres (q.v.) at whose request Angelram wrote a poetical life of St. Richarius.

Angelus Sabinus: See Sabinus, Angelus.

Angilbert: d. 814. Abbot of St. Riquier. Pupil of Alcuin (q.v.). Author and poet, he had a huge library of manuscripts, which he left to the monastery. A favorite of the Court Circle of Charlemagne and one of the figures in the "Carolingian Renaissance" (q.v.). Called the "Homer of the Court Circle." See *Karolus Magnus et Leo Papa.*

Angilomus of Luxeuil: 9th century exegetical writer; author of commentaries on Genesis, Kings, Song of Songs, etc.

Animae Ratione ad Eulalian Virginem, de: Treatise on the soul by Alcuin (PL 101).

Annales: Title of many works, in both prose and poetry, treating the history of Rome. Works of this title were written by Ennius (vid. s.v.), Accius, Cincius, Fenestella, Furius Bibaculus, Hortensius, Varro, and Tacitus. (See under the authors herein mentioned, and under *Annales,* Tacitus)

Annales: (Ennius) Great historical epic by Ennius (q.v.) in 18 books of hexameters, of which about 600 lines of fragments survive. Dealt with the glories of Rome from Aeneas to the present (ca. 170 B.C.). Among the subjects he covered were: Aeneas, Romulus, the Macedonian Wars, Pyrrhus, the Punic Wars, etc. Enough of the fragments have survived to show us that this is a work of more genius than art: it is vigorous, but crude. Of great importance, however, as the first Latin epic in hexameters. The oft-quoted lines: "O Tite, tute, Tati, tibi tanta, tyranne, tulisti!" and the violent tmesis "saxo cere comminuit brum" are balanced by the beauty of such lines as "simul aureus exoritur sol."

Annales: (Tacitus) Original title "Ab excessu divi Augusti." Written after the *Historiae,* which it precedes chronologically, the *Annales* is the greatest work of the greatest Roman historian. In spite of the great gaps, enough of the work has survived to reveal the genius of its author. (The lost portions cover part of the reign of Tiberius, all of Caligula, the first part of Claudius and the last part of Nero.) Among the unforgettable portions are: the picture of the cryptical Tiberius; Nero, the fire at Rome and the persecution of the Christians; the deaths of Seneca and Petronius; the fate of Paetus Thrasea, the death of Germanicus, and others. A fascinating and graphic account of one of the most interesting periods of all history. (Duff, Silver Age)

Annales Ecclesiastici: See Baronius.

Annales Pontificum: (also called Annales Maximi) Official Roman records, with the names of officials and records of memorable events, issued on a white tablet each year. When collected by the pontifex Scaevola in 130 B.C. there were eighty volumes. They were repeatedly destroyed by fire.

Annalista Saxo: A great historical compilation 741-1139, by an unknown author who collected such documents as chronicles of cloisters, histories of the Crusades, records of the bishoprics, and other such sources. He used, for example, the Annals of Fulda, the works of Ekkehard (IV), Lampert, Widukind, Adam of Bremen, etc. (qq.v.).

Annalists: See History. Annalists recorded events year by year.

Annianus: A minor poet of the time of Hadrian (see Neoterics). Wrote *Carmina Falisca*.

Annius, T.: A famed orator of the Gracchan period (last third of the 2nd century B.C.) Cicero mentions him as invincible in debate.

Annotationes: Notes, commentary, and corrections, specifically, those dealing with the Vulgate Bible by Lorenzo Valla (q.v.).

Anomaly: in language. See *Analogy and Anomaly*.

Anselm, St. (1): 1033-1109 (of Canterbury). Important theologian and Schoolman of the 11th century. One of chief figures in the development of Scholasticism. Developed the ontological argument (called Anselmian after him) for the existence of God, in the *Proslogium* and the *Monologium*. Reintroduced the spirit of Augustine into theology. Has been called the first original thinker of the Middle Ages.

Anselm the Peripatetic (2): Italian scholar and rhetorician of the 11th century. Wrote a work entitled *Rhetorimachia*.

Anselm (3): (of Mainz) German monk and poet of the 12th century. Wrote poetry on the life of Archbishop Adelbert II. Poem displays great learning and makes use of leonine (internal) rhymes.

Anselm of Liége (4): Middle of the 11th century. Wrote *Gesta Episcoporum Leodiensium* (history of the Bishops of Liége). The style is rather poetical, and sometimes almost metrical. (Manitius)

Anser: Minor poet, wrote erotic verses—mentioned by Ovid as a contemporary.

Anthologia Latina: Properly speaking, the title of a collection of poems made in the 6th century by one Octavianus of Carthage. Includes Virgilian centos (q.v.), poems on Roses, Dido's Letter, the Pervigilium Veneris (q.v.), etc.

Many other collections of minor works have been made, by Scaliger (1573), Baehrens, Riese-Buecheler, et al. The best collection for us today, perhaps, is that of J. W. and A. M.

Duff (Selections. Min. Lat. Poets, Loeb Classical Library, 1934). This has the added merit of a good English translation.

Antias, Valerius: Early Roman historian, used as a source by Livy, Plutarch and Pliny the Elder.

Antibucolica: Virgilian parodies by Numitorius (q.v.).

Anticato: (Anticatones) Lost work (or works) by Caesar in answer to eulogies of Cato Uticensis by Cicero, Brutus and others.

Anticlaudianus: Poem by Alan of Lille (q.v.) written in 1182/3. It is a long philosophical poem, depicting the ideal man allegorically, and it was tremendously popular in the Middle Ages. For its inclusion in medieval curriculum lists see *Laborintus*. "Contains a blend of literature and philosophy which was the basis of the humanism in the cathedral schools." (Manitius, Raby)

Anti-Lucretius: Work by Cardinal Polignac (q.v.) written in refutation of the *De Rerum Natura* of Lucretius (q.v.).

Antimachus: Greek poet whose epic *Thebais* was the principal source for the epic of the same name by Statius (q.v.).

Antiocheis: Twelfth century epic on the Crusades, especially the deeds of King Richard, by Joseph of Exeter (q.v.).

Antiopa: We possess this title of (lost) plays by Livius Andronicus and Pacuvius (qq.v.).

Antipater, L. Caelius: Early Roman historian whose work (now lost) dealt with the Second Punic War. Highly praised by Cicero, he was used as a source by Livy, Plutarch, etc.

Antiquitates Rerum Humanarum et Divinarum: Lost work by Varro (1) dealing with antiquities. 25 books were on the human, 16 on divine. Was widely used by the Christian Fathers for information concerning Roman life and worship. The work is usually called *Antiquitates*.

Antistius (1) Labeo: See Labeo, Antistius.

Antistius (2) Sosianus: Minor satirical poet of the Neronian Age.

Antonianae: See *Philippics*.

Antonine Itinerary: See under *Itinerary*.

Antonius (1) Iullus: Son of "Mark Antony," a minor poet of the Augustan Age. Wrote prose and epic poetry. Convicted of adultery in 2 B.C., he committed suicide.

Antonius (2) M: 143-87 B.C. One of the greatest orators of the pre-Ciceronian period, he was the grandfather of "Mark Antony."

Antonius (3), M.: 83?-30 B.C. ("Mark Antony") The triumvir and statesman, an excellent orator and fine soldier.

Antonius (4) Castor: Writer on botany during the early Principate. Source for the Elder Pliny.

Antonius (5) Liberalis: Rhetor of the Neronian period who is famous for his feud with Palaemon (q.v.).

Anulus: See Sextus.

Apella: Comedy by Naevius (q.v.).

Aper, Marcus: Famed advocate of Tacitus' day, one of the participants in the latter's *Dialogus de Oratoribus* (q.v.).

Aphrodisius, Scribonius: A slave, taught by Orbilius (q.v.), wrote on orthography and criticized the work of Verrius Flaccus (q.v.).

Aphthonius, Aelius Festus: Wrote a work, *De Metris,* in the 3rd century, incorporated into the *Ars Grammatica* of Marius Victorinus ca. 400.

Apicius: Famous gourmet under Augustus and Tiberius. A book on cookery *De Re Coquinaria* under his name was compiled much later.

"Apicius" de Re Coquinaria: A culinary compilation of the late Empire, falsely ascribed to Apicius (q.v.).

Apocalypse of Golias: Famous goliardic poem of the twelfth (or thirteenth?) century, variously assigned to Alan of Lille, Walter of Châtillon, and Hugh Primas (qq.v.). In the form of a vision, the poem is full of mordant satire against the clergy. (See Goliardic verse, etc.)

Apocolocyntosis Divi Claudii: "Pumpkinification of Claudius." A venomous and witty satire on the Emperor Claudius, written shortly after his death, by Seneca (2). In form it is a Menippean Satire (q.v.) with alternating prose and verse. It purports to tell what took place in Hell when Claudius died.

Hercules is sent to interview the uncouth, limping stranger who keeps mumbling unintelligibly. The final verdict is: Claudius is doomed to throw dice perpetually in a box without a bottom, a decision worthy of the Mikado! There has been some dispute as to Seneca's authorship, but it is now generally conceded.

Apollinaris (1): Literary critic of the Flavian period.

Apollinaris (1) Sidonius: See Sidonius Apollinaris.

Apollo: The only god in the Roman pantheon that was taken directly over from the Greek, rather than being identified with an Italian deity (cf. Jupiter, Venus, etc.). He is the god of music, light and healing. He appears as the sun god (not in Greek Mythology) through an identification or confusion with Helios.

Apollodoreans: Roman school of rhetoric, taking its name from Apollodorus (q.v.) the teacher of Augustus. The school stressed *narratio,* or the statement of the case. Quintilian belonged to this school.

Apollodorus of Pergamum: 104-22 B.C. Rhetor, teacher of the emperor Augustus. His work on rhetoric was translated into Latin by Valgius Rufus (q.v.).

Apologeticum: A fervent indictment of paganism by Tertullian (q.v.).

Apologia: (*Pro se de Magia*) Speech by Apuleius (q.v.)—his defence when he was accused of having won the love of one Prudentilla by the use of magic. Chiefly interesting for the light it throws on ancient superstitions.

Apologists: (Christian) Early defenders of Christianity against the attacks to which it was subjected. See Tertullian, Arnobius, Cyprian, Minucius Felix, and Lactantius.

Apophoreta: Little poems by Martial that were distributed to guests at a party along with the "party-favors." See Xenia.

Apophthegmata: Collection of witty sayings by Caesar (now lost). (Also called *Dicta Collectanea*)

Apotheosis: Poem by Prudentius (q.v.) on the incarnation and resurrection of Christ.

Appendix Virgiliana: Series of minor poems which have

all been, at some time or other, attributed to Virgil and incorporated with his works. The problem of their authorship is still undecided. The poems include: *Culex, Dirae, Copa, Ciris, Priapea, Lydia, Moretum, Aetna, Epigrammata* and/or *Catalepton*. There is a strong probability that some of these are Virgilian (e.g. Culex, Ciris, Catalepton, and others). See under the individual poems.

Appius Claudius Caecus: (cos. 307, 297 B.C.) One of the first of the Roman orators, a man of great vigor and integrity, he left his imprint on law, finance, engineering (the Appian Way), grammar, and poetry. Priscian (q.v.) quotes some lines of his poetry.

Apto Genere Scribendi, de: See Marbod of Rennes.

Apuleius, Lucius: fl. 150. African rhetor and novelist. Author of *Metamorphoses* or the *Golden Ass* (q.v.), one of the two novels that we have in the Latin language. Based on Greek tales, the work has a strange Latinity (see *elocutio novella*). The charming story of *Cupid and Psyche* is from the Metamorphoses. Other works by Apuleius: *Apologia* (q.v.), *Florida* (excerpts from declamations—some of them very good), *De Dogmata Platonis, De Mundo, De Deo Socratis,* translations from Plato, Menander, and (lost) works on agriculture, fish, natural science, trees, arithmetic, astronomy, arboriculture, political science, etc. He is, of course, most famous for his novel, the *Metamorphoses*, which alone is sufficient to grant his immortality as a Latin writer. (OCD)

Aquae Caldae: There were two plays of this title, both lost. One was a *togata* by T. Quintius Atta, the other a mime by Laberius (qq.v.).

Aquila Romanus: Rhetorician of the 3rd Century A.D., author of a work *De Figuris Sententiarum et Elocutionis,* based partly on Greek works, partly on Cicero, whom he often quotes and misquotes.

Aquilius (1): An early Roman comic poet. Wrote a comedy called *Boeotia.*

Aquilius Gallus (2): Jurist, pupil of the great Scaevola (q.v.).

Aquinas, Thomas: See Thomas Aquinas.

Aquis Urbis Romae, de: Treatise on aqueducts by Frontinus (q.v.). An interesting work, which, perhaps, belongs rather to the fields of archaeology and engineering than to literature. It is full of pride in Rome, and contains a great deal of useful information about the capacity, elevation, etc., of the aqueducts.

Aratea: Translations of the *Phaenomena* of Aratus by (1) Cicero, (2) Varro of Atax, (3) Germanicus, (4) Avienus.

Arator: Christian poet of the 6th century, pupil of Ennodius (q.v.). Wrote an epic *Acts of the Apostles* on the deeds of Peter and Paul—a work full of allegory and mysticism which delighted medieval readers, though it is generally held to be a rather inferior poem. (Duckett)

Aratus: Author of a Greek didactic poem on astronomy, *Phaenomena,* which was translated into Latin by Varro of Atax, Cicero, Germanicus and Avienus.

Arbiter, Petronius: See Petronius.

Arboribus, de: See Columella, Apuleius.

Archaizing period: In the second century there was a conscious attempt to return to classical diction. Best examples of the school are Fronto, Gellius, and Apuleius (qq.v.).

Archetype: See Textual Criticism.

Archia, pro: Cicero's famous speech in defense of the Greek poet Archias, whose citizenship was at stake. Transcending the original topic, the speech, one of Cicero's greatest, becomes a glowing eulogy of literature. (Duff, Golden Age)

Archias: Greek poet defended by Cicero. See *Pro Archia.*

Architectura, de: See Vitruvius.

Architrenius: (Chief Mourner) A poem by John of Hanville (late 12th century). It is an allegorical satire, obscure in style, and inferior in construction. The poet satirizes gluttony, sloth, vanity, cupidity, ambition, and the vices of the clergy. (Raby, SLP)

Archpoet: Twelfth century unknown author of secular Latin lyrics. One of the Wandering Scholars. The poems are in turn scurrilous, ribald, hauntingly beautiful, bitterly satiric, and nostalgic. The author tells us that he is a consumptive. He has sometimes been identified with Primas of Orleans, or Primas of Cologne. See Vagantenstrophe, Goliardic verse, Primas, *Carmina Burana*. (Manitius, Waddell, Raby)

Aretino, Leonardo: Humanist and historian of the Italian Renaissance.

Argentarius (1): A Greco-Roman epigrammatist. **2.** An Augustan rhetor. 1 and 2 may be identical.

Argonautica **(1):** Epic by Valerius Flaccus (q.v.). In eight books, the author tells the story of Jason and Medea, of the Argo and the Golden Fleece, one of the most romantic and popular of all Greek myths. The tale is too well known to need retelling. Some of the finer portions deal with the abduction of Hylas, the actual taking of the Fleece, the love of Jason and Medea, etc. The work breaks off and it is not known how it was to have ended. Perhaps with the revenge of Medea, perhaps with the death of Jason. It shows echoes of Homer, Virgil, Ovid, Lucan and Seneca. Despite certain imperfections, it is one of the best of the post-Virgilian epics.

Argonautica **(2):** Greek epic by Apollonius of Rhodes, translated into Latin by Varro of Atax (q.v.), it influenced Valerius Flaccus.

Argument: A summary or synopsis of the plot of a play. Used for the acrostic summaries of Plautus (q.v.).

Argumentum ex silentio: Literally, Argument from silence. A proof by the fact that something is not mentioned. E.g. The *Aetna* (q.v.) must have been composed before 79 A.D. because the eruption of Vesuvius is not mentioned (as it certainly would have been, had it occurred before the time of writing). Another example is the (inferred) mutual dislike of Martial and Statius, because neither mentions the other. One is also reminded of Doyle's "curious incident of the dog in the night-time." ("But the dog did nothing in the night-time." "That is the curious incident.")

Aristaeus: "Epyllion" (q.v.) by Virgil. Occurs in the Fourth

Book of the Georgics. In the story, Aristaeus offends the nymphs by pursuing Eurydice, and they in revenge destroy his bees. He goes to Proteus for advice. Cyrene, his mother, tells him to sacrifice cattle to the nymphs, which he does, and after nine days, he finds bees in the carcasses. The story is unknown except in Virgil.

Aristotle: Greek philosopher. Translated into Latin by Boethius, Aristotle became the basis of most of the medieval philosophy and theology. See Scholasticism, Thomas Aquinas, etc. He was known as *"The* Philosopher" in medieval times.

Armorum Iudicium: ("The Judgment of Arms") This story, dealing with the death of Ajax, was a popular subject for plays. Tragedies of this title were written by Accius and Pacuvius, and it was burlesqued by Pomponius (qq.v.).

Arnobius of Sicca (1): Christian rhetor and apologist (fl. ca. 300). In his *Adversus Nationes* (q.v.) he refutes the charge that the evils of the world have been caused by Christianity. (Rand, Labriolle)

Arnobius the Younger (2): ca. 450. Author of commentaries on the Psalms and other exegetical works; not to be confused with the Apologist (Arnobius 1).

Arnold of St. Emmeram: Wrote homilies, poetry, hymns, antiphons and responses, as well as an account of the miracles of St. Emmeram, a *Dialogus de memoria b. Emmerammi.* The literary value of the works is slight, but the historical worth considerable. (Manitius)

Arnulf (1): Cistercian monk of the 13th century. Abbot of Villers-en-Brabant. Wrote a hymn (*De Passione Domini*) of devotion to the wounds of Christ.

Arnulf (2): ca. 1050. French monk, composed *Delicie Cleri,* a collection of poems, consisting chiefly of proverbial lore, from the Bible, the *Disticha Catonis* (q.v.), etc.

Arnulf (3): Bishop of Lisieux 1141. Wrote lyric poetry, and a satire, *ad Lascivos Sodales.*

Arnulf of Mailand (4): Wrote (middle of the 11th century) a history of the bishopric of Mailand. The style is Biblical. (Manitius)

Arnulfus Rufus: Teacher of the 12th century. Lectured at Orleans on Ovid's *Fasti*.

Arria (1): Arria Major, wife of Caecina Paetus. When her husband was condemned to death by Claudius, she stabbed herself and gave the dagger to him, saying "Paete, non dolet" ("It doesn't hurt, Paetus").

(2) Arria Minor, daughter of the above. Wife of Thrasea Paetus, she was forbidden to die beside her condemned husband. Was a friend of Pliny the Younger.

Arruntius, L. (1): Historian of the Augustan period. He wrote a work (now lost) on the Punic Wars, in the Sallustian manner.

Arruntius Celsus (2): Grammarian of the 2nd century. Wrote commentaries on Terence and Virgil.

Arruntius (3) Stella: See Stella.

Ars: Art, or Study. In the singular, appears in titles of various types of handbooks (e.g. Ars Dictaminis, Ars Grammatica, etc.). In the plural (Artes) means the "Liberal Arts."

Ars Amatoria: "Art of Love" by Ovid (q.v.). The "carmen" which was perhaps instrumental in causing Ovid's exile in 8 A.D. An amazing collection of practical hints (e.g. how to instigate jealousy, never ask a woman's age, cosmetics, etc.) and flippancy, sensuousness and lovely poetry. In elegiac couplets, it consists of two books of instructions for men and one for women.

Ars de Nomine et Verbo: See Phocas.

Ars Dictaminis: Compilations of Latin law, literature, etc., a sort of correspondence business-course of the Middle Ages, designed to turn out The Compleat Secretary. Contained forms for all sorts of letters, business, dunning, requests, etc. See Alberic of Monte Cassino, Bernard of Meung, Buoncompagno. (Curtius)

Ars Grammatica: Title of numerous textbooks on grammar. See Victorinus, Aphthonius, Charisius, Cledonius, Cominianus, Dositheus, Diomedes, Palaemon, etc.

Ars Lectoria: See Aimeric.

Ars Metrica: See Atilius Fortunatianus.

Ars Poetica: Traditional title for Horace's *Epistula ad Pisones*. It should be remembered that Horace did not call it an *Ars Poetica*. Too often, it is criticized as if he had. It is a somewhat unsystematic treatment of poetry, drama, in short, of all literature. Had tremendous influence, especially in the 17th and 18th centuries. The *locus classicus* for such concepts as the *deus ex machina*, division into five acts, chorus, etc. Horace seems to have been trying deliberately to revive the almost-defunct Roman drama. Title "Ars Poetica" originates with Quintilian. Many of the stock phrases about drama and literature originate in this work: the purple patch (purpureus pannus), the plunging directly into a narrative (in medias res), the "polishing with a file" (limae labor), the "bathos born of bombast" (parturiunt montes, nascetur ridiculus mus), and the function of good literature, to mix that which is pleasant with that which is useful (omne tulit punctum qui miscuit utile dulci). These, and other stock elements of literary criticism, are to be found in the Ars Poetica, which deals with artistic unity, vocabulary, style, the uselessness of mediocrity and the necessity for painstaking work, and other subjects. (OCD, Duff, Golden Age)

"Ars Poetica" of St. Omer: A didactic poem on the Art of Poetry, by an unknown monk of the monastery of St. Omer.

Ars Versificatoria: Twelfth century work on poetry by Matthew of Vendôme (q.v.). See also *Laborintus*.

Arte Musica, de: See St. Augustine.

Artes Liberales: The Liberal Arts of the late classical and medieval periods. Studies worthy of a free man, hence "liberales." Consisted of the *trivium* (q.v.) i.e. Grammar, Rhetoric, Logic, and the *quadruvium* or *quadrivium* (q.v.), comprising Music, Arithmetic, Geometry, and Astronomy. To these seven, Varro in his *Disciplinae* added Medicine and Architecture. These *artes* were the basis of all education in the Middle Ages. (See Education, Nicolas de Orbellis)

Arulenus Rusticus: Stoic philosopher. Wrote a panegyric

on Thrasea and Helvidius Priscus which cost him his life (ca. 93 A.D.).

Arundel Collection: One of the collections of medieval Latin lyrics. (Cf. Carmina Burana, Cambridge Songs.) For best treatment of these lyrics, see Waddell and Raby, SLP. This collection contains religious as well as secular pieces and was made before 1250, perhaps in the latter part of the twelfth century.

Arusianus Messius: 4th century grammarian who compiled an alphabetical list of nouns, verbs, adjectives, prepositions, entitled *exempla elocutionum.* Valuable for its quotations from the *Historiae* of Sallust (q.v.).

Ascanius: In Roman mythology, the son of Aeneas (q.v.) and Creusa, a Trojan princess. Accompanies his father from the burning Troy and shares his adventures. Virgil changes his name to Iulus, to provide a plausible divine genealogy for the Julian gens, hence for Augustus. See *Aeneid.*

Asclepius: 1. (Aesculapius) Greek God of medicine.

2. Treatise handed down among the works of Apuleius (q.v.), but almost certainly not by him.

Asconius Pedianus, Q.: Great scholar of the Neronian Age. His works (lost) include a *Life of Sallust,* a *Symposium* in imitation of Plato's, a *Contra Obtrectatores Vergilii,* commentaries on Cicero's orations. A fifth century commentary on the Verrine orations included with his works will be found under Pseudo-Asconius (q.v.).

Asellio, Sempronius: Officer under the younger Scipio, wrote a history of his times whose most notable feature is that it was *not* composed along annalistic lines, but in the tradition of Thucydides and Polybius. Said that there was a difference between writing history and telling stories for children. (This famous fragment is preserved by Gellius.)

Asianism: Extremely flowery style of oratory. Most famous practitioner was Cicero's rival Hortensius (q.v.). The opposing school was called Attic or Atticist. Cicero's own style was a blend of the two. See Rhetoric and Oratory.

Asinaria: Comedy by Plautus. Not among his greatest

plays. Deals with a fake steward and how he got paid for his donkeys. See Plautus.

Asmonius: 5th century author of works on grammar and meter who was used by Priscian (q.v.). His works are now lost.

Asper, Aemilius: Learned grammarian of the 2nd century. Wrote commentaries on Sallust, Terence, and Virgil. Included many parallels from Greek and Roman authors. Used by Donatus (q.v.).

Aspiratione, de: Work on aspiration falsely ascribed to Phocas (q.v.).

Asser, Bishop of Sherborne: Wrote *Gesta* or *Res Gestae Alfredi Regis* (Deeds of Alfred the Great).

Assonance: A general term for similarity of sounds in prose or poetry though usually reserved for similarity of vowel sounds, includes:

1. Alliteration, a favorite device from Ennius onwards (see the line quoted under Ennius).

2. Homoeoteleuton, or similarity of *endings* in successive words.

3. Rhyme (q.v.) may be subdivided into conscious and unconscious. Sedulius and Fortunatus were among the first to use conscious rhyme as a poetical device. It became popular in the Middle Ages, and was used internally (leonine verses) as well as at the end of lines.

Astris, de: Lost work on astronomy by Julius Caesar (q.v.).

Astrologia, de: Work by Hyginus (2) q.v.

Astronomica: Didactic poem on astronomy and astrology by Manilius (q.v.). See also didactic poetry.

Atacinus: See Varro (2) of Atax.

Atalanta: The fleet-footed maiden of Greek mythology, who lost a famous race to her suitor Hippomenes because she stooped to pick up the golden apples which he threw. Title of two works. 1. An Atellan farce. 2. A tragedy by Pacuvius (q.v.).

Ateius Praetextatus "Philologus": Scholar, friend of Sallust and Pollio. A tremendously prolific writer, he claimed to have written 800 books. Among the titles that we possess are a *Breviarium Rerum Romanorum,* a *Liber Glossematorum* and a work entitled *An amaverit Didun Aeneas?* (Did Aeneas love Dido?)

Atellan farce: See Fabula Atellana.

Athenaeum: School established at Rome by the emperor Hadrian. See Education.

Atilius, M. (1): An early writer of *comoediae palliatae* (see Fabula Palliata). Very few fragments remain. Perhaps identical with an Atilius mentioned by Cicero who translated the *Electra* of Sophocles into Latin. Had a reputation for harshness, and for stirring the emotions. (OCD)

Atilius Fortunatianus (2): 4th century author of an *Ars Metrica* dealing with general principles of meter, and with the meters of Horace. Depends on earlier writers on the subject, e.g., Caesius Bassus.

Atratinus: One of the ablest orators of the Augustan Age.

Atreus: Three tragedies of this title, by (1) Accius, (2) Mamercus Scaurus, (3) Rubrenus Lappa. See under these authors.

Atrius: Minor prose author, contemporary with Pliny the Younger.

Atta, T. Quintius: 77 B.C. Writer of *Togatae,* or native Italian comedies. Roscius (q.v.) was very successful in his plays. Atta was especially adept in the portrayal of female characters.

Attic Nights: See Gellius, Aulus.

Atticism: (in oratory) A dry, unadorned style, the opposite of the florid Asian style of rhetoric. Cicero, although he claimed to be "Attic" in his oratory, was in reality an eclectic, combining the two styles, in the Rhodian manner. Calidius was an "Atticist," as were Caesar and Brutus.

Atticus, Julius: See Julius Atticus.

Atticus, T. Pomponius: Friend of Cicero, famous for the correspondence preserved in the *Ad Atticum* letters. One of the wealthiest men in Rome. He had a publishing and copying firm. His writings, on chronology, etc., are lost.

Atticus: Biography of above by Cornelius Nepos (q.v.).

Attis: See Catullus.

Attius: See Accius.

Atto of Vercelli: b. ca. 885. Bishop of Vercelli, author of many varied works, including letters, sermons, *de Pressuris Ecclesiasticis,* commentaries on the New Testament, and a work entitled *Polipticum,* of a political or historical nature. The latter is an extremely difficult work to understand, because of the crabbed and obscure style, strange word-order, and unusual vocabulary. Characterized by Manitius as "of a crazy and perverse artificiality." In general, the *Polipticum* is a complaint against the foreign domination of Italy, by an Italian patriot. (Manitius)

Auctor ad Herennium: See Rhetorica ad Herennium.

Auctores: Authors, i.e., Curriculum authors (q.v.), hence, authorities on any given field in the Middle Ages. These "auctores" might be medieval or ancient, pagan or Christian. Mostly the term is used of technical authorities, e.g., on medicine, horticulture, grammar, history, etc. Sometimes also used of fields such as philosophy and ethics. (Curtius)

Aucupio, de: Fragments on bird-catching, ascribed to Nemesianus (q.v.).

Aufidius Bassus (1): Historian under Tiberius, he wrote on the wars with the Germans. His work was continued by Pliny the Elder, hence the title "A Fine Aufidi Bassi."

Aufidius Chius (2): Writer on jurisprudence, at the time of Domitian. Mentioned by Martial.

Aufidius, Modestus (3): 1st century commentator on Virgil and Horace.

Augmentis Scientiarum, de: See Bacon, Francis.

Auguriis, de: Work on auguries, now lost, by Cicero (q.v.).

Augurinus, Sentius (or Serius): A friend of Pliny the Younger, author of poems (poemata) quoted and praised by Pliny. Imitated Calvus and Catullus, with a mixture of tenderness and satire.

Augustan Age: The great flowering of literary genius that arose under the patronage and sympathy of the emperor

Augustus. To it belong such figures as Virgil, Horace, Ovid, Propertius and Tibullus, Pollio and Livy (qq.v.). Also called the Golden Age, though this term more properly includes the age of Cicero.

Augustan History: See Historia Augusta.

Augustine, (1) St. of Hippo: (Aurelius Augustinus) 354-430. The greatest of the Church Fathers, preacher and writer, who exerted more influence on Christian thought than perhaps any other. Born in Numidia in 354 of a pagan father and Christian mother, he was proficient in Greek and Latin. Became a member of the Manichean sect. Went to Rome in 383, and had a professorship in rhetoric at Milan, 384. Due to the influence of Ambrose (q.v.) he was converted to Christianity in 386, and received holy orders in 391, at Hippo in Africa, where he subsequently became bishop. The remainder of his life was devoted to his preaching and his writing. He died in 430. His works are exceedingly numerous. They include the *Confessions* (describing his conversion), the *Retractiones* (a review of his writings to 427 and a correction of the errors in them), the *De Doctrina Christiana, De Catechizandis Rudibus* (a manual of Christian education), *De Trinitate* (on the Trinity), *De Consensu Evangelistarum,* and the great *De Civitate Dei,* in which he shows that the destruction of Rome is due to the pagan, not the Christian influence, and that God's City alone is eternal (this has been called the death-blow to ancient paganism); other works: *De Beata Vita, De Quantitate Animae, Contra Academicos, De Arte Musica, Enarrationes in Psalmos,* 125 sermons on the fourth Gospel, 500 miscellaneous sermons and 300 epistles. He is also important for revisions of the text of the Bible, in which respect he is second only to Jerome (q.v.). Much of his writing and thought shows Neo-Platonic influence. He is one of the most important links between antiquity and the Middle Ages—between Virgil and Dante. More than perhaps any other, Augustine helped to turn the Roman Empire into the Holy Roman Empire. He developed a comprehensive philosophy of Christianity, original sin, predestination, etc., and may be said truly to be one of the Founders of the Middle Ages. (Rand, Labriolle, OCD, Ferm-Encyclopedia of Religion)

Augustine (2), St. of Canterbury: The emissary of Pope Gregory the Great (q.v.), he arrived in England in 597, and was responsible for the conversion of the inhabitants of that island to Christianity. He died in 604.

Augustus: (C. Iulius Caesar Octavianus) Roman emperor (more properly Princeps), important as patron of arts and letters (see Augustan Age). For the account of his own deeds, see *Monumentum Ancyranum* and *Index Rerum Gestarum*.

Aulularia (1): One of the best comedies of Plautus (q.v.). It tells of the miser Euclio, who, for all the exaggeration in the depiction of his character, deserves to rank with Shakespeare's Shylock, Molière's Harpagon and Jonson's Volpone as one of the great misers in literature. The plot develops as he keeps digging up his pot of gold to avoid discovery, in an ever-increasing frenzy of grief and apprehension, wreaking vengeance upon a rooster who digs too near his treasure. It is a comedy of character, as well as of plot. (Duff, Golden Age)

Aulularia (2): Title of a lost mime (fabula riciniata) by Laberius (q.v.).

Aulularia (3): A medieval "comoedia" by Vitalis of Blois (q.v.).

Aulus Gellius: See Gellius, Aulus.

Aurelian of Moutier-St.-Jean: 9th century author of the *Musica Disciplina*.

Aurelius (1), Marcus: Roman emperor and Stoic philosopher. His famous "Meditations" were written in Greek.

Aurelius (2) Opilius: Author of a Plautine index, perhaps author of the acrostic summaries or *argumenta*.

Aurelius Victor (3): 4th century author of *Liber de Caesaribus*, treating the lives of the emperors from Augustus to Constantine, in a fashion not unlike that of Sallust. Also included in his works, but not by him, are an *Origo Gentis Romanae* (q.v.), and a *De Viris Illustribus*.

Aurora: Allegorical Biblical poem by Peter Riga, written ca. 1200. See *Laborintus* for its inclusion in medieval curriculum lists. Full of mannered affectation. One passage of 23 lines is in the "lipogrammatic" manner, i.e., in the first line the letter "a" does not appear, in the second, the letter "b", and so on.

Ausonius, Decimus Magnus: Gallic-Roman poet, fl. ca. 350 A.D. One of the greatest poets of the later period. He was a professor of grammar and rhetoric at Bordeaux. Called by emperor Valentinian to be the tutor of his son Gratian. A friend of Paulinus of Nola (q.v.), he could never understand why his friend "deserted Apollo for Christ." Works: *Mosella*, a long and rather charming poem about the river Moselle, describing the fish, vineyards, buildings, to be seen in and around that river; the *Ephemeris* or Diary, including many poems in many meters, the *Parentalia, Ordo Nobilium Urbium, Technopaegnion* and *Logodaedalia, Idylls, Eclogues,* etc. Important for the history of education is the *Commemoratio Professorum Burdigalensium. The Cento Nuptialis* (see Cento) is interesting for its ingenuity. (OCD)

Auspicius of Toul: 5th century poet, Bishop of Toul. Wrote poetry interesting for the metrical patterns. Rhyme is only occasional, but the strophe pattern is like that of the Ambrosian hymns.

Autobiography: (Memoirs) Usually by political figures, wholly or partly in justification of their actions. Among the names of those who wrote memoirs, mention should be made of the following (qq.v.): C. Gracchus, Rutilius Rufus, Sulla, Catulus, Varro, Cicero (who wrote prose and poetical accounts of his own consulship), Caesar, Augustus, Tiberius, Claudius, Agrippa, Agrippina the Younger, Hadrian, St. Augustine, and Guibert de Nogent.

Avancini, Nicolaus von: 1612-86. Austrian-Latin poet and dramatist. 27 of his plays are preserved.

Ave Maria: (Hail Mary) A popular devotion like the Credo and Pater Noster (Lord's Prayer). Composed in the 6th century.

Averroes: (Mohammed Ibn Roshd) Arabian scholar and

commentator on Aristotle in the 12th century. Known as "The Commentator." One of the chief sources of medieval Aristotelianism. There was a controversy between the Thomists and the Averroists. (Runes, Dictionary of Philosophy)

Averroists: Philosophic followers of Averroes (q.v.). They maintained the eternity of the material world. See Siger of Brabant.

Avianus, Flavius: Author of 42 fables of the Aesopean type, ca. 400. His fables are based on those of the Greek Babirius. Much imitation of Virgil and Ovid. Style is not very pure. His fables are dedicated to Macrobius (q.v.). See Fable.

Avicenna: (Ibn Sina) Persian-Arabian scholar. Wrote a comprehensive encyclopedia in 18 volumes. His philosophy is mainly Aristotelian, and he was, in fact, called "the Third Aristotle." Translated into Latin by Gundissalinus. Albert the Great and Aquinas both greatly admired Avicenna. (Runes, Dictionary of Philosophy)

Avienus, Festus Ruf(i)us: Latin writer of the 4th century. Made a poetical version of Aratus' *Phaenomena* (see Aratea). Also wrote a *Descriptio Orbis Terrae,* an *Ora Maritima* and various shorter works. In the Middle Ages, he was regarded as an authority on geography and astronomy.

Avitus, Alcimus Ecdicius: Christian-Latin poet of the 5th-6th centuries. Wrote an epic on the creation of man, *De Spiritalis Historiae Gestis,* Miltonian in character, full of allegory and tragic declamation. Also wrote a poem on chastity (*De Laude Virginitatis*), and numerous letters and sermons. He was Bishop of Vienne.

Axamenta: Litanies chanted by the Salian priests, in Saturnians. Some of the most ancient Latin belongs to this category. See Carmina Saliaria.

Aymon: Monk of Fleury, ca. 1000, wrote poems about angels who guided St. Benedict, and about three crows.

Aynard of St. Èvre: Monk and grammarian of the mid-10th century. Wrote a *Glossarium Ordine.*

Azo: Late 12th century author of a *Summa* on law.

Babio: English "comoedia" or versified tale of the 12th century.

Bacchides: A comedy by Plautus (q.v.). The plot deals with love and chicanery. Two amusing characters are the wily slave Chrysalus and the old pedagogue Lydus, who is perpetually bemoaning the demise of the older type of Roman education. The central point of the plot is the means used by the youth to get necessary 200 minae. He pretends he has been captured and demands the ransom from his own father.

Bacchus: Another name for the Greek god Dionysus, the god of fertility and wine. Also known to the Romans as Liber.

Bacon, Francis: 1561-1626. English scientist and philosopher, author of *Novum Organum* (the title taken from Aristotle's *Organon*), an extremely important work for the development of logic and the scientific method. Also wrote *De Augmentis Scientiarum* in Latin.

Bacon, Roger: 1214?-94. English Franciscan friar, scholar, philosopher and scientist. Studied at Oxford under Grosseteste (q.v.). An excellent experimental as well as theoretical scientist, he constructed instruments of all sorts. Studied optics, astronomy, geometry, chemistry and alchemy, and mechanics. One of the earliest exponents of the scientific method, he knew the importance of the experimental verification of hypotheses. Wrote a work, *Maius Opus,* an encyclopedia of the sciences of his day. Attacked Albert the Great and Aquinas (qq.v.).

Baebius Italicus: See *Ilias Latina.*

Baebius Massa: Orator and *delator* (informer) mentioned by Pliny the Younger.

Baeda: See Bede.

Baehrens, E.: German scholar, edited the *Poetae Latini Minores* and the *Fragmenta Poetarum Latinorum.*

Balbillus, Tiberius Claudius: Minor historian of the Neronian period. Wrote on Egypt.

Balbín, Bohuslav: 1621-88. Czech Jesuit, wrote poetry and history (*Epitome Rerum Bohemicarum*) in Latin.

Balbo, pro: Speech by Cicero (q.v.).

Balbulus, Notker: See Notker Balbulus.

Balbus (1) Cornelius: Wrote a praetexta (*Iter*) about Caesar. It has not survived.

Balbus (2): Writer (ca. 100 A.D.) on gromatics (q.v.) and geometry.

Balde, Jakob: 1604-68. German-Latin poet, called "the German Horace." Wrote *Silvae, Lyrica,* plays (*Jephthias*), epic, satires, and religious poetry.

Balderic of Liége: Bishop of Liége 1008-1018. His biography, written about 1050, by an unknown monk, throws considerable light on the political position of the bisphoprics of that day. (Manitius)

Balderich: 12th century German author of a life of Albero, Archbishop of Trier, which was later versified by an unknown author.

Baldus: An epic parody (1517). See "Macaronic epic."

Balneis Puteolanis, de: Famous poem on the Baths of Pozzuoli by Peter of Eboli (q.v.).

Balzac, Guez de: See Forgeries.

Bangor Antiphonary: Famous Irish collection of hymns.

Banquet of Trimalchio: See *Cena Trimalchionis, Satyricon.*

Baptismo, de: Work by Tertullian (q.v.).

Barbarismis et Metaplasmis, de: Grammatical work by Consentius (q.v.).

Barbaro, Francesco: 1390-1454. Italian humanist. Author of *De Re Uxoria.*

Barclay, John: 1582-1621. English writer of a Latin romance *Argenis,* satires, and other Neo-Latin works.

Bardo of Mainz: Biographies of this archbishop were written by (1) Vulculd, (2) an unknown monk of Fulda.

Baronius, Caesar: 16th century ecclesiastical historian, author of *Annales Ecclesiastici.*

Barthélemy, Nicolas: 1478-1540. French humanist and Neo-Latin poet. Friend of Erasmus and Budé; author of epigrams and a religious tragedy *Christus Xylonicus.*

Bartholomaeus Anglicus: 13th century English encyclopedist. Wrote an encyclopedia on natural history (*De Proprietatibus Rerum*).

Basle Collection: MS D iv 4 of the University of Basle—collection of Latin poems varying in nature from the satirical *O mores perditos* to the debate of Ganymede and Helen and love poems. Some of the poems are in the Goliardic meter, some in leonine verses. (Raby, SLP)

Bassus (1), Aufidius: See Aufidius Bassus.

Bassus (2): An iambic poet of the Augustan Age, friend of Ovid.

Bassus (3), Caesius: 1. Author of a metrical work *De Metris*.

2. Lyric poet, friend and editor of Persius, highly praised by Quintilian. It is quite likely that (1) and (2) are identical.

Bassus (4), Saleius: See Saleius Bassus.

Baucis et Thraso: Anonymous English "Comoedia" or versified tale written in the second half of the 12th century. Has some of the stock figures of Plautine comedy, such as Thraso, the soldier.

Baudri de Bourgeuil: 1046-1130. Abbot of monastery of Bourgeuil, archbishop of Dol in Brittany. Author of some rather fine poetry, showing a great sensitivity to nature. He imitates Ovid, his favorite poet. Wrote many poetical letters, and (in prose) the history of Jerusalem, a work on the sword and shield of Michael, etc. One of the most attractive figures of his time for his humanity and his humanism. (Waddell, Raby, SLP)

Bavius: Poetaster of the Augustan Age. Like Mevius, he was an enemy of Virgil which is ironical, as this is his only claim to fame.

Beatus Rhenanus: (Bild aus Rheinau) 16th century Alsatian humanist, author of *Rerum Germanicarum Libri III*.

Beaufort, Louis de: 18th century French scholar and historian. One of the first to challenge the unquestioning acceptance of the early legends.

Bebel, Heinrich: 1472-1518. German humanist. Made a collection of German proverbs which he translated into Latin; *Facetiae;* etc.

Bebo of Bamberg: 11th century. Author of various poetry, and of a long letter to Henry II.

Becket, Thomas a: See Thomas a Becket.

Bede, the Venerable: (Baeda) 673-735. Saxon monk who spent his entire life at the double monastery of Wearmouth and Jarrow. His most important work is his *Ecclesiastical History of the English People,* a fascinating amalgam of history, tradition and legend, one of the chief source books for the history of the English Church. Bede wrote an astonishingly pure Latin, and was highly esteemed both for his piety and for his learning. His works fall into three categories: scientific, historical, and theological. In the first category may be cited *De Natura Rerum, De Temporibus, De Temporum Ratione*; his main historical work has already been mentioned; in addition he wrote many treatises and commentaries on the books of the Old and New Testament.

Bella Parisiacae Urbis: Historical epic by Abbo of St. Germain (q.v.).

Bellarmine, Robert (St.): 1542-1621. Italian Jesuit, Archbishop of Capua, and Cardinal. Wrote *De Controversiis Christianae Fidei* on the Protestant position.

Bello Aegyptiaco, carmen de: See Rabirius.

Bello Civili, de: Caesar's account of his wars with Pompey. Noted for its restraint, the work contains no account of the crossing of the Rubicon, etc. (This may be found in other authors, e.g., Lucan, Plutarch, Suetonius.)

Bello Civili, de: (Lucan) See Pharsalia.

Bello Gallico, de: Account by Caesar (q.v.) of his campaigns in Gaul. In seven books. Both a public record and a personal apologia, the *Commentaries* are written in a clear, lucid style. Caesar nearly always refers to himself in the third person. One of the greatest military narratives of all literature. Tells of the wars with the Veneti, Helvetii, Germans, the campaign in Britain, with interesting anthropological digressions on the ways of the Britons and Germans. The style is completely free from adornment (see Atticism). There exists an eighth book, not by Caesar himself (see Bellum Gallicum VIII), probably by one of his lieutenants.

Bello Gallico de: Book VIII. A continuation of Caesar's

commentary by one Hirtius, who appears to know more of literary than of military matters.

Bello Troiano, de: Latin epic on the Trojan War by Joseph of Exeter (q.v.) based on the account in Dares Phrygius (q.v.).

Bellona: Roman goddess of war.

Bellorum Germaniae libri XX: (Lost) history of the German Wars by Pliny the Elder, quoted by Tacitus.

Bellum Africum: Account of Caesar's African war (47-46 B.C.). Good military history, though rather monotonous to read. Certainly not by Caesar, probably not by Hirtius either, its authorship is still in dispute. Pollio has been suggested as the author.

Bellum Alexandrinum: Account by an unknown author (Hirtius?) of Caesar's Alexandrian campaign—a continuation of the book on the Civil War. The style is pleasant and straightforward.

Bellum Catilinae: Sallust's vivid account of the Catilinarian conspiracy. Differs from that of Cicero in many respects. Noteworthy for the speeches of Caesar and Cato in the Senate. See Sallust.

Bellum Hispaniense: Badly-written, semi-illiterate account of the Spanish campaign ending with the battle of Munda, and the overthrow of the sons of Pompey.

Bellum Histricum: A lost epic on the war of 129 B.C. by Hostius.

Bellum Jugurthinum: Sallust's narrative of the war with Jugurtha. See Sallust.

Bellum Punicum: Great epic poem by the early Poet Naevius (q.v.). The first Roman epic. Written in Saturnian meter (q.v.). Influenced Ennius and almost certainly Virgil. One unsolved question about the work, of which only scanty fragments remain, is whether Naevius included the Dido episode (see *Aeneid*).

Bellum Sequanicum: Lost epic on Caesar's war with Ariovistus, by Varro (2) of Atax.

Bembo, Pietro: Italian humanist of the Renaissance, wrote Latin poetry.

Benedict (1), St. of Nursia: 480?-547? Founder of Western monasticism and the Rule of Benedict. An extremely important figure in the transmission of culture in medieval Europe.

Benedict (2) of St. Andrea: Middle of 10th century. Author of a chronicle from the birth of Christ to 965, characterized by Manitius as "a monstrosity, both as regards form and content." The work is full of inaccuracies and confusions. (Manitius)

Benedict Biscop (3): 7th century monk and teacher at Wearmouth and Jarrow whose principal claim to renown is that he was the teacher of the Venerable Bede (q.v.).

Benedictus Crispus: Author of a poem on medicine. Perhaps identical with Crispus (q.v.).

Benediktbeuern: Benedictine monastery in upper Bavaria where the MS of the *Carmina Burana* (q.v.) was found.

Beneficiis, de: Seneca's work on benefits and ingratitude. In seven books. Among others, the following topics are treated: the right and wrong methods of conferring benefits; importance of the right attitude in giving; can one prosecute for ingratitude; should one benefit the ungrateful; and others. The work is full of Stoic paradoxes, such as the question whether an unintentional benefit is really a benefit, how one can benefit a wise man who has everything, etc.

Bentley, R.: English classical scholar of the 18th cent. Of the greatest importance for the history of textual criticism (q.v.), he was one of the first to insist on the importance of having sound texts.

Benzo of Alba: Nothing known of his life. Wrote *Libri vii ad Heinricum:* A miscellaneous collection of historical, political, theological and poetical writings, dedicated to Henry IV. Full of vainglory and invective. Quotes Cicero, Sallust, Gellius, Boethius, Persius and the *Disticha Catonis,* as well as the more usual Virgil and Horace. (Manitius)

Berengarius (1) of Tours: ca. 1010-1088. A teacher, scholar and heretic of the 11th century. Had a famous controversy with Lanfranc (q.v.).

Berengarius (2): A disciple of Abelard (q.v.), fl. ca. 1140.

Bernard (1) of Angers: Pupil of Fulbert of Chartres (q.v.). Wrote on the Miracles of St. Fides.

Bernard (2) of Chartres: d. ca. 1126. Teacher and humanist of the school of Chartres, early 12th century. A Platonist in philosophy, Bernard is chiefly remembered as the author of a bit of verse in which he says that the moderns are dwarfs on the shoulders of giants, and thus can see farther.

Bernard (3) of Clairvaux: 1091-1153. Famous abbot and mystic, chiefly remembered as the man who broke Abelard by charging him with heresy. The last guide of Dante in the Divine Comedy. Wrote a famous prayer to the Virgin Mary, and other poetry and hymns. A man of great piety and principles.

Bernard (4) of Cluny: (Bernard of Morlaix) 12th century monk, fl. 1140. Author of *De Contemptu Mundi,* a satirical poem about the wickedness of the world; *Mariale,* a poem in praise of the Virgin Mary, and various hymns and theological treatises.

Bernard (5) of Meung: Second half of the 12th century. Wrote an *Ars Dictaminis,* or letter-writers' handbook.

Bernard (6) Sylvestris of Tours: Humanist of the 12th century (fl. 1140), author of *De Mundi Universitate* (q.v.), one of the most important books of the Middle Ages. Also wrote commentary on Virgil. A Platonist in his philosophy. Wrote a great *summa,* or treatise on prose composition, which was abridged by Bernard of Meung; a commentary on the *Aeneid* and perhaps a prose-verse work on astronomy. (Manitius)

Bernard (7) of Utrecht: Grammarian of the late 11th century. Sometimes confused with the great Bernard Silvestris. Wrote a commentary on Theodulus.

Berner: Monk at St. Remi in Reims. Wrote a *Vita et translatio Hunegundis,* about the middle of the 10th century.

Berno of Reichenau: d. 1008. Writer of works on various subjects: theological (On the Advent, the Mass, Sermons, etc.), biographical (Life of St. Udalric), and musical

(On the Psalms, on tonalities, as well as hymns, tropes, and Sequences).

Bernold: 1054-1110. Wrote a work *De Prohibenda Sacerdotum Incontinentia,* on clerical marriages, *De Damnatione Scismaticorum, De Emtione Ecclesiarum,* on simony, and numerous others dealing with various aspects of the Church-State struggle at the end of the 11th century. (Manitius)

Bernold of St. Blasien: Author of a *Chronicle* (late 11th century), with a completely clerical viewpoint. Also wrote a work *De Divinis Officiis.*

Berter of Orleans: 12th century poet, author of a poem on the Crusades.

Bertha: Nun at Vilich, wrote a biography of the Abbess Adelheid, with an appendix on the miracles performed at her grave.

Berthold (1) of Regensburg: 1220-1272. A Franciscan preacher and missionary.

Berthold (2) of Reichenau: Pupil of Hermann of Reichenau, whose biography he wrote. Also wrote a *Chronicle,* of which only excerpts survive. Nothing is known of his life. (Manitius)

Bèze, Théodore de: 1519-1605. French humanist, theologian; friend of Calvin; numerous religious writings in Latin and French.

Bibaculus, Furius: See Furius Bibaculus.

Biblical epic: A popular form of literature from the 5th and 6th centuries onwards. Biblical themes (Creation, the Gospels, etc.) were treated in the Virgilian manner. Early writers of this genre were Arator (*Acts of the Apostles*), Prudentius (the *Hexaemeron* and *Psychomachia*—the latter being an allegorical epic), Dracontius (*De Laudibus Dei*), and Juvencus (*Evangelorum Libri iv*). Peter Riga, author of *Aurora,* an allegorical Biblican poem; Hildebert of Le Mans, who wrote hexameter poetry on Biblical subjects; Laurence of Durham, and others, are later writers of epic or epic-like poetry on Biblical subjects.

Bibliomancy: The practice, in late antiquity and the Middle

Ages, of consulting a book (e.g., the Bible, Virgil, etc.) at random to get prophetic advice. See *Sortes Virgilianae*.

Bibulus: Minor historian of the Augustan Age who wrote about Brutus.

Bidermann, Jakob: 1578-1639. German Latin dramatist. Wrote tragedies, verse, and a novel *Utopia*.

Biographies of the Abbots of Cluny: Among the most important, the following may be mentioned: biographies of (1) Odo, two versions, (2) Majolus, (3) Odilo, (4) Hugo. Among the authors may be mentioned: Nalgod, Jotsald, Gilo, Hildebert of Lavardin, and Rainald.

Biography: A favorite form of literature from Republican times onward. Countless works were written *De Viris Illustribus* from the earliest times. See Varro, Nepos, Hyginus, the Elder Pliny, Tacitus, Suetonius. Later authors: Sulpicius Severus, Jerome, Einhard, etc. (qq.v.). The medieval lives of saints, kings, popes and bishops are even more numerous, extending into the hundreds or even thousands. See also under *Gesta*, Autobiography.

Biography, medieval: The field of medieval biography is extremely wide, embracing hundreds of *Vitae* of abbots, bishops, popes, counts, kings. Many are without either historical or literary importance. For the important ones, see under the name of the subject (e.g., Charlemagne, Gregory VII, *Gesta Friderici*, etc.).

Biondo, Flavio: 1392-1463. Italian humanist, historian. Author of *Historiarum ab Inclinatione Romanorum Decades*, in 32 books. Also wrote works on the Latin language. Secretary to four popes, and one of the founders of modern historiography.

Birgitta: (or Brigitta) A mystic of the 14th century, who had a number of revelations, chiefly concerning reforms of Church and State. Her writings were published in Lübeck in 1492.

Birk, Sixt: 1500-1554. German dramatist. Wrote plays: *Susanna, Sapientia Salomonis*.

Blandus, Rubellius: Augustan rhetor and teacher of equestrian rank.

Blitho, Sulpicius: (1st cent. B.C.) Early historian who wrote on Hannibal. One of the sources mentioned by Cornelius Nepos (q.v.).

Blondus, Flavius: See Biondo, Flavio.

Bobbio: One of the most famous of Italian monasteries. Located between Milan and Genoa, founded ca. 600 by the Irish monk Columbanus (q.v.).

Boccaccio, Giovanni: One of the most important figures of the Italian Renaissance. In addition to his works in Italian, he wrote in Latin *De Genealogia Deorum Gentilium*.

Bocchus: Roman geographer and historian. Lived under Claudius. Wrote on Spain and on chronology.

Boece, Hector: 1465-1536. Scottish historian. Author of *Scotorum Historia ab Illius Gentis Origine*.

Boeotia: Comedy by the early playwright Aquilius. Varro thought it was by Plautus but this seems most unlikely.

Boethius, Anicius Manlius Severinus: 480-524. Scholar and philosopher. Called "last of Roman authors and the first of the Schoolmen." One of the links between antiquity and the Middle Ages. Imprisoned by Theodoric, he wrote his most important work, the *Consolatio Philosophiae* in prison. Much influenced by the Greek philosophers, particularly Plato's Theory of Ideas. Began the application of Aristotelian logic to problems of Christianity, paving the way for Aquinas. Set himself the task (which his early and violent death rendered impossible) of translating all the works of Plato and Aristotle and reconciling the differences between them. Translated Porphyry's *Isagoge* and Aristotle's *Organon* into Latin, inventing many philosophical terms, as had Cicero and Lucretius before him. Rand (Founders of the Middle Ages) says that but for his untimely death, Boethius would have gone on to do most or all of what Aquinas did. Wrote, in addition to the *Consolatio* (which ranks as one of the great pieces of prison literature), the theological tractates *De Fide Catholica, Contra Eutychen,* and *De Trinitate.* Also wrote on the trivium and quadrivium (qq.v.). His work *De Musica* was still being used as a text at Oxford in the 18th century. In addition he wrote on arithmetic and geometry and translated Euclid. (Rand, OCD)

Boletinus, Paganus: See Paganus Boletinus.

Bolland, Jean: 1596-1665. Dutch Jesuit, editor of *Acta Sanctorum*.

Bonaventure, St.: 1221-1274. Franciscan friar, theologian and philosopher. Chiefly concerned with Aristotelian and Augustinian philosophy.

Bonefons: Renaissance author (16th century) of Latin epigrams.

Bonfini, Antonio: 1427-1505? Italian scholar, historian. Wrote *Rerum Hungaricarum Decades*, speeches, Latin translations of Greek historians, etc.

Boniface (1), St.: 680-755. Anglo-Saxon monk chiefly responsible for the reform of the Frankish Church. Important precursor of the Carolingian Renaissance. Wrote poetry. It was Boniface who destroyed the sacred oak of Thor at Geismar.

Boniface (2), St., Pope: Author of many letters. Another pope of this name (Boniface VIII) is important in connection with the Papal Bull *Unam Sanctam* (q.v.) of 1302.

Bonitho of Sutri: b. ca. 1045. Wrote a *Liber ad Amicum* relating the history of the Church from the earliest times, telling of Constantine, Charlemagne, etc. and culminating with the papacy of Gregory VII and his struggle against simony and clerical marriages. Tells of Henry's humiliation at Canossa, always from the Church's viewpoint. The work has little historical value, because of the partisan position of its author. (Manitius)

Books: The Greek model was chiefly followed in early times, i.e., papyrus rolls. Linen books were also known (see the *libri lintei*). The Latin word Liber (book) implies that bark was used. Many ancient authors mention books (e.g., Martial, Catullus, Propertius, Tibullus, etc.). In late antiquity the change was made from papyrus to codex of vellum. In addition, wax tablets were used as notebooks and there are many references to this also. It is probable that several of these tablets tied together first inspired the idea of the Codex as a book-form. See Libraries.

Bordeaux, University of: One of the earliest centers of learning. See Universities, Ausonius.

Bore, the: (Horace; Sat. I, 9) One of the best-known and wittiest of Horace's Satires (q.v.). It describes the familiar bore (a prototype for this character in literature) fastening himself to the poet; the latter's unsuccessful effort to shake him off. Eventually the bore is hauled off to court and Horace ends: "Thus Apollo saved me." The work is based on a similar one by Lucilius (q.v.).

Borup, Morten: 1446-1526. Danish-Latin poet. Wrote *Carmen Vernale* and other works.

Bourbon, Nicolas: 1. (the Elder) 1505-post 1548. French-Latin poet and humanist; author of *Nugae*.

2. (the Younger) 1574-1644. Also wrote Latin poetry, including the famous *Dirae*, a curse on the murderer of Henry IV.

Bourne, Vincent: 1695-1747. English Latin poet, teacher of Cowper.

Bovo of Corvey: Abbot of Corvey 900-916. Wrote a commentary on Boethius' *Consolatio Philosophiae*, stressing the Christian philosophy.

Bracciolini, Poggio: See Poggio Bracciolini.

Bradwardine, Thomas: First half of 14th century. English theologian and philosopher. Taught at Oxford, wrote *De Causa Dei*. Later became Archbishop of Canterbury.

Brant, Sebastian: 1457/8-1521. German poet and satirist; *Liber Faceti, Carmina Varia*, etc.

Braulio: Bishop of Saragossa. d. 651. Spanish clergyman and poet. Wrote rhymed hymns.

Breakspear, Nicholas: 1100-1159 (Pope Adrian IV). The only Englishman to become a Pope. A monk, scholar and humanist, first at St. Albans, then at St. Denys, then became bishop of Albano. In 1154 he was elevated to the Papal See. Took a firm stand against the encroachment of the temporal powers on the prerogatives of the Church.

brevis brevians: In Latin prosody, the rule that a short syllable may shorten a long one following it if preceded or followed by the accent. Useful for understanding of Plautine meters.

Brevitate Vitae, de: Philosophical essay by Seneca (2) on the brevity of life. One of his best works. It shows how people waste their lives and hoard land and money but spend freely the one thing they should conserve: time. It is necessary for the philosopher to know the proper use of leisure.

Brice, Germain: ante 1500-1538. French scholar and Neo-Latin poet. Most famous work: *Chordigera*, a naval epic. Also wrote *Carmina*.

Broekhuizen, Joan van: 1659-1704. Dutch Neo-Latin poet; edited Propertius and Tibullus.

Bromyarde, John de: fl. 1400. Chancellor of Cambridge University. Wrote sermons.

Browne, Isaac: 1705-1760. English Neo-Latin poet. Author of *De Animi Immortalitate*.

Brülow, Caspar: 1585-1627. German Latin dramatist (*Andromeda, Elias, Gaius Julius Caesar*, etc.).

Brunellus: The name of the donkey in Nigel Wireker's *Speculum Stultorum* (q.v.).

Bruno (1): Saxon clergyman, late 11th century. Wrote a history of the Saxon war (*de bello Saxonico*). Style is rhetorical and owes a great deal to Sallust. (Manitius)

Bruno (2), Giordano: 1548-1600. Renaissance philosopher and poet who was burned at the stake. A firm anti-Aristotelian and pro-Copernican. Some of his works are in Latin (e.g., *de Monade*).

Bruno (3) of Querfurt: Wrote, ca. 1000, a prose life of St. Adalbert, and a *Vita Quinque Fratrum*.

Bruno (4), Bishop of Segni: Wrote many exegetical works, and one *De Symoniacis* (on simony, q.v.) ca. 1100.

Bruno (5) of Wurzburg: d. 1045. Bishop of Wurzburg. Author of a huge commentary on the Psalms and other works of lesser note.

Bruttedius Niger: Rhetor and historian, quoted by Seneca (1). Wrote an account of the death of Cicero.

Brutus, M. Junius: 85-42 B.C. The "tyrannicide." A renowned orator of the Attic school (q.v.) and the inventor of the Latin prose dialogue. He wrote three books *De Iure Civili*, for his son.

Brutus: 1. A tragedy (praetexta) by Accius.

2. A dialogue (also called *De Claris Oratoribus*) by Cicero. Consists of an historical sketch of Greek and Roman eloquence. About 200 Roman orators are named and characterized.

Brynolf, Algotsson: 1250?-1317. Swedish writer of hymns.

Buchanan, George: Scottish scholar of the 17th century. Wrote Latin poetry of considerable merit.

Bucolics: (Virgil) Another name for the *Eclogues* (q.v.). *Bucolica* is given as the name for the whole work, *Eclogue* for the individual poems.

Budaeus: (Budé, Guillaume) 1468-1540. Great French scholar and humanist, important for the history of Classical Scholarship (q.v.).

Buechler: See Anthologia Latina.

Buoncompagno: Italian scholar, professor at Bologna in the first part of the 11th century. Wrote an *Ars Dictaminis* (q.v.) or Letter-Writer's Manual.

Burana, Carmina: See *Carmina Burana*.

Burchard of Worms: Bishop of Worms ca. 1000. Authority on church law. Wrote a *Decretum* (Migne PL CXL) which is one of the most important compilations of canon law before Gratian (q.v.).

Burchard of Worms, Life of: Biography of the famous Bishop of Worms (d. 1025) by an unknown monk of Worms. Important and unimportant features are mixed together, and only a very superficial picture of the bishop is given. Some general history included as a framework. (Manitius)

Buridan, John: 14th century nominalist, student of Ockham (q.v.). To him is attributed the story of "Buridan's Ass" who starved to death because he was unable to choose between two equivalent sources of food. The story, however, is not found in his writings (*Compendium Logicae, Quaestiones in Decem Libros Ethicorum Aristotelis,* etc.). Chiefly interested in the problem of free-will.

Burleigh, Walter (Burlaeus): d. 1343. Author of *De Vita et Moribus Philosophorum.*

Bursian: Compiler of the *Jahresbericht über die Fortschritte der klassischen Altertumswissenschaft,* a monumental work in nearly 300 volumes, giving collections of critical reports on all the main fields of classical studies. Editors after Bursian are: Müller, Kroll, Munscher, Thierfelder, and Reisland.

Bury, J.: 1861-1927. English historian and classical scholar. Edited Valerius Flaccus, wrote an excellent History of Greece and a History of the Roman Empire. Also very proficient in the writing of Greek and Latin verse. (See Neo-Latin)

Byrhtferth: Anglo-Saxon monk of the 10th century. Wrote commentary on Bede's *De Natura Rerum* and *De Temporum Ratione,* an *Enchiridion* or handbook, a *Life of St. Dunstan,* etc.

Caecilius (1) Africanus: 2nd century. Roman jurist, pupil of Salvius Julianus (q.v.). Wrote nine books of *Quaestiones.*

Caecilius (2) of Novum Comum: A friend of Catullus. His poem about Cybele is mentioned in Catullus' poem no. 35.

Caecilius (3) Statius: ca. 219-166 B.C. Early writer of *palliatae* (comedies in Greek dress). Only fragments survive. Seventeen titles are the same as Menander's. The characters are the standard ones of the New Comedy (q.v.). Caecilius was a friend of the poet Ennius.

Caelio, pro: Speech by Cicero. Deals with the notorious Clodia and her allegations of attempted poisoning. Contains some good narrative portions.

Caelius (1) Antipater: See Antipater.

Caelius (2) Rufus: One of the Catilinarians. Lover of Clodia after Catullus (qq.v.). Defended successfully by Cicero (see Caelio, pro) on a poisoning charge. We have several of his letters to Cicero. He was famous for his wit and his invective.

Caelius (3) Sabinus: A noted jurist of the Flavian period, under Vespasian. He belonged to the Sabinian School of jurisprudence (q.v.).

Caepio: Botanist in the first century of the Empire (under Tiberius). Used as a source by Pliny the Elder (q.v.).

Caesar (1), C. Julius: 102-44 B.C. Great Roman statesman, general, and man of letters. The details of his life, his consulship, his conquest of Gaul, his dictatorship and assassination are not of concern here, except as they affect or are affected by his writings. His *Commentaries* (the *De Bello Gallico* and *De Bello Civili*, qq.v.) are familiar to everyone who has studied Latin. They are a marvel of compression, and combine military narrative with political propaganda. A man of great versatility in his writings as well as in his other abilities, Caesar wrote letters, speeches (he was second only to Cicero among orators of the day), a work on grammar (*De Analogia*), one on astronomy (*De Astris*), and various other works, including a tragedy (*Oedipus*), a collection of witticisms, etc. (*Apophthegmata* or *Dicta Collectanea*), *Anticatones*, *Iter*, love-poetry, etc. See under the individual titles. (Duff. Golden Age)

Caesar (2), C. Julius Strabo: See Strabo.

Caesar (3), L. Julius: The consul of 64 B.C. Wrote a work *de Auspiciis*.

Caesarianiae: Three speeches by Cicero characterized by excessive hypocrisy and adulation of Caesar. They are: *Pro Marcello, Pro Ligario,* and *Pro Rege Diotario.*

Caesarinus: Bishop of Arles in 502. A Burgundian clergyman and theologian who wrote on the Trinity, and also a book of rules for monks and nuns.

Caesarius of Heisterbach: ca. 1170-1240. Wrote *Dialogus Miraculorum,* a collection of tales about miracles, visions, monks, etc.

Caesellius Vindex, L.: Roman grammarian, ca. 100 A.D. Wrote an alphabetical collection or miscellany called *Antiquae Lectiones* or *Stromateus.* It has not survived.

Caesius Bassus: See Bassus, Caesius.

Caiado, Henrique: d. 1508? Portuguese Latin poet; author of epigrams, elegies, *Sylvae*, etc.

Calepino, Ambrogio: 1440-1510. Italian humanist and lexicographer. Wrote *Cornucopia*, a Latin dictionary.

Calidius, M.: Roman orator of the 1st century B.C. He led a reaction against the florid Rhodian style of Cicero, favoring the simpler "Attic" styles. See Oratory, Atticism.

Caligula: Roman emperor after Tiberius. His insane jealousy led him to attempt to destroy the works of Homer, and he severely criticized Virgil and Livy. A capable orator. Characterized the younger Seneca's style contemptuously as "sand without mortar."

Callimachus: Alexandrian poet. He had a tremendous influence on the "Cantores Euphorionis" and on Catullus (q.v.). Many of the works produced by this school (e.g., the *Coma Berenices* of Catullus) are in direct imitation of Callimachus, as is Ovid's *Ibis*.

Callimachus and Drusiana: See Hroswitha.

Callistratus: Roman jurist of the third century. Wrote *Institutiones, Quaestiones,* and *De Iure Fisci.* His Latin is full of Grecisms.

Calpurnius (1) Flaccus: 2nd century author of *Declamationes* (q.v.). Excerpts from fifty-three of them have survived.

Calpurnius (2) Piso: 1. Consul of 1 B.C. Made a famous speech about corruption.

2. Elegiac writer mentioned by Pliny (2).

Calpurnius (3) Siculus: Author of seven pastoral poems or eclogues, and allegedly of four which have been proven to be by Nemesianus (q.v.). His date is inferred to be the middle of the 1st century from internal evidence. Nothing is known about his life. The poems owe much to Virgil's *Eclogues,* and contain the usual contest between shepherds in amoebean verse. See Pastoral Poetry.

Calvin, Jean: 1509-1564: The great religious reformer wrote many works in French and in Latin (*Christianae Religionis Institutio*).

Calvus, C. Licinius: Roman poet of the "Alexandrian" School. One of the Cantores Euphorionis (q.v.). A member of Catullus' circle and mentioned in the latter's poems. A lawyer of great eloquence, he was the author of a (lost) epyllion *Io*.

Cambridge Songs: A collection of 49 Latin lyrics probably dating from the 11th century. In various meters, and dealing with various subjects, both sacred and secular, the collection has been called a Goliard's song-book, but it is probably too early to be so termed. See Vagantenlieder, Goliardic poetry, etc.

Camenae: Italian goddesses identified with the Muses.

Camilla: (Roman Mythology) Legendary Volscian maiden thrown by her father Metabus across a river, attached to a javelin.

Camillus, M. Furius: Early Roman hero who saved Rome from invasion by the Gauls. Livy tells of him.

Campion, Edward, S.J.: Teacher of rhetoric and Jesuit of the 16th century. Wrote a treatise on *Imitation* and a *Compendium of Rhetoric*.

Campion, Thomas: 1567-1619. Skillful Latinist, advocate of quantitative verse.

Candidus of Fulda: Author of *Lives of the Abbots of Fulda*, and of an *Expositio Passionis Domini*.

Canidia: A witch. See Horace, Epodes.

Caninius, Rufus: Minor writer of epic poetry, ca. 100 A.D.

Canius Rufus: Tragic poet of the Flavian period.

Cano, Melchior: 16th century Spanish humanist and theologian. Wrote *De Locis Theologicis*.

Canon: This term means

1. A catalogue of writers (e.g., the ten Attic orators) established by someone in authority. See Conrad of Hirsau, Walter of Speyer.

2. Church law. (Cf. canonization, etc.) See Canon Law, Gratian, Burchard of Worms.

Canon Law: The law of the Roman Catholic Church, the *Corpus Iuris Canonici*. Various collections of Canon Law were made. Gratian's *Concordantia Discordantium Canonum* is one of the most important (q.v.). A good treatment of the subject is to be found in Ferm's Encyclopedia of Religion.

Cantemir, Dimitrie: 1673-1723. Rumanian author of a (Latin) description and chronicle of Moldavia, and a history of the Ottoman Empire.

Canterbury: Cathedral school in England. A leading center of education in the Middle Ages.

Canticum: The sung, or recitative, portion of the Roman comedies. Usually accompanied by flutes. See Diverbium.

Cantores Euphorionis: The "Alexandrian" circle of poets in Rome in the first century B.C. The group is characterized by excessive artificiality, great erudition, and by its imitation of the Greek models of Callimachus (q.v.). A favorite literary form was the epyllion or toy-epic (q.v.). Among the Cantores, mention should be made of Catullus, Valerius Cato, Calvus, Cinna, Furius Bibaculus, and Cornificius. The school takes its name from Euphorion, an Alexandrian poet.

Canus: See Julius Kanus.

Capella, Martianus: See Martianus Capella.

Caper, Flavius: Latin grammarian of the second century. Wrote treatises *De Latinitate* and *De Dubiis Generibus* which were widely used by later grammarians. He was supposed to have written an *Orthographia* and a *De Verbis Dubiis*.

Capgrave, John: 1393-1464. English friar; author of sermons, commentaries, historical works, all in Latin.

Capito (1), C. Ateius: 34 B.C.-22 A.D. Roman lawyer and jurist. His opposition to Labeo (q.v.) on personal and political grounds was the occasion for the split of jurists into opposing schools. Labeo's adherents were known as Proculians, Capito's as Sabinians after Sabinus, a disciple of Capito.

Capito (2), Sinnius: Wrote on grammar and literary history in the Augustan Age.

Captivi: Comedy by Plautus. Lessing calls it the best play ever staged! The story revolves around a man and his servant who are captives and who change places. Nice examples of fidelity and self-sacrifice. There is dramatic irony in the punishment of the slave Tyndarus by Hegio, as the slave turns out to be his long-lost son. One of Plautus' finest plays.

Carmen: A song, or poem. Often appears in titles, even where the work is frankly didactic, e.g., *Carmen de Ponderibus et Mensuris* (Song of Weights and Measures).

Carmen ad Flavium Felicem de Resurrectione Mortuorum: Poem by an unknown African author, probably in the 6th century, dealing with the resurrection of the dead. The poem is interesting for its use of rhyme.

Carmen Apologeticum: See Commodianus.

Carmen Arvale: One of the earliest specimens of Latin. The ritual of the Arval Brotherhood, or Fratres Arvales, whose duty it was to supervise agricultural festivals.

Carmen de Bello Aegyptiaco: Fragments of a papyrus found at Herculaneum. Epic poem on Antony's defeat. See Rabirius (1).

Carmen de Bello Mediolanensium adversus Comenses: Historical epic in 2030 hexameters (early 12th century) about the war between Milan and Como.

Carmen de Bello Saxonico: Historical epic on the Saxon War, by an unknown author of the latter part of the 11th century.

Carmen de Christi Jesu Beneficiis: See Rusticius Helpidius.

Carmen de Figuris: Anonymous poem, written ca. 400 on figures of speech.

Carmen de Leda: Mythological poem by an unknown Englishman, about the middle of the 12th century. (Manitius)

Carmen de Moribus: Lost work by Cato (1).

Carmen de Ponderibus et Mensuris: Anonymous "ode on Weights and Measures" which has been incorrectly attributed to Priscian.

Carmen in Victoriam Pisanorum: A poem celebrating the end of a war between the people of Pisa and an African town (Dalmatia). Late 11th century.

Carmen Laureshamense: A poem in 143 hexameters, sent by the monks of Lorsch to the king (Henry V) to appeal to him for a righting of the wrongs done by the monks of Hirsau. It is full of invective against the latter monks, who are accused of everything from growing their beards too long (they sweep the floor every time they bow in greeting) to practicing free love! The poem is important for the contrast between the old and new type clergy. (Manitius)

Carmen Nelei: Iambic fragments belonging to the time of Livius Andronicus. Possibly from a tragedy, the precursor of the Praetexta.

Carmen Paschale: See Sedulius (1). Poem dealing with the miracles of the Old and New Testaments, ending with the Resurrection and Ascension.

Carmen Saeculare: Official ode by Horace. As is often the case with formal poetry written for an occasion, this is far from being his best work.

Carmina: (Horace) See Odes, Horace.

Carmina Burana: Collection of rhymed lyrics of the 12th or 13th centuries. See Goliardic verse. Found in German monastery of Benediktbeuren, hence the name. The poems are on the one hand full of satire, invective and ribaldry, and on the other hand, deal with the joys of love and spring. They tell of the delights of wine, woman and song. Called by Waddell "the last flowering of the Latin tongue." (Waddell)

Carmina Figurata: See Figure-Poems.

Carmina Hoeufftiana: Publication of Neo-Latin poems each year since 1845; the result of an annual competition. See Neo-Latin.

Carmina Saliaria: Chanted by the Salian priests every March as part of their ritual. Quoted by grammarians. One of the oldest extant specimens of Latin. Quintilian says that they were so archaic that they could not be understood even by the priests who chanted them.

Carneades: Greek philosopher of the New Academy. fl. 180 B.C. Had considerable influence in shaping Roman thought through Cicero.

Carolingian Renaissance: Flowering of letters and revival of classical literature and learning that centered in the court of

Charlemagne and the Palace School. The central figure was Alcuin of York, under whose guidance monastic libraries were developed and books were copied. The period is thus important in the transmission of texts. Besides Alcuin, Einhard, Theodulf, Paulus Diaconus, Hrabanus Maurus and Walafrid Strabo (qq.v.) are important figures in the Carolingian Renaissance.

Carpenter, Alexander: fl. 1420. English scholar (Oxford); author of *Destructorium Viciorum,* a description of various vices.

Cartesius: See Descartes.

Carthage: Phoenician colony in N. Africa. Arch-enemy of Rome during the 3rd-2nd centuries B.C. (Punic Wars). In mythology, the home of Queen Dido (q.v.).

Casaubon, Isaac: 1559-1614. Great scholar and humanist of the 16th-17th centuries. Edited Persius.

Casina: Comedy by Plautus. One of his most ribald; the last scene, in which a man is disguised as a bride, is particularly so.

Cassian: (Joannes Cassianus) ca. 360-435. Christian monk and author of the 4th-5th centuries. Founded the monastery of St. Victor at Marseilles. Wrote *Dialogus, Collationes,* and a handbook on monasteries and the eight principal vices (*De Institutis Coenobiorum et de Octo Principalium Vitiorum Remediis*).

Cassiodorus, Flavius Magnus Aurelius: ca. 490-583. Writer, teacher, grammarian, theologian, he linked the study of Christian and secular learning with monasticism. Established a great library at Vivarium and wrote handbooks for the monks, whom he taught to copy manuscripts. Cassiodorus is thus one of the greatest single contributors to the transmission of classical texts. Also wrote exegetical works on the Psalms, theological works, commentaries, etc.

Cassius (1) Hemina: Early Roman historian, contemporary of Cato (1).

Cassius (2) Longinus: 1. Orator of the 1st century B.C. Shakespeare's "lean and hungry Cassius."

2. Rhetor and jurist of the Neronian period.

Cassius (3) of Parma: Roman writer of tragedies. Only his name survives.

Cassius (4) Severus: See Severus, Cassius.

Castor, Antonius: Antony's freedman. Wrote a work on botany which was used by Pliny the Elder (q.v.).

Catachannae: Lost collection of verse by the emperor Hadrian (q.v.).

Catachthonion: Lost work by Lucan. A description of a descent to the Underworld.

Catalepton: (or, less correctly **Catalecta**) Collection of short poems attributed to Virgil (see *Appendix Virgiliana*). Some, if not all, may be genuine. They show the influence of Catullus on the author.

Catechizandis Rudibus, de: See Augustine of Hippo.

Cathedral Schools: The centers of literary activity, in the late Middle Ages, began to shift from the monasteries to the Cathedrals. See Chartres, Fulbert, Gerbert, Canterbury, etc.

Cathemerinon: Collection of lyrical hymns by Prudentius, the first great Christian Latin poet (q.v.).

Catilinae Coniuratione, de: See Sallust.

Catilinam, in: See Catiline, Cicero.

Catiline: (L. Sergius Catilina) Conspirator whose plot was detected and overthrown by Cicero in 63 B.C. The four orations by Cicero against Catiline are among the great masterpieces of invective, irony, and forceful exposition, and rank with the world's finest forensic rhetoric.

Catius, T.: Writer on Epicureanism, mentioned by Cicero. Source for Lucretius (q.v.).

Cato, M. Porcius (1): "Cato the Censor," 234-149 B.C. Prototype of the frugal, stern and stoical Roman of the Republic. Father of Roman prose. Staunchly opposed to the influence of Hellenism. Important for history, oratory, and technical subjects. Works: *Origines* (lost), historical work; Oratory: He published 150 speeches, and we have fragments of 80; Technical: He wrote an encyclopedia for his son, which dealt with jurisprudence, agriculture, military science, rhetoric, and medicine. The treatise on agriculture (*De Agri Cultura*) is the only work which survives in bulk. It consists of information on farming, and abounds in the practical, hard-headed shrewdness so typical of the Roman of the Punic Wars. We have, besides the famous "Carthage must be destroyed," two quotations that reveal his character: his description of the orator as "vir bonus dicendi peritus" (a *good* man who has skill in speaking), and his motto "rem tene, verba sequentur" (Know your facts, and the words will come). His style is simple but not uneffective. We know also of a collection of maxims, the *Carmen de Moribus,* but the *Disticha Catonis* (q.v.) is of much later date. (Duff, OCD)

Cato, M. Porcius (2): "Cato Uticensis," 95-46 B.C. Great-grandson of Cato (1). Stern and uncompromising opponent of Caesar, a powerful orator and religious Stoic. Sallust has given us examples of his rhetorical ability (Catiline). His suicide after the battle of Thapsus is proverbial. He is the real hero of Lucan's epic (q.v.), and that poet's admiration for Cato knew no bounds. Plutarch is also highly laudatory.

Cato (3) or **Catunculus:** An unknown author, probably of the third century whose collection of practical and philosophical maxims, falsely attributed to Cato (1), was extremely popular in the Middle Ages. See *Disticha Catonis.*

Cato: 1. Biography by Cornelius Nepos.

2. Cicero's encomium on Cato Uticensis.

3. Historical play (praetexta) by Curiatus Maternus (q.v.).

Cato Maior: See *Senectute, de* (Cicero).

Catullus, C. Valerius (1): 84-54 B.C. One of the great lyric poets of Rome and of all literature. Born ca. 84 in Verona of a noble family, he came to Rome ca. 62, and speedily became a member of the fashionable literary clique. Many of his poems deal with his love, despair, and finally, his disgust with the notorious Lesbia (Clodia). He is one of the most deeply personal of Roman poets, whether he is rejoicing in his beloved yacht, mourning on the death of Lesbia's sparrow, attacking Caesar, expressing the ambivalence he feels for the fickle Lesbia ("odi et amo") or grieving at his brother's death. His meters range from the hendecasyllables of "Vivamus, mea

Lesbia, atque amemus" to sapphics ("Ille mi par esse"), elegiacs and hexameters. The Alexandrian influence was strong, especially in the longer poems, the *Peleus and Thetis*, the *Attis*, and the *Coma Berenices* (in imitation of Callimachus). But it is in the shorter poems that his genius is most clearly seen: the clear and unabashed revelation of the poet's heart that is remembered long after one has forgotten the mannered artificiality and erudition of the longer Alexandrian poems. Mackail and Duff (OCD) rank Catullus with Sappho and Shelley among the greatest of lyric poets. (Duff, J. W. and A. M.)

Catullus (2): Writer of mimes under Caligula and Nero. One of his lost plays was *Phasma* (the Ghost); another, *Laureolus*, featured the crucifixion, on the stage, of a bandit.

Catulus, Q. Lutatius: Consul 102 B.C. An accomplished orator, he wrote memoirs and epigrams.

Catulus: One of the 2 books of Cicero's *Prior Analytics* (now lost).

Catunculus: See Cato (3).

Causa Dei, de: See Bradwardine.

Causis Corruptae Eloquentiae, de: Lost work by Quintilian; a study of the reasons for the decadence in Roman oratory.

Celano, Thomas of: See Thomas of Celano; *Dies Irae*.

Celsus (1) Albinovanus: Minor Augustan poet; accused by Horace of plagiarism.

Celsus (2), A. Cornelius: Nothing known of his life. Lived during reign of Tiberius. Wrote an encyclopedia (cf. Varro, Cato 1) which treated agriculture, medicine, law, military tactics, philosophy and rhetoric. Only the *De Medicina* survives. It contains much superstition, but also a good deal of practical wisdom and common sense. Celsus keeps abreast of the latest discoveries and practices in medicine. He deals with the diseases, symptoms, remedies, drugs, surgery, diet, exercise, etc. For the importance of this work in later times, cf. *Paracelsus*.

Celsus (3), P. Juventius: An important jurist of Hadrian's time. Wrote *Epistulae, Commentaries, Quaestiones,* and *Digesta* (39 books). Enough fragments have survived to judge his style, which is excellent.

Celtes, Conrad: 1459-1508. Lyric poet. First "Poeta Laureatus" of Germany. Wrote poetry in the style of Horace and Ovid; edited Tacitus and Hroswitha.

Cena Cypriani: A Biblical parody by an unknown author. Recast in Charlemagne's time by John the Deacon.

Cena Trimalchionis: The central portion of Petronius' *Satyricon* (q.v.). It is a vivid and scintillating description of a Roman banquet, with Trimalchio the perfect type of the nouveau-riche; vulgar, ostentatious, ignorant in his outrageous misquotations of Homer. The work is particularly valuable for the insight it gives us into the *sermo plebeius* or everyday speech (q.v.).

Censorinus: 3rd century grammarian and excerptor. Wrote *De Die Natali* (q.v.) and *De Accentibus* (lost).

Centauri: (The Centaurs) Lost work—either a play by Livius or part of the *Erotopaegnia* of Laevius.

Cento: A "patchwork" or "crazy-quilt." A poem made by piecing together bits or lines of other poetry (usually Virgil's). The form seems to have been invented by Proba (q.v.). It was used by Ausonius (the famous and obscene *Cento Nuptialis*), Hosidius Geta (*Medea*), Pomponius, Pseudo-Sedulius (*de Incarnatione Verbi*), Columban, Waldram, and many others. The *Ecbasis Captivi* is partly made up of tags from Horace, and the anonymous *De Alea* is another example of the genre.

Cento Nuptialis: An ingenious and obscene patchwork by Ausonius. Lines and half-lines are taken from Virgil and pieced together to form a new poem. As literature, it is deplorable, as a tour de force, remarkable, and as an indication of the depths to which literature can sink when genius gives way to artificiality, it is significant.

Centuriae Magdeburgenses: See Magdeburg Centuries.

Cerberus: In mythology, the three-headed dog (50, according to Hesiod) who guarded the entrance to the underworld. Mentioned by Virgil, Horace, et al.

Cerealis, Julius: See Julius Cerealis.

Ceres: In mythology, the goddess of grain, identified with the Greek Demeter, and mother of Proserpina (q.v.).

Cestius Pius: Rhetorician and teacher from Smyrna. Lived in the Augustan Age. Seneca (1) mentions his wit, his vanity, and his hatred of Cicero.

Chalcidius: Partially translated Plato's *Timaeus*, with a commentary, into Latin. Extremely important for the Middle Ages, as this was the chief source of medieval Platonism.

Champeaux, William of: See William of Champeaux.

Charisius, Flavius Sospater: Late 4th century grammarian, author of an *Ars Grammatica* which is largely extant. Chiefly valuable for the quotations from early authors such as Cato (1), Ennius, Lucilius, etc.

Charon: In mythology, the ferryman over the river Styx. There is a famous description of him in the *Aeneid* (Book VI).

Chartier, Alan: 1385-1429. Author of *Tractatus de Vita Curiale* and other Latin treatises.

Chartres: French cathedral town. Great center of 12th century humanism and Platonism. Such figures as John of Salisbury, Fulbert, Bernard of Chartres, William of Conches, Walter of Mortagne, Gilbert de la Porrée, and others are associated with Chartres.

Chiampel, Durich: 16th century Swiss poet; wrote, in Latin and Romansch, historical-geographical works.

Chorographia: See Pomponius Mela.

Chorographia, de: Geographical poem by Varro of Atax (q.v.).

Christi Vitalia Gesta: Epic treatment of the life of Christ by Juvencus (q.v.).

Christian of Stablo: 9th century exegetical writer. Commentary on Matthew, etc.

Christian-Latin literature: See Apologists (Tertullian, Minucius Felix, Cyprian, Arnobius, Lactantius); Hymns: Hilary, Ambrose; Church Fathers: Jerome, Ambrose, Augustine, Isidore; Exegetical works, Scholastics: Aquinas, John Scotus, Abelard, John of Salisbury, Anselm, etc.; Hagiography (numerous lives of saints and accounts of miracles); Church History (Bede, Adam of Bremen, et al.); poetry (Prudentius, Biblical epic, etc.); Sequence, Religious drama, Passion Plays, etc.

Christian-Latin poetry: Early period 400-600. Biblical epics (Prudentius, Juvencus, Dracontius, etc.) and hymns (Ambrose, Hilary, etc.). Mostly, the early poetry consisted of treating Biblical subjects in a Virgilian manner. See the above authors, and Sedulius, Fulgentius, Ennodius, Carolingian Revival or Renaissance. A later development was the Sequence (q.v.). Epic poetry on religious subjects and rhymed lyrics continued to flourish throughout the Middle Ages. The allegorical epic (q.v.) is a subdivision. (Raby, Labriolle, Duckett, Rand)

Christianus: 10th century Czech chronicler of Wenceslaus.

Chronica: See Isidore of Seville.

Chronicae Polonorum: History of the Poles, written in the 12th century by an unknown author, probably French. Style rather bombastic. (Manitius)

Chronicon Salernitatum: A chronicle written by an unknown monk of Salerno, in the last quarter of the tenth century. Tells of the Lombard kingdoms in South Italy, beginning where Paulus Diaconus leaves off. Actually more a collection of source material than a real history. (Manitius)

Chryses: Title of a lost play by Pacuvius (q.v.). Presumably it dealt with the Trojan War.

Cibis Iudaicis, de: See Novitian.

Cicero, M. Tullius: 106-43 B.C. Life. Born at Arpinum. Father an equestrian. Studied literature and rhetoric. The latter early became his forte. Made a name for himself by his prosecution of Verres. Studied at Athens and Rhodes. Married Terentia. In politics, Cicero was a "novus homo." He went through all the usual stages and was elected consul for the year 63. During his consulship he detected and overthrew the Catilinarian conspiracy, a fact which he never forgot, and, incidentally, which he never allowed anyone else to forget, either. He incurred the enmity of Clodius, by whom (at Caesar's instigation) he was exiled. After a period of great suffering and self-pity he was recalled and re-entered the city in triumph. There followed a period of vacillation between Pompey and Caesar. In 46 he divorced his wife Terentia, and the following year his beloved daughter Tullia died. In his bereavement, Cicero turned to philosophy, and most of his works in this field were written in the last two years of his life. After the assassination of Caesar, Cicero was an outspoken opponent of Antony. This cost him his life. The story of Augustus and his grandson is a touching example of the esteem in which Cicero was held, even though he was on the opposite side of the political fence. The emperor found his young grandson reading Cicero, and as the youth sought to conceal the dangerous document, Augustus took it, studied it for a long time, then returned it to the lad, saying, "An eloquent man, my boy, eloquent and a patriot."

Works: *Speeches.* 58 survive, including the *Catilines,* the *Verrines,* the *Manilian Law,* the *Pro Archia, Pro Quincto, in Pisonem, Pro Murena, in Rullum, in Caecilium, Pro Sulla, Pro Milone, Pro Rabirio Postumo. De Provinciis Consularibus,* the *Philippics, Post Reditum,* and many others. See under separate titles, also *Caesarianae.*

Rhetoric, works on: *De Oratore, Brutus, Orator, Partitiones Oratoriae, de Inventione, De Optimo Genere Oratorum, Topica* (qq.v.).

Political: *Republic* and *Laws.* The famous *Somnium Scipionis* is from the first of these. See *Republica, de, Legibus, de.*

Philosophical, Dialogues: *De Officiis, de Finibus, Tusculan Disputations, Academics, Paradoxes, De Fato, De Natura Deorum, De Amicitia, De Senectute, de Divinatione.* Lost works on *Cato, Auguries, Virtues, Timaeus.* See under titles.

Letters: We possess four collections, those to (and from) Atticus, Brutus, his brother Quintus, and the miscellaneous *Ad Familiares.*

Poetry: An epic on his consulship, translations from Homer and the Greek dramatists, Xenophon, Plato, and others. Except for fragments, his poetry is lost, but it was probably not as bad as Juvenal would have us believe.

It is as a man of letters, not as a statesman, that Cicero has had his most lasting results. He is responsible for the molding of Latin prose into an orderly and harmonious instrument for the expression of human thought. In his rhetorical, philosophical and other works, his language is clear, melodious, and forceful. From his letters we get the picture of a man of many facets, patriotic, intelligent, honest, but capable of abysmal self-pity and odious egotism, as well as of downright hypocrisy. But his failings are all human ones and are far outweighed by his virtues; i.e., his warmth, wit, tolerance, geniality, and humanism. His philosophical writings are of particular importance for the Middle Ages. Most of what later ages knew of the Greek philosophers, they culled from Cicero. He invented many important philosophical terms. In the truest sense of the word, Cicero was a humanist. His impact on the Latin language was a lasting one. He ranks with Demosthenes among the great orators of all time. (Duff, OCD)

Cicero: Lost biography of the orator by Nepos (q.v.).

Cicero, Quintus: The brother of the orator. Wrote four tragedies in sixteen days. One does not regret their loss.

Ciceromastix: Lost work of the Flavian period by Largius or Larcius Licinus.

Ciceronian Age: Takes its name from its greatest author, Cicero (q.v.). Roughly, the last half-century of the Republic. It was during this period that the Latin language was developed into the instrument of precise expression that it remained for many centuries. Most important authors of the period are, besides Cicero himself, Caesar, Sallust, Lucretius, Catullus (qq.v.).

Ciceronianus: Work by Erasmus (q.v.) in 1528, illustrating his importance as a humanist.

Cicuta: A collection of biting epigrams by Domitius Marsus, a minor poet of the Augustan Age.

Cid, the: The great hero of Spanish epic. A Latin poem by an unknown author was composed ca. 1100.

Cincinnatus: The familiar semi-legendary figure of Roman history who laid down his plow, became dictator, vanquished Rome's enemies in 16 days, and returned to his farm.

Cincius (1) Alimentus: Early Roman historian who wrote in Greek; a prisoner of Hannibal.

Cincius (2): A later author of historical works is quoted by Livy. Apparently not identical with Cincius (1). He wrote on constitutional and military antiquities, and his works were erroneously ascribed to the earlier Cincius.

Cinna, C. Helvius: Dean of the "Cantores Euphorionis" (q.v.). Roman poet, friend of Catullus. Wrote an epyllion (or toy epic) called *Zmyrna*, and epigrams. Apparently this is the same Cinna who was lynched by the mob after the death of Caesar, being mistaken for the conspirator of the same name.

Ciris: Poem of the Augustan Age, attributed to Virgil and found in the *Appendix Virgiliana* (q.v.). It tells of Scylla's love for her enemy Minos, and her cutting of the fateful lock of hair from the head of her father. It is a good example of the Alexandrine "epyllion." There are many Virgilian echoes in it, but whether they are imitations by another poet of Virgil, or vice versa, or whether Virgil himself wrote it and imitated *himself*, is unknown. (Duff, OCD)

Cisneros, Cardinal Ximenes de: See Ximenes.

Cistellaria: Minor comedy by Plautus (q.v.).

City of God, the: See *Civitate Dei, de*; Augustine of Hippo.

Civitate Dei, de: Augustine's greatest work, in which he shows that the new religion, Christianity, is not responsible, as had been alleged by its detractors, for the decline of Rome, but that the "Eternal City" of Rome was an ephemeral one, and that the City of God alone is truly eternal. Extremely important for medieval philosophy and theology.

Classical, Classic: The term appears to have been invented by Aulus Gellius, and originally meant art of the first class. Pertaining to Greek and Roman antiquity, the word denotes a certain perfection of form, but can be properly used of Racine and Goethe, Mozart and Raphael, as well as of Virgil and Sophocles.

Clastidium: Title of a lost historical drama (praetexta) by Naevius. It was a dramatization of contemporary events, and its hero was one Marcellus.

Claudian: (Claudius Claudianus) fl. ca. 400. The last great poet of the pagan Roman world. Wrote an epic on the Gothic Wars, glorifying the general Stilicho and the latter's victory over Alaric in 402. Other works: *De Raptu Proserpinae,* an unfinished mythological epic, *Contra Rufinum, Fescennine Verses,* and others. His Latin, in spite of the late date, is as good as almost any of the Silver Age writers. He writes with grace and elegance, a wealth of mythological detail and allusion, and above all, he loves Rome. Generally, his writings fall into three categories: political (panegyric and invective), mythological, and the smaller miscellaneous verses, including some nice landscape descriptions, the Fescennines, etc.

Claudianus Mamertus: 5th century. Christian author, poet, orator, dialectician, theologian, mathematician and musician. Wrote many letters. He has been credited with the authorship of the famous *Pange lingua,* but this hymn is almost certainly by Venantius Fortunatus.

Claudius: Roman emperor 41-54. His works, which were varied and numerous, are all lost. They include a treatise on gambling, speeches, an autobiography, a work on orthography, on Carthaginian and Etruscan history, and others. He was particularly interested in Livy and Roman antiquities.

Claudius of Turin: d. ca. 827. Spanish biblical scholar, favored by the court of Charlemagne. Opposed cults of crosses, saints. Wrote commentaries on Genesis, Kings, Matthew.

Claudius, Appius: See Appius Claudius.

Claudius Quadrigarius: One of the early historians of

Rome. Omitting the mythological period, he wrote on Roman history beginning with the fire of 390 B.C., and going down to his own times.

Cledonius: Late grammarian (5th century?). Wrote an *Ars Grammatica* which survives in a 6th century manuscript, one of the oldest of its kind.

Clemens Romanus: (?) Early patristic writer. Several identities may be merged here, including Pope Clement and Flavius Clemens, who was put to death for "maiestas" and who may have been a Christian.

Clemens Scotus: An Irish grammarian of the early 9th century.

Clementia, de: Philosophical essay by Seneca (2). Deals with the necessity for clemency, particularly in a ruler. The second book has Seneca's definitions of mercy, pardon, clemency, etc.

Clodia: Voluptuous and disreputable woman, beloved by Catullus (q.v.), the "Lesbia" of his poems; afterwards, mistress of Caelius. Cicero gives a graphic picture of her in the speech *Pro Caelio*.

Clodius (1) Pulcher: A disreputable Roman, brother of the famous Clodia. Enemy of Cicero, he passed a law, probably at the instigation of Caesar, which resulted in the exile of Cicero.

Clodius (2) Quirinalis: A rhetor of Nero's day. Came from Arles in Gaul.

Clodius (3) Servius: Famous Plautine scholar of ca. 100 B.C. Said to be able to recognize any line of Plautus by its sound.

Clodius (4) Turrinus: There were two rhetors of this name, father and son. Seneca (1) mentions them. The elder lost much of his force because he did not deviate from the rules of Apollodorus (q.v.). Seneca treated the younger as his own son.

Cluny: Renowned French monastery. See Peter the Venerable, Odo, Alcuin. One of the chief centers of learning in the Middle Ages.

Cluvius Rufus: Historian of the first century. Used as a source by Tacitus.

Cockneys, Roman: Catullus tells of one Arrius who said "hinsidiae" for "insidiae." Presumably this was a reaction against the practice of omitting the initial "h." (Catullus, 84)

Codex: See Books. A manuscript, with leaves arranged in quires, in the modern way. Legal Codex: Earliest collection was the *Codex Gregorianus* in 291 A.D., the *Hermogenianus* was a supplement. In the fifth century the *Codex Theodosianus* was the official collection of imperial constitutions. The most famous was the Code of Justinian (q.v.).

Codex Iuris Canonici: See Canon Law.

Codex Iuris Civilis: Justinian's Code. Includes the *Digesta,* the *Codex Repetitae Praelectionis,* and the *Novellae Constitutiones.* It includes a summary of all the imperial constitutions before Justinian. See Justinian, Tribonianus.

Codrus (Cordus?): Flavian poet. Wrote an epic "Theseid."

Coelius Antipater: See Antipater.

Coffin, Charles: 1676-1749. French Neo-Latin poet; author of a poem on Champagne.

Coincidentia Oppositorum: See Nicholas of Cusa.

Colax: We know of three Roman plays with this title; by Naevius, Plautus, and Laberius. Probably they are all based on one by Menander.

Colet, John: English humanist of the Renaissance, dean of St. Paul's, friend of Erasmus (q.v.). He rejected the allegorical method of scriptural interpretation.

Collationes: See Cassian.

Collectanea Rerum Memorabilium: See Solinus, Theoderich of St. Trond.

Colloquies: Dialogues by Erasmus (q.v.). First intended as textbooks, they soon came to have a wider significance. They are full of local and topical allusions, i.e., to the shortcomings of the Church, and as such they played a great part in the Reformation, and had a lasting influence on European literature. Rabelais, Shakespeare, and Cervantes are all indebted to the *Colloquies.*

Colman: Irish poet of the 9th century.

Colonna, Francesco: 1432?-1527? Italian Dominican friar, author of *Hypnerotomachia Pophilii,* an allegorical work.

Colores: See Rhetoric, Seneca (1), Onulf of Speyer.

Coluccio Salutato: Important figure of the Italian Renaissance, friend of Petrarch. Noted for his excellent Latinity.

Columba, St.: (521-597) Irish monk. Trained in Latin and Celtic, he wrote poetry in both languages. Wrote a *Liber Hymnorum,* founded schools and abbeys. See Altus Prosator.

Columbanus, St.: (543-615) Irish monk who founded monasteries of Bobbio and St. Gall. Columban was chiefly responsible for the transmission of Irish monastic culture to the mainland of Europe. Also wrote poetry, hymns. (Duckett, Raby)

Columella, L. Junius Moderatus: Author of *De Re Rustica,* a handbook of agriculture. A Spaniard from Gades (Cadiz). Also wrote on trees and against fortune-tellers. The former work is didactic rather than artistic, but has a fine feeling for the land of Italy. It is full of interesting and useful information. It contains a powerful indictment against absentee landlords as one reason for the decline of Italian agriculture. See *Re Rustica, de.*

Columna Rostrata: Inscription on a column to one Duilius, the victor of a naval battle against Carthage in 260 B.C. It may be either a copy of the original inscription or an antique-style composition of a later date. (Duff)

Coma Berenices: Catullus' epyllion or mock-epic on the theft of a lock of hair. Imitation of Callimachus (Cf. Pope's *Rape of the Lock*). A good example of the Alexandrine influence in Roman poetry.

Comedy, Roman: See Palliata, Atellan farce, Mime, Togata, Plautus, Terence, and other individual names. Comedy never again attained the height it had reached in the times of Plautus and Terence. In the ensuing decline, the mime became more and more popular. For medieval comedies, see Vitalis of Blois, Hroswitha, *Baucis et Thraso,* Matthew of

Vendôme, Babio, and Richard of Venosa. For the early canon of writers of comedy see Sedigitus.

Cominianus: 4th century grammarian, author of a (lost) *Ars Grammatica.*

Commemoratio Professorum Burdigalensium: See Ausonius.

Commentaries: (1) See *Bello Gallico, de.* (2) Title of many exegetical works, both on classical subjects and on the Bible.

Commentariolum Petitionis: Title of a work by Quintus Cicero.

Commentarium in Metra Terentiana: See Rufinus (2).

Commentum in Ciceronis Libros de Inventione: See Grillius.

Commodianus: Christian author of the fifth century, wrote in accentual verse (q.v.). Works: *Carmen Apologeticum,* a versified defense of Christianity; *Instructiones,* a collection of short poems.

Commonitorium: See Orientius.

Commorientes: Lost comedy by Plautus, based on an original by Diphilus.

Comoedia: In classical times, the word means what we mean by "comedy." In the Middle Ages, it came to mean a versified tale. See *Milo, Alda, Pamphilus, Geta.*

Comoediis Plautinis, de: Lost work by Varro (q.v.). Valuable because it established a sound canon of authority for the Plautine plays. Varro listed 21 and we possess 21. The inference that they are the same plays is inescapable.

Compendiosa Doctrina, de: Work by Nonius Marcellus (q.v.). Deals with grammar and other minutiae, in more or less alphabetical order. Valuable for its many quotations from the early poets.

Compendium: See Velleius Paterculus, Florus.

Compitalia: Two lost works of this name. (1) a comedy by Afranius; (2) a mime by Laberius.

Complutensian Polyglot: Great achievement of Biblical scholarship in Spain, under Cardinal Ximenes (q.v.). It consists of the Old and New Testaments in the original languages, with the Vulgate in parallel columns.

Compositione et de Metris Oratorum, de: See Rufinus (2).

Conches, William of: See William of Conches.

Concordantia Discordantium Canonum: See Canon Law, Gratian.

Concordia Novi et Veteris Testamenti: See Joachim of Floris (Fiori).

Confessio: See Patrick.

Confession of Golias: A work describing the life and nature of the Wandering Scholars. See Goliardic poetry. Perhaps by the Archpoet (q.v.).

Confessions: See Augustine of Hippo.

Conflictu Virtutum et Vitiorum, de: Short poem (52 lines) dating from the middle of the 11th century. See Streitgedicht.

Conflictus Veris et Hiemis: (Debate between Spring and Winter) An example of the "Streitgedicht" (q.v.) or poetical debate. Previously attributed to Alcuin. Now this attribution is generally rejected, but the work is thought to belong to the period of the Carolingian Revival.

Conrad of Gelnhausen: 1320-90. Professor of theology at the University of Paris, Chancellor of Heidelberg. His *Epistola Concordiae* advocated conciliar methods for ending the great schism. (Ferm)

Conrad of Hirsau: First half of the 12th century. German monk. His *Dialogus super Auctores* is one of the valuable indications of what authors were studied in his day. It includes: Donatus, Cato, Aesop, Avianus, Sedulius, Juvencus, Prosper of Aquitaine, Theodulus, Arator, Prudentius Cicero, Sallust, Boethius, Lucan, Horace, Ovid, Juvenal, "Homer," Persius, Statius, and Virgil. Conrad also wrote an *Epithalamium Virginum.*

Consentes Di, or Di Consentes: The twelve chief gods of the Roman pantheon. They were: Jupiter, Neptune, Mars, Apollo, Mercury, Vulcan, Juno, Venus, Minerva, Diana, Ceres, and Vesta.

Consentius: Grammarian of the 5th century. His extant works are: *De Nomine et Verbo, De Barbarismis et Metaplasmis*. He is important for the light he sheds on the "sermo plebeius" (q.v.).

Consolatio: A literary genre possibly introduced into Rome by Cicero. Mostly a consolation on another's death or exile. Certain "loci communes" or common expressions appear in nearly all, such as: all men are mortal, time heals wounds, etc. See Cicero, Seneca (2), Ambrose, Jerome, Agius of Corvey.

Consolatio: Now fragmentary work by Cicero. On the death of his daughter Tullia, and of other people.

Consolatio ad Liviam: A poem incorrectly assigned to Ovid. It has also been assigned to the 15th century. Probably was written in the 1st century.

Consolatio Philosophiae: See Boethius. His greatest work. Written in prison in the prose-verse form of the Menippean Satire, it describes the visit to the author of the allegorical figure of Philosophy, who tells B. that he is not the first to suffer for his love of truth (she mentions Socrates, Zeno, and Seneca), and helps him to count his blessings. It is a noble work, dealing as it does with the concept of the summum bonum, and is Platonic in spirit. God is identified, as in Plato, with the Good. This work is one of the bridges between antiquity and the Middle Ages.

Consolations: (of Seneca) See Seneca (2).

1. *Ad Helviam Matrem.* Consoles his mother on his own exile. Contains much Stoic philosophy and some fine writing.
2. *Ad Marciam.* Contains the usual "loci communes" of the genre. Seneca mentions other mothers who have mourned for their sons, as Marcia is doing.
3. *Ad Polybium.* A consolation on the loss of P's brother.

None of the three may be called a spontaneous consolation; they are really all literary exercises, following a definite pattern.

Constantia Sapientia, de: Work by Seneca (2) to one Serenus (q.v.). It is an attempt to convert the latter to the philosophy of Stoicism. Its basic premise is that the wise man can never be injured or insulted.

Constantine: Abbot of St. Symphorian in Metz. Wrote a biography of Adalbero II of Metz, ca. 1000.

Consulatu Suo, de: Cicero's poem on his own consulship. The horrible "O fortunatam natam me consule Romam!" which Juvenal mentions scathingly, occurs in it.

Consultationes Zacchei et Apollonis: See Firmicus Maternus.

Contaminatio: The theory, that two plays were combined to produce one new one, has been convincingly rejected by W. Beare, on linguistical and dramatic grounds. Beare (The Roman Stage, et s.v. Oxford Classical Dictionary) maintains that this interpretation is an impossible one, and that the term simply means "spoiling" a play.

Contemptu Mundi, de: Long satirical poem by Bernard of Morlaix (q.v.).

Contest between Cook and Baker: See Vespa; *Streitgedicht.*

Contra Eutychen: See Boethius.

Contra Symmachum: Poem by Prudentius (q.v.) against the heathen gods. See Altar of Victory.

Controversia: See Seneca (1), rhetoric, suasoria. A standard form of rhetorical exercise. Many examples in the *Controversiae* of Seneca.

Controversiis Agrorum, de: Lost treatise by Frontinus (q.v.) on gromatics. Commentary by Aggenius Urbicus. See also Gromatics.

Copa: Poem in the Appendix Virgiliana. Almost certainly *not* by Virgil. A short elegiac description of a barmaid. Contains the famous line "Mors aurem vellens, 'Vivite,' ait, 'venio.'" (Death plucks the ear and says: 'Live, for I am coming.')

Copernicus, Nicolaus: 1473-1543. Father of modern astronomy (*De Revolutionibus Orbium Coelestium*), he also wrote odes on the Infancy of Jesus (*Septem Sidera*).

Corbulo, Domitius: Minor historian of the Neronian period. Used by Tacitus.

Cordus (1), Aelius Junius: Biographer, follower of Suetonius.

Cordus (2), Euricius: 1486-1535. German humanist; author of Latin epigrams which Lessing praised highly.

Cordus (3), Cremutius: See Cremutius Cordus.

Corinna: See Ovid's *Amores*.

Coriolanus: Legendary Roman; hero of the Corioli. In a well-known story, he leads his army against Rome, but the entreaties of his mother prevent him from taking the city ("You have saved Rome, Mother, but you have destroyed me.").

Corippus, Flavius Cresconius: African poet of the 6th century. Wrote an epic in eight books, *Johannis,* on the exploits of the Magister Militum against the Mauretanians. Actually, the poem is a panegyric, thinly disguised as an epic (Cf. Claudian's "epic" on Stilicho). Corippus also wrote a panegyric on Justinian (*In Laudem Justini*).

Cornelia: The prototype of the Roman mother. Her sons were the Gracchi. A woman of great culture, she was the daughter of Scipio Africanus, and is supposed to have had twelve children. There are fragments of two letters attributed to her, but their authenticity is doubtful. She also wrote memoirs.

Cornificius, Q. (1): One of the Cantores Euphorionis (q.v.). Author of a toy epic, or epyllion, called *Glaucus.* Cornificius was a friend of the poet Catullus. He died in 42 or 41 B.C.

Cornificius (2): See *Rhetorica ad Herennium.*

Cornutus, L. Annaeus: Either a freedman or relative of Seneca. A Stoic teacher, and friend of the satirist Persius. He was a grammarian, tragic poet and commentator. Persius dedicated his fifth satire to C. Exiled in 66, either because of his being involved in the conspiracy of Piso, or because he had the temerity to say that 400 books were too many for Nero's epic on Rome. His one surviving work is a Stoic exposition of Greek mythology, in Greek.

Coronatus: A minor poet of the African Anthology (q.v.).

Corpus Grammaticorum Latinorum: Keil's collection of the works of Latin grammarians.

Corpus Iuris Canonici: The great body of Church Law (see Canon law). Based on compilations like that of Gratian (q.v.).

Corpus Scriptorum Ecclesiasticorum Latinorum: (CSEL) Great collection, made in Vienna, of medieval Church writings, poetry, etc.

Corpus Tibullianum: Together with the poems of Tibullus, the MSS. contain elegies by one "Lygdamus," Sulpicia, the *Panegyric* on Messalla. These appear in Book III, along with some works that are probably by Tibullus himself. All the works belong to the circle of Messalla, which included Tibullus. (See Tibullus, "Lygdamus," Sulpicia.) Duff, OCD.

Correctorium Fratris Thomas: See William de la Mare.

Coruncianus, Ti.: Consul of 280 B.C. Reputed to have been the first professor of Jurisprudence at Rome.

Corvinus, Laurentius: 1465-1527. Silesian humanist. Author of *De Apollone et Novem Musis, Hortulum Elegentiarum, Geographica.*

Corvinus, Messalla: See Messalla.

Corydon: A typical pastoral figure in the Greek eclogues (Theocritus), as well as the Roman ones (e.g. Calpurnius Siculus and Virgil).

Cosconius, Q.: A scholar and grammarian of the 1st century. He wrote on law as well as on grammar. None of his works has survived.

Cosmas Iapygus: Early 11th century. A monk from Apulia who wrote on the Passions of Theopompus and Senesius. He wrote in elegiac distichs which were not only epanaleptic (q.v.) but which had the same rhyme in the hexameter and pentameter. (Manitius)

Cosmas of Prague: Wrote a *Chronica Boemorum*—a history of the people and land of Bohemia to the year 1125. It was continued after his death by various hands. (Manitius)

Cotta, Aurelius (1): A great orator of the 1st century B.C. None of his speeches has survived. It is at his house that Cicero's dialogue *De Natura Deorum* is represented as taking place. Cotta, in the dialogue, is the exponent of Academic philosophy.

Cotta, Aurelius (2): The son of Messalla (q.v.); an orator.

Cotton, Bartholomew: d. ca. 1300. English monk, author of *Historia Anglicana*.

Council of Love at Remiremont: An anonymous poem of the 12th century. It is a rather cynical description of the orgies in a convent.

Crashaw, Richard: 1612/3-1649. English poet. Wrote poetry in Latin and Greek (epigrams, etc.).

Crassicius, L.: Teacher and scholar of the Augustan Age. Wrote a commentary on Cinna's *Zmyrna*.

Crassus (1), L. Licinius: Uncle of the triumvir Crassus. One of the greatest of the pre-Ciceronian orators. Like Cicero, he probably paid for his rhetorical skill with his life. Cicero greatly admired him.

Crassus (2), Ninnius: 1st century B.C. (?). Translated the *Iliad* into Latin.

Crates of Mallos: Head Librarian of Pergamum. His visit to Rome in 168 B.C. was a great stimulus to the Roman interest in grammar.

Cremutius Cordus, Aulus: Historian of the first century, wrote under Augustus and Tiberius. Did not glorify the Emperors, but took his life into his hands by praising Brutus, Cicero, and Cassius, whom he called "the last of the Romans." He gave offense to Sejanus, was prosecuted, and committed suicide by starving himself to death.

Cricius (Krzycki), Andrzej: 1482-1537. Polish-Latin poet, wrote satires, epigrams, panegyrics.

Crispinus: Wrote books on Stoic philosophy, in verse, during the Age of Augustus.

Crispus (1), Vibius: Orator and informer in the Julio-Claudian and Flavian periods.

Crispus (2): Archbishop of Milan 681-725. Wrote poems, epitaphs, etc.

Crotius Rubienus: ca. 1480-1539. German humanist. One of the authors of the *Epistolae Obscurorum Virorum* (q.v.).

Crucifixo, in: Religious poem by Froumond of Tegernsee (q.v.).

Cruindmelus: 9th century Irish grammarian; author of *De Metrica Ratione*.

Csezmiczey, Janos: See Pannonius (his Latinized name).

Culex: (the Gnat) A poem in the Appendix Virgiliana (q.v.). A gnat stings a sleeping shepherd, who first kills the insect, then realizes that it was only warning him against a snake, which he also kills. The ghost of the gnat appears to the shepherd, accusing him of ingratitude. Finally a tomb with an epitaph is erected to the gnat. Several authors (Statius, Donatus, etc.) tell us that Virgil wrote a *Culex*. The problem: is this the one? There are many Virgilian echoes in the poem, which can be explained in any one of three ways: they are imitated *from* Virgil by another author; they are imitated *by* Virgil; or, possibly, Virgil imitated himself. Duff thinks the poem may be the Virgilian one. Enk (OCD) emphatically denies this.

Cultu Feminarum, de: A diatribe by the apologist Tertullian (q.v.) on how women ought to dress. Fiercely satiric.

Cultura Hortorum, de: "*Hortulus*"—See Walafrid Strabo.

Cupid and Psyche: The well-known story of the god of love and his too-curious mortal wife. See Apuleius.

Cupiditate, de: See Servasius.

Cupido Amans: An anonymous poem in sixteen hexameters, written in the third century. Duff J. W. and A. M. Minor Latin Poets. (Loeb)

Cupuncula: Lost comedy by Ennius (q.v.).

Curculio: ("The Parasite") One of the minor comedies of Plautus (q.v.).

Curiatus Maternus: Poet and dramatist under Vespasian. Wrote praetextae, or historical plays, *Cato* and *Domitius,* and tragedies, *Thyestes* and *Medea.* He is one of the interlocutors in Tacitus' *Dialogue on Orators* (q.v.), and it is at his house that the dialogue is represented as taking place.

Curio, Scribonius: Orator of the early first century B.C. Cicero mentions him as one of the greatest speakers of his (Cicero's) youth.

"Curriculum Authors": Latin authors, pagan and Christian, whose works formed part of the standard curriculum in the Middle Ages. See Conrad of Hirsau, Walter of Speyer, and Laborintus.

Curtius: Legendary Roman hero of an aetiological myth in which he leaps into a chasm that has appeared in the Forum. The story was presumably invented to explain the name of the *Lacus Curtius,* a pond in the Forum.

Curtius, Ernst R.: Author of "European Literature and the Latin Middle Ages," a work of great importance, especially for its concept of the literature of Europe as a continuous, organic whole, in which Homer and Dante, Virgil and Goethe, are all viewed as parts of a literary unity, and such topics as the influence of rhetoric, the Curriculum Authors, the "loci communes," and other important topics and curiosa are well treated.

Curtius Montanus: A satirical poet of the Neronian period; mentioned by Tacitus.

Curtius, Rufus, Q.: Author of a history of Alexander the Great in ten books. Nothing is known of his life; his dates are by inference (reign of Claudius). In spite of its faults (over-credulity, poor geographical knowledge, and no real attempt to estimate the historical importance of Alexander) the work is extremely readable and entertaining. Many of the incidents, such as the Gordian Knot; the siege of Tyre; the entrance of Alexander into India and the description of that country; the death of the conqueror; and other passages, are vividly and memorably depicted. Curtius has a flair for the romantic and adventurous, and an almost unexcelled gift of character-delineation. As history, the work falls short of first-rank status; as adventure, it rates highly. (Duff, Silver Age)

Cybele: A nature or mother-goddess of Asia Minor. Her cult was widespread in Greece, Rome, and especially the provinces of Gaul and Africa.

Cynegetica: Books by Grattius and Nemesianus (qq.v.) on hunting and hunting-dogs.

Cynthia: The mistress of Propertius (q.v.). In reality, the lady was one Hostia, perhaps the granddaughter of Hostius (q.v.).

Cyprian, St.: One of the Christian Apologists (ca. 200-258, in which year he was martyred). Bishop of Carthage. Wrote letters, *Testimonia ad Quirinum, Ad Fortunatum, Ad Donatum, De Ecclesiae Unitate*. His style, which is better than that of Tertullian (q.v.) shows the influence of Cicero, Virgil and Seneca.

Cyprianus Gallicus: An early Christian-Latin poet.

Cytheris: See "Lycoris," Gallus.

Damasus, Pope: Friend of St. Jerome. Wrote epigrams.

Damiani, Peter, St.: 1007-1072. Italian clergyman, scholar and humanist of the 11th century. A passionate lover of the classics, he wrote, in his youth, much very fine lyric poetry. Also wrote a book on the duties of monks (*De Perfectu Monachorum*), and a *Liber Gomorrhianus*.

Danaë: In mythology, the mother of the hero Perseus. Title of two lost Latin tragedies, one by Livius Andronicus, the other by Naevius.

Dante Alighieri: 1265-1321. In addition to his chief works, which do not concern us here, since they were written in Italian, Dante wrote a treatise on poetry in the vernacular (*De Vulgari Eloquentia*). The treatise was written in Latin, as was his work on monarchy (*De Monarchia*) and minor works, including two Latin eclogues, and a *Quaestio de Aqua et Terra*. (Curtius)

Dantiscus, Joannes: Polish-Latin poet of the 16th century; author of satirical verse (*De Nostrorum Temporum Calamitatibus*, etc.).

"Dares Phrygius": In Homer, the name of a priest of Hephaestus at Troy. The reputed author of a pre-Homeric diary of the Trojan War. The name is also attached to a Latin "translation" of this diary, *De Excidio Troiae Historia,* written in the 4th or 5th century. Its only merit is that it is one of the two sources used by medieval authors for the Trojan War. It contains an alleged "dedication" by Sallust to Cornelius Nepos. Tells the story of the war from the Trojan point of view. See also Dictys Cretensis.

Dati, Leonardo di Piero: 1408-1472. Italian humanist. Wrote Latin poems, tragedy (*Hiempsal*).

David of Dinant: Philosopher and theologian of the 12th century. Wrote *Quaternuli,* summing up his philosophy, which may be termed materialistic pantheism. This book, naturally enough, was condemned by the Church at the Council of Paris in 1210. (Ferm, Encyclopedia of Religion)

Davus: A satirical work by Matthew of Vendôme (q.v.).

de: (Lat. "of, concerning") For titles beginning with this word, see under next word. Thus, for *De Rerum Natura,* see *Rerum Natura, de.*

Decembrio, Pier Candido: 1392-1477. Italian humanist, author of biographies, historical works.

Decius: Title of a lost praetexta, or historical drama, by Accius.

Decius Mus: Legendary Roman hero of the Samnite War, who charged into the enemy to insure the Roman victory, and was killed.

Declamationes: Series of declamatory exercises attributed to Quintilian. Some are romantic, dealing with pirates, wizards, and the like, some concern legal technicalities, others are material for "thrillers," dealing with adultery, murder, tyrannicide, etc. Jerome, Lactantius, and Isidore are all unquestioning in their attribution of the Declamationes to Quintilian himself. There are 19 long declamations and 145 short ones.

Declamations: Rhetorical exercises. See Controversia, Seneca. They were composed by, and for, students of rhetoric. For one group see "Declamationes" of Pseudo-Quintilian.

Defensor Pacis: See Marsilius of Padua.

Defloratio: See Robert of Cricklade.

Delatores: Professional informers. These flourished in the first century and afterwards. Their activities were encouraged by the government, which gave them a share in the confiscated property.

Delia: See Tibullus.

Deliciae: Name given to various collections of Neo-Latin poetry.

Dellius, Q.: Minor historian of the Augustan Age. Wrote a eulogy of Mark Antony.

Delrio: 17th century Jesuit scholar who wrote a *Syntagma Tragoediae Latinae*.

Dentatus (1) Lucius Sicinius: The "Roman Achilles"—a legendary hero embodying the virtues of the plebeians.

Dentatus (2) Manius Curius: Plebeian hero of early Rome, famous for his incorruptibility. If Dentatus (1) is the "Roman Achilles," Dentatus (2) might be termed the "Roman Robespierre."

Deo Socratis, de: Work by Apuleius (q.v.) on the "inner voice" or *daimonion* of Socrates.

Descartes, René: 1596-1650. Great French philosopher. Wrote some of his works in Latin (*Meditationes de Prima Philosophia, Principia Philosophiae,* etc.). Mentioned here only to show the post-Renaissance persistence of Latin as the language of scholarship and philosophy.

Descriptio Orbis Terrae: See Avienus.

Desiderius: Famous abbot of Monte Cassino in the 11th century. A sort of clerical Maecenas, who gathered around him a great band of scholars, poets, and authors. See Alberic, Amatus, Alphanus, Guaiferius.

Destruction of Milan: Dialogue by an unknown Italian poet of the 12th century.

d'Etaples, Lefèvre: See Lefèvre.

Devotio Moderna: Religious movement in the Netherlands. Leaders were Groote, Thomas a Kempis, Radewijns, Zerbold (qq.v.).

Dhuoda: Poetess of the Carolingian Revival. Wrote a manual of instruction for her son.

Dialects, Italic: Divided into P-Italic and Q-Italic, depending on the development of certain labio-velars. (Thus, Lat.

quis, Quinctius, coquina; but Oscan-Umbrian pis, Pompeius, popina) Latin and Faliscan are examples of Q-Italic; Oscan and Umbrian of P-Italic. The term "Italic Dialects" is usually used to signify Osco-Umbrian, however.

Dialogue, Latin: (See under names listed below) Since the time of Plautus and Terence, the dialogue form was exceedingly popular in Rome. It was used by Ennius and Lucilius. Marcus Brutus, the tyrannicide, is thought to have invented the Latin prose dialogue with his three books on law. The form was perfected by Cicero, many of whose philosophical, political, and rhetorical works are cast in dialogue form. Varro and Seneca also wrote dialogues, though the latter are not really deserving of the name. Tacitus wrote a dialogue on oratory in the Ciceronian manner. The use of the form for Christian literature is exemplified by the *Octavius* of Minucius Felix and the *Dialogues* of Gregory the Great. See also Boethius, Fulgentius, Conrad of Hirsau, Caesarius of Heisterbach.

Dialogues: (Cicero) See *De Republica, De Oratore, Tusculan Disputations, De Finibus, De Natura Deorum,* etc.

Dialogues: (Gregory the Great) See Gregory the Great.

Dialogues: (Seneca) See separate titles (*de Providentia, de Constantia Sapientiae, de Ira, de Otio, de Tranquillitate Animi, de Vita Beata, de Brevitate Vitae,* and *the Consolationes*).

Dialogus de Oratoribus: Work by Tacitus. Date unknown. An inquiry into the reasons for the decadence of oratory. This is a dialogue after the manner of Cicero. Prominent Romans are engaged in the discussion: Curiatus Maternus the poet, Marcus Aper, and others. Each of the interlocutors takes one viewpoint and defends it. There has been considerable doubt as to Tacitus' authorship of the work, but now its authenticity is pretty generally conceded.

Dialogus Miraculorum: See Caesarius of Heisterbach.

Dialogus super Auctores: See Conrad of Hirsau.

Diana: In mythology, the virgin goddess of the hunt and of the moon. Sister of Apollo, identified with the Greek Artemis.

Dicta Catonis: See *Disticha Catonis.*

Dicta Collectanea: (Julius Caesar) See *Apophthegmata.*

Dicta Gratiani: Commentaries of Gratian (q.v.) on canon law.

Dictatus Papae: Also known as *Dictatus Hildebrandini.* Statement of papal rights and prerogatives formerly attributed to Gregory VII.

"Dictys Cretensis": A Cretan, companion of Idomeneus, who was supposed to have written a diary on the Trojan War. This was allegedly translated into Latin in the second or third century by one L. Septimius *(Ephemiris Belli Troiani).* This "translation" was one of the two chief sources used by medieval writers for the story of the Trojan War, the other being "Dares Phrygius" (q.v.).

Dicuil: Geographer and astronomer of the early 9th century. Wrote a *Liber de Astronomia* and a *Liber de Mensura Orbis Terrae,* in which he used Pliny the Elder.

Didactic Poetry: (See under the separate authors and works) One of the oldest and most prevalent forms of Latin literature. In the Republic, mention should be made of Ennius and Accius, both of whom wrote didactic poetry as did Varro of Atax. The greatest of Republican, and perhaps of all didactic poets was Lucretius (q.v.). In the field of didactic poetry, his name is rivaled only by that of Virgil (*Georgics*). Other practitioners of this genre are Horace (*Ars Poetica*), Ovid *(Ars Am.)* Macer (on birds and serpents), Manilius (Astronomy), Grattius (Hunting) Columella, Nemesianus, Avienus, the *Aetna,* Serenus Sammonicus, the various translations of the *Phaenomena* of Aratus, the *Ora Maritima.* See also Ausonius, Dhuoda, Odo of Meung, Geoffrey of Vinsauf, Alexander of Villedieu, Matthew of Vendôme, Marbod of Rennes, and Eberhard of Bethune for medieval didactic poetry.

Didascaliae: Records of performances, commentaries, all sorts of significant data on the Plautine and Terentian plays, appearing in various forms in the different MSS.

Didascalica: See Accius.

Didascalion: Work by Hugh of St. Victor (q.v.), a great Scholastic of the 12th century.

Dido: The Carthaginian queen who figures in Virgil's Aeneid (q.v.). She may have appeared in Naevius' epic.

Die Natali, de: Work by Censorinus (q.v.), dedicated to Q. Caerellius on the latter's birthday. It deals, though not very profoundly, with such subjects as the planets, their effect on human life, etc.

Dies Irae: One of the most famous and majestic of all medieval Sequences (Raby). Incorporated into the Catholic Requiem Mass. A hymn on the Last Judgment. See Thomas of Celano.

Digest: See Justinian, Salvius Julianus.

Diomedes: A 4th century grammarian. Wrote an *Ars Grammatica,* which dealt with grammar and metrics or poetics.

Dionysius the Carthusian: 1402-1471. "The Ecstatic Doctor"—Flemish theologian, philosopher and exegetical writer.

Dirae: ("Curses") A poem in the *Appendix Virgiliana* (q.v.). It deals with the curses of a poet when he was evicted from his land by a veteran. It probably belongs to the Augustan Age, but is almost certainly not by Virgil himself.

Disciplinae: (More properly, *Disciplinarum libri IX*) Work by Varro (1), treating of the scheme of education in Rome. There are nine branches of learning: the trivium and quadrivium (qq.v.) and medicine and architecture besides.

dispositio: "Arrangement of material"—one of the five branches of rhetoric (q.v.).

Disputatio adversus Abaelardum: See William of Thierry.

Disputationes Metaphysicae: See Suarez.

Disticha Catonis: Versified collection of moral and philosophical maxims, aphorisms, etc. Immensely popular in the Middle Ages. Probably dates from the third century. "Cato" is possibly merely a recognition of Cato's position as one of Rome's first moralists.

Dittochaeon: A collection of hexameter quatrains by Prudentius (q.v.). The topics are Biblical.

Diverbium: The spoken part of a Plautine comedy, as opposed to the sung portion (*canticum*).

Diversitate Fortunae et Philosophiae Consolatione, de: See Henry of Settimello.

Divinae Institutiones: Polemic against pagan religion by Lactantius (q.v.).

Divinatione, de: Treatise on divination by Cicero (q.v.).

Divisione Naturae, de: See John Eriugena.

Divisiones: See Rhetoric.

Dlugosz, Jan: 15th century Polish-Latin chronicler, who imitated Livy.

Docta Ignorantia: "Learned ignorance," i.e., man's knowledge of God. Title of a work by Nicholas of Cusa (q.v.).

Doctors of the Church: The four original Latin Doctors are Ambrose, Jerome, Augustine, and Gregory the Great. Later additions: Anselm, Aquinas, Duns Scotus, Bernard of Clairvaux, and other learned theologians of the Middle Ages. The title is bestowed, usually by a Pope, for a combination of holiness and erudition.

Doctrinale: A didactic poem on grammar by Alexander of Villedieu. Together with the *Grecismus* of Eberhard of Bethune, it supplanted the older grammars of Priscian and Donatus in the later Middle Ages. For its inclusion in the Curriculum Authors, see *Laborintus*.

Documentum de Arte Versificandi: See Geoffrey of Vinsauf.

Dogmate Platonis, de: Study of Plato's philosophy by Apuleius (q.v.).

Dolet, Étienne: 1509-1538. French humanist and poet, author of *Commentarii Linguae Latinae*. Dolet was burned at the stake.

Dolopathos: See John of Haute-Seille.

Domitian: This emperor wrote poetry in his youth, and fostered literary competition with the Alban and Capitoline literary contests.

Domitius: Title of a lost praetexta by Curiatus Maternus.

Domitius (1), Afer: A delator or informer, and a lawyer of considerable skill. Wrote a legal treatise *De Testibus*. Teacher of Quintilian.

Domitius (2), Marsus: See Marsus.

Domo Sua, de: Speech by Cicero, dealing with the confiscation of his house by Clodius (q.v.).

Donation of Constantine: A forged document, purporting to be a grant made by Constantine the Great to Pope Sylvester. The forgery was made, possibly by one Christopher, during the reign of Pepin. It was proved to be a forgery by Lorenzo Valla (q.v.). See also Forgeries.

Donatus, Aelius (1): Grammarian of the mid-4th century. His commentary on Virgil is well known. He was perhaps the outstanding grammatical authority of the Middle Ages, together with Priscian. In fact, the word Donat came to be synonymous with Textbook. Also wrote a commentary on Terence. Donatus was the teacher of St. Jerome.

Donatus (2): Irish scholar and poet, Bishop of Fiesole, ca. 850.

Doniro: (or Donizo) Monk of Canossa, wrote a biography of the Countess Matilda.

Dositheus "Magister": 4th century grammarian. Wrote a bilingual *Ars Grammatica* (Greek and Latin). There exists a textbook called *Pseudo-Dositheana Hermeneumata*.

Dossennus: "The Hunchback"—one of the stock characters of the Atellan Farce or Fabula Atellana (q.v.).

Dousa, Janus: 1545-1609. Dutch humanist, poet, and historian. Wrote epigrams, satires, *Silvae,* and *Annales* in prose and in verse.

Draco Normannicus: See Stephan of Rouen.

Dracontius, Blossius Aemilius: fl. late 5th century. A lawyer, "vir clarissimus," and poet. Wrote secular works, *Romulea,* and mythological epyllia on the subjects of Helen, Medea, and Hylas. His Christian works are of far greater importance. They comprise the *Satisfacio* (an elegiac poem written in prison) and the *De Laudibus Dei*. This is marked by some rather fine passages, but also by obscure language, poor syntax and a lack of unity.

Drama, religious: See religious drama.

Drama, Roman: See Tragedy, Comedy, togata, palliata, praetexta, Atellana, mime, etc. Drama at Rome came into swift bloom with the comedies of Plautus and Terence, and the tragedies of Ennius, Accius, and Pacuvius, and nearly everything after these authors was in the nature of an anticlimax. Certainly the frigid pieces of Seneca were never meant for the stage. The works of Varius, the *Medea* of Ovid, the plays of Pomponius Secundus, Curiatus Maternus, etc., and the *Octavia* (the one surviving example of the praetexta) complete the picture. In the Middle Ages, the religious drama, passion plays, mystery plays, and "comœdiae" carry on the tradition. By the time of the Empire, drama had given way to the mime and the pantomime. For a later example, see Mussato's *Ecerinus*.

Dream of Scipio: See *Somnium Scipionis*.

Drepanius: See Panegyric.

Du Bellay, Guillaume: 1491-1543. French statesman, author of *Peregrinatio Humana*, an allegorical poem.

Du Bellay, Joachim: 1522-1560. French poet; wrote Latin *Xenia, Amores*.

Dubiis Generibus, de: See Caper, Flavius.

Dubius Sermo: Grammatical work by Pliny the Elder (now lost). It dealt with doubtful forms in speech.

Du Cange, Charles: 1610-1688. Author of a medieval Latin dictionary (*Glossarium ad Scriptores Mediae et Infimae Latinitatis*).

Duchesne, Louis: See *Liber Pontificalis*.

Dudo of St. Quentin: 11th century monk, author of the first history of the Normans (*De Moribus et Actis Primorum Normanniae Ducum*). The work is in form a "prosimetron" (see Menippean Satire), and is marred by excessive credulity and bad chronology.

Duff, J. Wight: Author of *Literary History of Rome to the Close of the Golden Age*, and of *Literary History of Rome in the Silver Age*. The two volumes together represent perhaps

the best treatment of Latin literature from the beginnings
to the Age of Hadrian.

Dulcitius: See Hroswitha.

Dulorestes: Lost play by Pacuvius, in the Greek style.

Dungal: Irish poet, ca. 800. Wrote primarily on astronomy.

Duns Scotus: (John Duns Scotus) 1265(?)-1308(?). 13th
century Franciscan friar. Lectured at Oxford and Paris. Theologian, philosopher, and scholastic. He agrees, in part, with
Aquinas. Was involved in the controversy on universals as
well as metaphysical speculation on the nature of God. Works
include *De Primo Principio, Quaestiones in Metaphysicum,
Opus Oxoniense.* Duns Scotus was called "Doctor Subtilis" or
the "Subtle Doctor."

Dunstan, St.: 908-988. Abbot of Glastonbury, scholar and
philosopher. Brought about complete reform of the church.
Later became Archbishop of Canterbury.

Duodecim Abusivis Saeculi, de: Anonymous work from
Ireland (6th century), dealing with the 12 abuses or contra-
dictions of the age: e.g., the youth without obedience, the old
man without religion, the wife without chastity, the king without righteousness, etc.

Durandus of St. Pourcain: A Dominican friar who held
views sharply opposed to those of Thomas Aquinas. His views
are Platonic and Augustinian, and he was an adversary of the
Nominalists, cf. Nominalism.

Eadmer of Canterbury: Wrote (a) *Historia Novorum in
Anglia,* dealing with recent events in England; (b) *de Vita et
Conversione Anselmi.* Eadmer died ca. 1134.

Ealhwine: See Alcuin.

Earliest Latin: ca. 500-240 B.C. Primarily interesting from
a linguistic and historical, rather than a literary viewpoint.
Little remains that antedates the Gallic invasion of 390 B.C.
Among the oldest specimens may be cited: the Praenestine
Fibula, the Duenos Bowl, the *Carmina Saliaria* and *Carmen
Arvale,* the epitaphs of the Scipios, the Laws of the Twelve
Tables, the Atellan farce and the Fescennine verses.

Early literature of the Republic: This category includes nearly all the Roman Drama. See Plautus, Terence, Caecilius Statius, Ennius, Livius, Naevius, Lucilius, Accius, Pacuvius, and Cato (1), for the fields of comedy, epic, tragedy, satire, and prose.

Easter Sequence: See Sequence; Wipo.

Ebarcius of St. Amand: End of 8th or beginning of 9th century. Author of *Scripturarum Claves*, an alphabetical lexicon of Biblical and other glosses, compiled piecemeal from various glossaries, in other words, a lexicographer's crazy-quilt. Uses great wealth of sources, only some of which are ascertainable. (Manitius)

Eberhard (1) of Bethune: d. 1212. Wrote *Graecismus*, a didactic poem on grammar, which, together with the work of Alexander of Villedieu (q.v.), became the chief grammatical authority of the later Middle Ages. See also *Laborintus*. Eberhard also wrote an *Antiheresis*.

Eberhard (2) the German: Late 13th century. Teacher, author of *Laborintus*, a didactic poem on rhetoric, which contains a complete listing of the Curriculum authors. See *Laborintus*.

Ecbasis Captivi: Anonymous work of the 10th century, probably by a monk. It is a sort of beast-epic, about a calf that has escaped from its mother. The style is obscure and labored. There is a great deal of leonine rhyme. (Raby, SLP)

Ecclesia, de: A Virgilian cento by Mavortius (q.v.). Probably dates from the 6th century.

Ecclesiae Historia: See "Magdeburg Centuries."

Ecclesiale: Work on canon law and chronology by Alexander of Villedieu (q.v.).

Ecclesiastical History of England: See Bede.

Ecclesiastical Latin: (Church Latin) Latin has always been, and still is, the official language of the Roman Catholic Church. One of the great deviations brought about by the Reformation was the discontinuance of the use of Latin for Protestant services. It is interesting to note that in a recent papal edict (August 1954) Pope Pius XII gave the American Church permission to use English instead of Latin for the rites of baptism, marriage, and Extreme Unction (not, however, for the Mass).

Ecerinus: Title of a Latin tragedy by Alberto Mussato (q.v.).

Eckhart, Meister: 1260-1327. German theologian, Scholastic, and mystic. Has been called "Father of German mysticism."

Ecloga de Calvis: See Hucbald.

Eclogues: (Virgil) A group of ten pastoral poems by Virgil. They were written during the years 42-39 B.C. They show the influence of Greek pastoral poetry, particularly that of Theocritus, and of the Alexandrine school. They are thus rather artificial and imitative, but nevertheless they are far better than later pastoral poetry (e.g., the eclogues of Calpurnius Siculus and Nemesianus). They are marked by a smoothness of expression and, above all, by a great love of Nature, which characterizes all Virgil's works. Among other aspects of pastoral poetry, the *Eclogues* feature the use of amoeban verse (q.v.). See *Messianic Eclogue.*

Eclogues: See also Calpurnius Siculus, Nemesianus, *Einsiedeln Eclogues, Bucolics,* Pastoral Poetry.

Editions of Classical texts: The best modern editions are: (German) Teubner, Leipzig; (British) Oxford; (French) Budé—text with French translation; (American-British) Loeb Classical Library—text with English translation. These are now published by Harvard. For medieval authors, Migne (PL) and the CSEL (See *Corpus Scriptorum Eccl. Lat.*). For Latin poetry, the most comprehensive is Postgate's *Corpus Poetarum Latinorum.*

Education: Duff enumerates three stages in the development of Roman education: (1) to the end of the Punic Wars; (2) to the time of Hadrian; (3) to ca. 500 A.D. In general, there were the following branches of education: first, the "litterator" or primary school, where children learned the "3 R's" and moral principles; second, the "grammaticus" or secondary school, where the poets were studied, as well as other authors, along with such subjects as natural science, music, mathematics, etc.; and thirdly, the "rhetor," corresponding roughly to what we would call a college or university education. Here the subject was logic and dialectic, and the *controversia* and *suasoria* and declamatory exercises were learned. The following authors (qq.v.) give us important information about various aspects of Roman education: (*a*) Cicero (*de Oratore*, etc.), who recognized the importance of a good all-round education, as did Plato and Quintilian; (*b*) Varro, whose *Disciplinae* outlined the subjects of importance to contemporary education: i.e., the Liberal Arts: the trivium (grammar, rhetoric, logic or dialectic), the quadrivium (arithmetic, geometry, music and astronomy) plus medicine and architecture; (*c*) Quintilian, who gives us perhaps the best picture of the education of his day, embodying many principles which even today are recognized as educationally sound; (*d*) Seneca (1), who shows the type of rhetorical exercises which were current; (*e*) St. Augustine and Boethius, each of whom planned a systematic treatment of the curriculum subjects, or Artes (liberal arts); (*f*)Martianus Capella, whose *Wedding of Mercury and Philology* is an exceedingly good summary of ancient education. The interest of the State in education may be seen from the following items: Julius Caesar enfranchised teachers of the "Arts"; Vespasian and Hadrian appointed professors of rhetoric and created state-supported chairs; Pliny (2) endowed a school at his home town of Novum Comum; Antoninus Pius made schools exempt from taxation; Alexander Severus established scholarships; Diocletian fixed the salary of teachers. The *Codex Theodosianus* regulated all matters concerning schools, teachers and pupils, and shows to what extent the conduct of schools came within the imperial purview. In the Middle Ages, control of education was lodged first with the monasteries, due to the work of such men as Benedict and Cassiodorus; then with the Cathedral Schools; finally with the Universities. Until the 4th century, Greek kept pace with Latin as the language of the schools, but after that it was gradually superseded and finally disappeared altogether, just as the study of pagan authors gradually gave way to that of Christian authors.

See: Artes, Trivium, Quadrivium, Nicolas de Orbellis, Martianus Capella, Universities, Cathedral Schools, Cassiodorus, Varro, Quintilian, and other names herein mentioned. (Duff; OCD)

Egbert: Archbishop of York; teacher of Alcuin (q.v.).

Egbert of Liége: Teacher in the Cathedral school of Liége; wrote poetry: *Fecunda Ratis* ("the well-laden ship") is a curious collection of Biblical and classical lore. The two parts are called *Prora* and *Puppis* (prow and stern). Egbert was a teacher of the subjects of the trivium (q.v.).

Eginhard: See Einhard.

Einhard: An East Frank, d. 840. Most famous for his Life of Charlemagne (*Vita Karoli*). Einhard was probably the best prose writer of the Carolingian Renaissance. He was well fitted for his task, being the friend and secretary of Charlemagne. His Latin is clear and graphic, and is modeled on that of Suetonius. He also wrote *Annales*.

Einsiedeln Eclogues: Two short pastoral poems of 49 and 38 lines, respectively, which were found in a 10th century MS. They date from the early part of Nero's reign, and have been attributed to Calpurnius Siculus, but with no great authority.

Ekkehard I: ca. 900-973. Abbot of the famous monastery of St. Gall. Author of the epic *Waltharius* (q.v.).

Ekkehard IV: d. ca. 1060. Abbot of St. Gall. Wrote *Casus S. Galli*—the chronicles of the monastery; as well as poetry (a *Liber Benedictionum*).

Elegiac Poetry: A line of dactylic hexameter, followed by two half-lines. Used by Ennius, Lucilius, and Catulus. Catulus developed the form to a perfection it had not previously enjoyed, and others of the Alexandrine School employed elegiacs. It was, however, in the Augustan Age that the genre reached its fullest development and refinement, and became identified with love-poetry. Tibullus brought the form to its greatest perfection, Propertius to its greatest intensity, and Ovid to its greatest facility. After the Augustan Age, the only writer of first rank is Martial, whose use of the form for barbed epigrams was foreshadowed by Catullus. See also *Appendix Virgiliana*, Claudian, Rutilius Namatianus, epigram, epitaph, Gallus.

Elegiae in Maecenatem: Two poems in the *Appendix Virgiliana*. Much dispute has been raised about their date. The attribution to Virgil is manifestly absurd, since they were written after Maecenas' death, and Maecenas died eleven years after Virgil.

Elizabeth I of England: Well-versed in the classics, she translated Boethius and Horace with no little ability.

Elocutio: "diction," one of the five branches of rhetoric (q.v.).

Elocutio Novella: The "New Speech." A conscious reaction against the style of Silver Latin (q.v.). Consists of a mixture of archaic style, vulgar Latin and foreign importations. See Fronto, Gellius, Apuleius. The expression was coined by Fronto. (Duff)

Embricho of Mainz: b. ca. 1010. Wrote a poem, *Vita Mahumeti* (Life of Mohammed), of 571 distichs, which was formerly attributed to Hildebert of Le Mans. (Manitius)

Emperors, literary activity of: Many of the emperors were cultured men, until the days of the so-called "Barracks Emperors." Augustus wrote the *Res Gestae* (see *Monumentum Ancyranum*); Tiberius was famous for his oratorical style; Claudius wrote memoirs, and dabbled in antiquities; Nero is known for his poetical accomplishments; Vespasian wrote memoirs and was a competent orator; Titus wrote a poem about a comet; Domitian also wrote poetry and fostered literary contests; we possess some of Trajan's correspondence with Pliny; Hadrian wrote a good deal of trash and one lovely little poem to his soul; Marcus Aurelius wrote the well-known *Meditations* (in Greek). Later emperors, such as Justinian and Theodosius are responsible for codifying laws and edicts.

Ena, Sextilius: Minor poet of the Augustan Age. Came from Corduba in Spain.

Enchiridion Militis Christiani: "Handbook for the Christian Knight" by Erasmus (q.v.).

Encyclical: A letter or communication from the Pope. Differs from a Papal Bull in that it is less dogmatic.

Encyclopedia: In both Classical and Medieval periods, there were many collections made of universal knowledge, sometimes for school use, sometimes for personal or family use. For examples, see Cato, Varro, Celsus, Pliny, Isidore of Seville, Boethius, Martianus Capella, Cassiodorus, Bede, Alcuin, Hrabanus Maurus, Thomas of Cantimpré, Vincent of Beauvais, Peter Comestor.

Endelechius: Friend of Paulinus of Nola (q.v.); probable author of the Christian eclogue *De Mortibus Boum.*

Ennius (1), Q.: 239-169 B.C. Greatest of the early Roman poets. Friend of the elder Scipio; there was a statue of the poet in the marble tomb of the Scipios. His genius was varied, leaving no field of literature untouched. He wrote 20 tragedies, 2 comedies, one or two praetextae, a huge epic on Roman history (the *Annales*), saturae, didactic verse, etc. His ability was by no means equal in all these fields. His greatest genius appears to have been for tragedy. Only fragments of the works survive, but there are enough of them to give us some indication of his style. His hexameters are rather crude, but much better than the Saturnians of Naevius. He had a real eye for beauty. His influence was felt by Lucretius, Virgil, Ovid, Cicero (who affectionately calls him "noster Ennius"), Horace, Quintilian, Fronto, Gellius, and others. The plays are much influenced by Euripides. They were still produced in the Augustan Age. The greatest single work was the *Annales* in 18 books. This definitely established the dactylic hexameter as the meter of the Latin epic. Ennius combined practical wisdom with emotional force and occasional flashes of real poetical genius which justify his being termed "Father of Roman Poetry." He may be said to have invented the form of the Satura or satire. Perhaps the best criticism of Ennius is that of Quintilian, who said that E.'s verses are like old trees, which have majesty rather than beauty. Works: *Annales;* Tragedies: *Thyestes, Telamo, Andromeda, Hecuba, Iphigenia, Medea Exsul, Melanippa, Alexander, Telephus, Andromache.*

Comedies: *Cupuncula, Pancratiastes.* Praetextae: *Ambracia, Sabinae, Saturae.* Minor works: *Hedyphagetica, Epicharmus, Euhemerus,* Epigrams, Epitaphs, etc.

Ennius (2): There existed a grammarian of this name, to be distinguished from the poet.

Ennodius: Magnus Felix, ca. 473-521. Christian poet. Bishop of Pavia. Wrote letters, speeches, poetry, hymns, epigrams, a biography of Epiphanius, an epithalamium, and other works. His work is full of rhetorical affectation and elegant style, but of little depth.

Epanaleptic Verse: Elegiac verses in which the latter half of the pentameter repeats the first half of the preceding hexameter.

Example: Sentio, fugit hiems; Zephyrisque amantibus orbem
         iam tepet Eurus aquis: sentio, fugit hiems.
See Pentadius.

Ephemeris (1): Alexandrine work by Varro (2) of Atax (q.v.).

Ephemeris (2): Poem by Ausonius (q.v.) describing a typical day in town. The poem has a mixture of Christian and pagan feeling which is to be expected in a poet like Ausonius.

Ephemeris Belli Troiani: See "Dictys Cretensis."

Epic, Roman: (See under the individual authors and titles)
1. Republic, Ennius, *Annales*; Naevius, *Bellum Punicum,* Livius Andronicus, Hostius, Furius Bibaculus, Cicero (on his Consulship), Varro of Atax (*Bellum Sequanicum*). Lucretius, *De Rerum Natura.*

2. Augustan Age. Virgil brought the epic to its highest peak of perfection with his *Aeneid* (q.v.). See also Albinovanus Pedo, Cornelius Severus.

3. First century of the Empire. Four writers are here to be distinguished: Lucan (*Pharsalia* or *de Bello Civili*), Valerius Flaccus (*Argonautica*), Silius Italicus (*Punica*), and Statius (*Thebais* and *Achilleis*).

4. Later authors: Claudian, Corippus, Sidonius.

5. Biblical epic: Prudentius, Juvencus, Dracontius, Sedulius.

6. Medieval epic: *Waltharius,* Wido (*Battle of Hastings*),

Carmen de Bello Saxonico, Gesta Friderici, Solimarius, Ligurinus.

See epyllion, historical epic, Biblical epic, allegory, mythological epic.

Epicadus: Freedman of Sulla; finished the *Commentarii Rerum Suarum* of Sulla after the latter's death.

Epicharmus: Poem on Nature by Ennius. Based on the work of the Sicilian Epicharmus. Has the traditional theory of the four elements: earth, air, fire and water.

Epicius: Noted teacher of late Republic. He numbered Augustus, Mark Antony, and Virgil among his pupils.

Epicleros: ("the Heiress") Lost comedy by Turpilius (q.v.).

Epictetus: Famed Stoic teacher, ca. 100 A.D. Arrian, his pupil, wrote his *Discourses* and *Enchiridion* (Manual or Handbook) in Greek.

Epicureanism: Greek system of philosophy preaching avoidance of pain and freedom from fear of death. Founded by Epicurus. For influence on Roman literature, see Lucretius.

Epideictic oratory: As opposed to legal, or forensic. Showpieces of oratory; ceremonial speeches. The Greek Gorgias first defined this type of oratory. Includes funeral orations, panegyrics, etc.

Epidicus: Play by Plautus, said to have been his favorite, but modern tastes find it too complex, and prefer such plays as the *Menaechmi, Rudens, Mostellaria, Amphitruo,* etc.

Epigram: (See under the individual authors) Originally an inscription for a tomb, the term came to be used for any short, pithy piece of verse. Elegiac meter became the standard form. An early practitioner was Q. Lutatius Catulus. Caesar and Cicero wrote epigrams, as did Varro (1), Furius Bibaculus, Cinna, Calvus and Catullus. The last-named poet gave the epigram its sting, in which respect he was surpassed only by Martial, the name that immediately leaps to mind when one thinks of epigram. In late antiquity, Ausonius and Claudian were known for their epigrams. In the Middle Ages, examples are to be found in the works of Godfrey of Cambrai, Peter

Damiani, Henry of Huntingdon, Marbod of Rennes, and the Goliardic poets. Sir Thomas More (q.v.) also wrote epigrams.

Epigrams: (Martial) Martial developed the form of the epigram to the extent that his name is almost synonymous with the genre. In his hands it was equally efficient as the instrument for the expression of tender sentiment, worldly philosophy, or biting satire. In his epigrams we get a wonderful picture of the society of the early Empire, with all the usual types, all the foibles of men and their society sharply delineated. He mentions many of his contemporaries, but not the poet Statius, from which it is inferred that Martial disliked the other poet. The two most obvious faults of Martial are his servility and his obscenity. From Martial's day onward, the term "epigram" came to mean the barbed, witty expression that Martial made it. (Duff, Silver Age)

Epigrammata: Title appearing in lists by Donatus and Servius of the works of Virgil. Probably identical with the Catalepton (q.v.).

Epigraphy: The study of inscriptions on stone, metal, etc. as distinct from those on parchment or papyrus, which come under the headings of paleography and papyrology. Belongs rather to the fields of history, law, philology, etc. than to literature.

Epirota, Q. Caecilius: Freedman of Atticus (q.v.). He lectured on Virgil and the new poets of the Augustan Age.

Epistles: (Horace) Book I. 19 letters. In hexameters. Almost a continuation of the Satires (q.v.). Mostly philosophical in nature, with Horace's usual genial reflections on life. His philosophy is eclectic. In spite of his calling himself "a porker from the flock of Epicurus," his leanings are often Stoic.

Book II. Two longer letters. Chiefly deal with literary criticism of contemporary and of earlier works. This book is also in hexameters.

Epistolae Obscurorum Virorum: ("Letters of Obscure Men") A series of letters, by Ulrich von Hutten, Reuchlin, Erasmus, and Crotius Rubienus, published in 1515 and 1517, containing powerful satire on monasticism.

Epistula ad Pisones: See *Ars Poetica* (Horace).

Epistulae ad Atticum, Brutum, etc. See Letters, Cicero's.

Epistulae ex Ponto: (Ovid) Like the *Tristia* (q.v.) this is a collection of elegiac poems written by Ovid from his place of exile on the Black Sea. Full of self-pity as they are, they nevertheless contain a good deal that is of autobiographical interest.

Epistulae Morales: (Seneca, 2) Series of letters by Seneca. In varying styles and of varying excellence, the Moral Epistles give us a good picture of the author. They deal with such subjects as the pleasure of philosophy, how to face death, Stoic doctrines of abstinence, etc., how to travel, kindness to slaves, gladiator shows, seaside resorts, and many other topics. Seneca preaches a sensible moderation in all things. The question has been raised whether these are genuine letters or not.

Epitaph: (See also epigram) As in the Greek, Roman epitaphs are often in two lines, and in the elegiac meter. Examples: Ennius' epitaph:

Nemo me lacrimis decoret nec funera fletu
  faxit. cur? Volito vivus per ora virum.

(Weep not nor mourn for me, because I shall live to flit on the mouths of men.)

Virgil's: Mantua me genuit, Calabri rapuere, tenet nunc
      Parthenope; cecini pascua, rura, duces.

(Born in Mantua, lived in Calabria, buried in Naples, I sang of pastures, fields, and warriors.) Martial's epitaph to the girl Erotion (Lie lightly on her, earth; she trod lightly on thee) is a good example. In the *Culex* there is an epitaph to the gnat who saved the shepherd's life.

Epitaphs of the Scipios: In Saturnian verse. Some of the earliest remains of Latin that we possess.

Epithalamium: A marriage-song. Probably came into Rome from Alexandria. Catullus and the Cantores Euphorionis (qq.v.) were among the first to write this type of poetry. Ovid, Statius and others down to the time of Claudian did so too. Ausonius' famous cento is another example. The Christian epithalamium (with an allegorical, or mystical note to it) is a development of late antiquity. Paulinus of Nola, Dracontius, Sidonius Apollinaris, Venantius Fortunatus are among those who wrote Christian epithalamia.

Epithalamium Fridi: A Virgilian cento (q.v.) by Luxorius. Like the Cento Nuptialis of Ausonius, it is obscene.

Epitome: The "Reader's Digest" of antiquity. Works of the size of Livy's history, etc., needed to be epitomized in late imperial times. Sometimes only the epitome has survived, and is therefore a useful clue to lost works, while sometimes the original has survived along with the epitome, as with Vitruvius. See Florus, Aurelius Victor, Festus, Epitome Caesarum, Eutropius.

Epitome Bellorum Omnium Annorum DCC: Florus' abridgement of Roman history. Deals with all the wars down to the time of Augustus. The work has little historical perspective.

Epitome Caesarum: An account of Imperial history from Augustus to Theodosius. Falsely attributed to Aurelius Victor (q.v.).

Epitome Rei Militaris: See Vegetius.

Epodes: (Horace) A group of 17 poems, mostly in iambic meter. On various subjects: love, invective, the witch Canidia, true and false loves, wine, woman and song, the praise of country life, and the eulogy of Maecenas. One of the Epodes is about garlic. The sixteenth is the most famous, with its expression of Horace's disgust with the wars and his plea that the Romans migrate to the shores of the Ocean where a new Golden Age will take place.

Eponymous hero: One who gives his name to something (e.g., a tribe). Just as Athena gave her name to Athens, and Poseidon to Posidonia, so did heroes give their names to places or tribes. The practice was a common one in Greece and Rome.

Epyllion: A toy epic. One of the products of the Alexandrine movement at Rome. Epyllia were written by Catullus (*Peleus and Thetis*), Calvus (*Io*), Cinna (*Zmyrna*), Cornificius (*Glaucus*), Cicero (*Alcyone*), and Virgil (the Aristaeus epi-

sode in Georgics, IV). The *Culex* and *Ciris* of the Appendix
Virgiliana are further examples. Ovid's *Metamorphoses* might
be called a succession of epyllia. After Ovid the form seldom
occurs. The *Aegritudo Perdicae* is a late example.

Equos Troianus: Plays of this title, dealing with the Wooden
Horse, were written by Livius Andronicus and by Naevius.

Erasmus, Desiderius: 1466?-1536. Great Dutch scholar and
humanist. Wrote the *Moriae Encomium* (Praise of Folly), the
Enchiridion Militis Christiani (Handbook for the Christian
Knight), *Adagia, Ciceronianus, De Libero Arbitrio, Colloquia
Familiaria*, etc. An excellent Greek scholar as well. A powerful
force in the Reformation. It was said that Erasmus laid the
egg of ecclesiastical reform and Luther hatched it.

Erbo: A clergyman who wrote, ca. 1189, a dirge on the fall
of Jerusalem (*Threni Captis Hierosolymis*).

Erchanbert of Freising: 9th century grammarian.

Eriphyla: Lost tragedy by Accius.

Eriugena: (Erigena) John Scotus. See John Eriugena.

Ermenrich of Ellwagen: 9th century grammarian, author of
grammatical treatise, hagiographical works. At various times,
he was associated with the monasteries of Fulda, Reichenau,
and St. Gall.

Ermoldus Nigellus: 9th century (fl. 825) poet. Wrote a
poem on the deeds of Louis the Pious, to which he appended
an entirely irrelevant description of St. Mary's in Strasbourg;
and other poetry. (Raby)

Ernald of Bonneval: Cistercian monk of the 12th century.
Wrote a biography of Bernard of Clairvaux. Criticized the
Platonic cosmology of Bernard Silvestris and Alan of Lille
(qq.v.).

Eros, Staberius: See Staberius Eros.

Erotopaegnia: See Laevius.

Essay, Philosophical: See Cicero (*De Senectute*, etc.) and
Seneca (*De Ira, de Vita Beata*, etc.). If Cicero invented the
form, Seneca developed it to its full fruition.

Est et Non: Minor poem in the *Appendix Virgiliana*. Probably written in the 4th century.

Etiological myth: See Aetiological myth.

Etruscans: A people who settled in the Italian peninsula, probably from Asia Minor, about 800 B.C. Their language is not Indo-European and is still a mystery. The Etruscans had a profound influence on Roman art, burial customs, architecture, etc.

Etymologiae: See Isidore of Seville.

Eucharisticon: Poem by Paulinus of Pella (q.v.). Written in his 84th year. In it the poet looks back on his long life and relates its blessings.

Euclerius: Minor poet of the 4th century.

Eugenius III: Bishop of Toledo, middle of the 7th century. Noted for the artificiality of his writings. Wrote a whole series of verses with tmesis, acrostics, and other such devices.

Eugenius Vulgarius: Poet and grammarian of Naples, fl. ca. 900. Wrote a work on rhetoric, figure poems (q.v.), acrostics, and the like.

Euhemerus (Sacra Historia): A work by Ennius, following the Greek rationalist Euhemerus, who attributed the existence of the gods to apotheosized heroes. The work is lost, and it is not even known whether it was in prose or verse.

Eulogius: Bishop of Cordova in the 9th century. Writer of various hagiographical works, Passions, etc.

Eumenius: See *Panegyric.*

Eunuchus: Play by Terence, in which a youth pretends to be an Ethiopian eunuch to win the favor of a slave girl. She proves to be free-born and the lovers are united at the end.

Euphemism: The practice of attributing a good name to a person or thing, hoping thereby to make it so. Examples: Eumenides (Furies). Previously called the Erinyes. Eumenides means "The Well-Disposed Ones," Euxine (Black Sea) or "Friendly to strangers," Faunus (woodland deity of Italy— the name means "kindly").

Eupolemius: Pseudonym for a French poet of the 11th century, author of a *Messiad,* an allegorical epic which shows the influence of Prudentius' *Psychomachia* (q.v.).

Eusebius (1): Ecclesiastical historian of the 4th century

(d. 339). Bishop of Caesarea. Wrote a universal chronicle, adapted by Jerome, and translated into Latin by Rufinus (see Rufinus 3).

Eusebius (2): Author of a collection of Riddles (*Enigmata Eusebii*).

Eusthenius: Minor poet of the 4th century.

Eutropius: fl. 350. Wrote an epitome of Roman history (see epitome) from Romulus to the emperor Jovian. The title is *Breviarium ab Urbe Condita.*

Evagrius (1): 5th century Gallic author of "*Altercatio Legis inter Simonem Judaeum et Theophilum Christianum.*"

Evagrius (2): Sixth century author of ecclesiastical history.

Evangelorum Libri: See Juvencus.

Everard le Moine: 12th century Anglo-Norman poet who wrote a version of the *Disticha Catonis* (q.v.).

Excessu Divi Augusti, ab: See *Annales*, Tacitus.

Excidio Troiae Historia, de: See Dares Phrygius.

Exempla Elocutionum: See Arusianus Messius.

Exemplum: "Example"—a story or parable to illustrate some particular point, as, "exempla virtutis" (examples of courage). In the Middle Ages, the story was usually to illustrate some theological doctrine. See also Valerius Maximus.

Exitus Inlustrium Virorum: See Titinius Capito.

Exordio Gentis Francorum, Carmen de: See Minor Carolingian Poetry.

Explanatio in Artem Donati: See Servius.

Explanationes in Donatum: See Sergius.

Expositio in Psalmum: See Ambrose.

Expositio Sermonum Antiquorum: A study of rare words by Fulgentius (1) (q.v.).

Expositio Vergilianae Continentiae Secundum Philosophos Moralis: A commentary on Virgil by Fulgentius (1). Full of allegorical interpretations, this work is, if nothing else, a good indication of the position and reputation of Virgil in late antiquity.

Eyb, Albrecht von: 1420-75. German humanist. Wrote *Margarita Poetica, Speculum Morum,* etc.

Fabianus, Papirius: Philosopher and teacher of rhetoric (rhetor) of the Augustan Age. Studied with Blandus and Arellius, and became a public lecturer on philosophy. The younger Seneca was his pupil.

Fabius Maximus: See Maximus.

Fabius Pictor (1), Q.: One of the earliest Roman historians. Wrote a history of Rome from Aeneas to his own day (Second Punic War). The history, which was written in Greek, was a source for Livy.

Fabius Pictor (2), Servius: Wrote on pontifical law. Not to be confused with Fabius Pictor the historian.

Fabius Rusticus: Author of a (lost) historical work, used by Tacitus.

Fable in Classical times: A very ancient form of literature in which beasts speak and act as men. The earliest collection is that of "Aesop," in Greek. These fables were usually satiric, in that they pointed out the foibles of men, and a moral was either explicitly drawn or at least implied. In Roman literature, the fable was used by Ennius, Lucillus, Horace, Phaedrus (who wrote a collection of fables in iambic senarii), "Romulus," Avianus, and others. See under the separate names.

Fable, medieval: There were many collections of "Aesopian" fables made in the Middle Ages. Among them should be mentioned: Walther (Galterus Anglicus), who versified the Romulus-fables (q.v.), the *"Novus Avianus,"* a new working, ca. 1100, of the Avianus collection, the *"Novus Avianus Vindobonensis,"* the fables of Alexander Neckham (q.v.), and the collection made by Baldo in the 12th century, called the *"Novus Aesopus."* See also *Ysengrimus* by Nivard of Ghent.

Fabula. From the Latin verb meaning "speak"—the word is used as a story, tale, or "fable," then becomes more or less standardized in the meaning of a play (Fabula Atellana, palliata, etc.).

Fabula Atellana: A sort of comic burlesque, or Punch-and-Judy show which was extremely popular in Italy. It had certain well-defined stock characters, such as Maccus, the fool; Pappus the graybeard; Manducus the guzzler; Dossenus the hunchback; and Bucco, a Falstaffian figure. We have titles of many of these burlesques.

The Literary Atellana is a development of the genre. For examples, see Pomponius and Novius.

Fabula crepidata: A Roman tragedy on a Greek theme (the name comes from "crepida"—the buskin worn by actors in tragedies), as contrasted with the "praetexta" or tragedy dealing with Roman history.

Fabula palliata: A Roman comedy based on a Greek model (e.g., Menander, Diphilus, Philemon, etc.). The comedies of Plautus and Terence fall into this category. See Plautus, Terence, Comedy, contaminatio.

Fabula praetexta (or praetextata): A Roman play on an historical subject (from "praetexta," the magistrate's toga). We possess many titles of praetextae by Ennius, Accius, Curiatus Maternus, and others. The one extant example of a praetexta is the *Octavia* (q.v.).

Fabula riciniata: i.e., the Mime (q.v.), so called from the "ricinium" or short cloak worn by the female character in this type of play.

Fabula saltica: The libretto for a pantomime (q.v.). The words were sung by a chorus, and the pantomime was danced in accompaniment thereto.

Fabula tabernaria: A comedy of tradespeople; a slight change from the fabula togata (q.v.).

Fabula togata: Native Italian comedy of manners, in which the "pallium" or Greek cloak (cf. Fabula palliata) is replaced by the "toga." Since none of the togatae have survived, it is impossible to form an estimate of this genre. We know, however, that it dealt with the lower classes. Cf. Aristotle's dictum ("Poetics") that comedy deals with men worse than the average.

Fabula trabeata: A form of togata (q.v.); a comedy representing the equestrian class. The genre was invented by one Melissus, the freedman of Maecenas.

Fabulae: See Hyginus (3).

Facta et Dicta Memorabilia: Work by Valerius Maximus

(q.v.). A veritable potpourri of illustrative examples for orators (see "exempla"). The headings are loosely arranged according to subject-matter, as: religion, omens and prodigies, games, customs, virtues, moderation, gratitude, filial piety, chastity, punishments, vicissitudes of fortune, etc. Under each general heading there are illustrative anecdotes. The work is thus a manual or repertory for the orator, furnishing him with examples of anything he may wish to illustrate. There are about twice as many Roman as Greek examples. The work was popular in antiquity and even more so in the Middle Ages. (Duff, OCD)

Fadius Gallus, M.: A friend of Cicero's. We possess five of his letters to the orator (Fam. vii. 23-27). He wrote eulogies of Cato.

False Decretals: A forged collection of Canon Law (q.v.) based on an earlier collection. See Forgeries.

Familiar Colloquies: Work by Erasmus (q.v.), published 1518. It is a textbook to be used in polishing the speech of the young pupil. See also *Colloquies*.

Fannius, C. (1): Consul 122 B.C. Wrote a history of Rome from its origins. Praised by Cicero, Brutus and Sallust.

Fannius, C. (2): Was engaged in writing a work on the victims of Nero. Contemporary and friend of the younger Pliny, who mentions him in glowing terms.

Farley, Robert: fl. 1640. Scottish Latin poet (*Lychnocausia*).

Fasti: "Dies Fasti" and "Dies Nefasti"—that is, auspicious and inauspicious days—the old Roman calendar, which also included lists of consuls and other magistrates, triumphs, priestly lists, etc. (These are separately known as Fasti Consulares, Fasti Triumphales, and Fasti Sacerdotales.) See Ovid, Verrius.

Fasti: (Ovid) A calendar for half the year, mingled with records of festivals, history, folklore, superstition, astronomy, religious observances, etc., in elegiac distichs. This is Ovid's one claim to being a national poet. His exile prevented him from completing the work. Although he says (*Tristia*) he has written 12 books.

Fates: The Roman Fates were called Parcae. It is likely that they were originally birth-goddesses (from parere- to bear), and that they were identified with the Greek Moirae (Fates) through a mistake in etymology. See Religion. (Rose in OCD)

Fathers of the Church: (Patres) Founders of the Roman Catholic Church, known for their orthodoxy, holiness, and antiquity.

Fato, de: Work on Fate by Cicero. The beginning and end are incomplete.

Faunus: A minor Roman deity of the forest, identified with the Greek Pan. Also, god of herdsmen. The name is a euphemism (q.v.), and means "kindly one."

Faustulus: In Roman mythology, the shepherd who reared Romulus and Remus.

Faustus: Tragedian of Nero's time. Wrote a *Thebae* and *Tereus*.

Faventinus, M. Cetius: Made an abridgement of Vitruvius, used by Palladius.

Favonius Eulogius: Contemporary of St. Augustine, wrote a *Disputatio de Somnio Scipionis.*

Fecunda Ratis: See Egbert of Liége.

Felix, Flavius: Poet of the African anthology, ca. 500 A.D. Wrote epigrams on the Baths of Allicana, which include an acrostic, telestich and mesostich (qq.v.). (Lindsay)

Feltre, Vittorino de: See Vittorino.

Fenestella: Antiquarian and annalist of the Augustan Age. Wrote a History of Rome, perhaps from the beginnings. A special authority for the age of Cicero. Used by Pliny (1).

Ferrières, Lupus of: See Servatus Lupus.

Fescennine Verses: See Versus Fescennini.

Festus, Sextus Pompeius: Made an abridgement of the work of Verrius Flaccus (*De Significatu Verborum*) in the second century. Festus in turn was abridged by Paulus Diaconus (q.v.).

Fichet, Guillaume: 15th century French rhetorician (*Rhetoricorum libri III*).

Ficino, Marsilio: 1433-99. Renaissance Platonist from

Florence. Translated Platonic dialogues into Latin, with commentary and exposition. Works: *Theologica Platonica, De Christiana Religione.* Translated various of the Neo-Platonists, as Porphyry, Proclus, etc. Of tremendous importance for the transmission of Greek philosophy to Latin civilization.

Fide Catholica, de: See Boethius.

Figulus, Nigidius: 98-45 B.C. A great scholar of the Ciceronian Age. Wrote on grammar, natural science, divination, etc. Next to Varro (1), he was the most learned man of his day.

Figure-Poems: (Carmina Figurata) Poems whose outline on the page represent some object. Cf. "The Mouse's Tale" in *Alice in Wonderland.* See Optatianus, Milo of St. Amand.

Figures of Speech: The most common used by Roman authors are the *simile* and *metaphor, metonymy, litotes* or understatement, *chiasmus* (interlocked word order: ab-ba, e.g. "Her eyes were blue and gold was her hair"), *synecdoche, hendiadys* (co-ordination of ideas usually subordinated one to the other: e.g., "crimes and madness" for "mad crimes"), *zeugma* (extension of a modifier to two or more words, with only one of which it makes sense), *anaphora* (repetition of a word at the beginning of successive clauses).

Figuris Sententiarum et Elocutionis, de: See Aquila Romanus.

Filelfo, Francesco: 1398-1481. Poet, scholar and humanist of the Italian Renaissance. Composed in round numbers (ten books of satires, each consisting of ten satires of 100 lines apiece, etc.).

Fine Aufidi Bassi, a: (Lost) Historical work by Pliny the Elder in 31 books, which continued the work of Aufidius Bassus (q.v.). Cited by Tacitus.

Finibus Bonorum et Malorum, de: Philosophical work by Cicero (q.v.) on the limits of good and evil. Deals with the four rival theories of the "summum bonum" propounded by the Epicureans, Stoics, Peripatetics and Academy.

Firmicus Maternus, Julius: 4th century author of a treatise on astrology (*Mathesis*), and later, upon his conversion to

Christianity, of *De Errore Profanorum Religionum,* pleading with Constans and Constantine to do away with paganism. Another work (*Consultationes Zacchaei et Apollonis*) has been attributed to him.

Fisher, John: 1469-1535. English clergyman, Bishop of Rochester, executed by Henry VIII. Wrote miscellaneous Latin works.

Fitz-Geffry, Charles: 17th century author of Latin epigrams, sermons, and epitaphs.

Flacco, pro: Speech by Cicero, refuting a charge of mismanagement and oppression in the province of Asia. The speech was delivered in 59 B.C.

Flaccus: See Horace, Valerius, Verrius, Persius.

"Flaccus, the slave of Claudius": Provided musical accompaniment for the plays of Terence, using four kinds of flutes.

Flaminio, Marco Antonio: 1498-1550. Italian humanist; author of Latin poetry (*Carmina, Lusus Pastorales*).

Flavian period: The period 69-96 A.D. Emperors Vespasian, Titus, and Domitian. During this period there flourished Pliny the Elder, Quintilian, Valerius Flaccus, Silius Italicus, Statius and Martial.

Flavius Caper: Grammarian ca. 100 A.D. Wrote on Virgil and early authors. Used by Charisius and Priscian (qq.v.).

Flavius Vopiscus: One of the six authors of the *Historia Augusta* (q.v.).

Flavus, Alfius: Minor Augustan rhetor and poet.

Flavus, Verginius: Rhetor of the Neronian period; teacher of Persius (q.v.).

Flemmyng, Robert: d. 1483. English humanist and Latin poet (*Lucubraciunculae Tiburtinae*).

Flodoard of Reims: (894-966) Wrote a work on the Triumph of Christ and the Saints in Palestine; a *Life of St. Pelagus; Annals;* and a *Historia Remensis Ecclesiae* (History of the Church of Reims). The last-named work accomplished for Reims what Bede and Adam (qq.v.) did for Britain and Hamburg-Bremen.

Florence of Worcester: d. 1118. English chronicler (*Chronicon ex chronicis*) in Latin.

Florentinus: African poet, ca. 500.

Florentius of Worcester: End of 11th, beginning of 12th century. Translated the great *Saxon Chronicle* into Latin. Begins with Bede and the earliest history and goes down to the year 1117. A later continuer brings the work down to 1154. The style is simple, sober, and unadorned. (Manitius)

Flores Rhetorici: See Alberic of Monte Cassino.

Florida: Excerpts from speeches and declamations of Apuleius. They range in interest and importance from the jejune to the beautiful.

Floridus Aspectus: Collection of poems of Peter Riga (q.v.).

Florus, Julius: Minor Augustan satirist.

Florus (1), P. Annius or L. Annaeus: It is now generally conceded that the historian, rhetor, and poet of this name are one and the same. Works: *Epitome* of Roman history; Dialogue *Vergilius an orator an poeta,* and various poetry. The famous *Pervigilium Veneris* (q.v.) has been assigned to Florus, but with no real grounds.

Florus (2) of Lyons: Theologian of the 9th century. Erudite and fanatical in his persecution of Lucretius. Wrote a Complaint on the partition of the Frankish kingdom; and religious poetry in hexameters.

Folcvin of Laubach (Lobbes): d. 990. Author of *Gesta Abbatum Sithiensium,* and *Gesta Abbatum Lobiensium,* which mingle general history with the history of the cloisters. Great fondness for Virgilian quotations. Distinguished neither by their style, Latinity, nor their composition. (Manitius)

Folengo, Teofilo: 16th century author of an epic parody. See Parody.

Folk-tale: There are many motifs of folk-tale common to Roman, Greek, Hebraic, Germanic and other peoples: Such elements as the Invulnerable Hero with the one vulnerable spot; the Exposed Infant who is saved and returns to kill or destroy those who exposed him (her); the Uninvited Guest who casts a curse; the Trial of Strength, in which the least likely competitor wins; the Difficult Question or Riddle; the Man who Sacrifices the First Thing he Meets (his son or daughter). The Beast-fable is another form of folk-tale. The story of Cupid and Psyche (Apuleius) is yet another example.

Fons Philosophiae: See Godfrey of St. Victor.

Fonteio, pro: Speech by Cicero on behalf of a defendant who was charged with oppression in Gallia Narbonensis. The speech is incomplete.

Forgeries: Examples: *Donation of Constantine*; "Dares Phrygius"; "Dictys Cretensis"; *Sulpiciae Sabella*; Guez de Balzac's forgery *Indignatio in Poetas Neronianorum temporum*; the 15th century—*De Progenie Augusti Caesaris*; Hildegar of Meaux; Aethicus Cosmographus.

Formando Studio, de: Work on Curriculum-reform by Rudolf Agricola (q.v.).

Fortescue: Sir John, ca. 1394-ca. 1476. English author and juristconsult. Wrote *De Laudibus Legum Angliae.*

Fortleben: German. The survival, influence in later times, etc. of an author or work.

Fortuna: Italian goddess of luck or chance, identified with the Greek Tyché. Rose (OCD) says that she was probably an old fertility deity.

Fortunatae Insulae: The "Islands of the Blessed." Many references to these islands appear in ancient literature. Homer, Hesiod, Pindar and others mention them. They have been variously identified with Madeira and the Canary Islands.

Fortunatianus: See Atilius.

Fortunatus, Venantius: 530?-610. Late Roman-Gallic poet. Wrote Life of St. Martin, a metrical paraphrase of the *Vita* of Sulpicius Severus (q.v. 4); elegics, panegyrics, occasional poems. One of the first to use rhyme. Has been called "Last of the Roman Poets." Probably the author of the famous Passion-hymn *Pange Lingua Gloriosi.*

Fourteenth Century: The century in which the Latin Language began to lose its struggle to compete with the vernaculars. Dante, Petrarch, and Boccaccio in Italy; Wolfram von Eschenbach and the *Nibelungenlied* and *Tristan* in Germany, Wycliffe and Chaucer in England; the *Roman de la Rose* in France—these are examples of the national literatures which by the 14th century had begun to supplant Latin.

Fra Giovannino: See Giovannino.

Franciscan Literature: Mention should be made of the vast body of writings that arose from the life and works of St. Francis of Assisi: Lives of the saint, the *Speculum Perfectionis, Sacrum Commercium,* etc.

Franco of Cologne: 11th century author of a treatise on counterpoint. Pupil of Fulbert of Chartres.

Franco of Liége: 11th century mathematician. Wrote *De Ratione Computi, De Quadratura Circuli,* and other mathematical works. (Manitius)

Fratres Arvales: See Carmen Arvale; Earliest Latin.

Frechulph of Lisieux: Probably a student of Alcuin (q.v.). Wrote a *History* from the Creation to his own day; and edited Vegetius (q.v.). (Manitius)

Fredegar: Historian and chronicler of the 7th (?) century.

Fredegard: 9th century poet of St. Riquier. Wrote a lovely poem about a thrush that sang so beautifully that he (the poet) lost his toothache.

Fredro, Andrzej, Count: 17th century Polish historian. Wrote works in Latin and in Polish.

Frischlin, Philipp Nicodemus: 1547-1590. German humanist and Neo-Latin dramatist. One of the last of the humanists, he wrote satirical plays: *Julius Redivivus,* and other works of satire (e.g. *Priscanus Vapulans*) against the barbaric Latin of the learned guilds.

Frithegode: 10th century author of a metrical life of St. Wilfrid.

Frontinus, Sextius Julius: ca. 30-104. Author of two extant works, the *Stratagems* and the *De Aquis Urbis Romae* (qq.v.), and of lost works on military science and gromatics.

Fronto, Cornelius: (ca. 100-166) African author of the "Archaizing School." See *Elocutio Novella,* Gellius, Apuleius.

Frontoniani: Archaizing followers of Fronto. See Elocutio Novella.

Froumond of Tegernsee: ca. 960-1008. Teacher and poet of the late tenth century. Collated the MSS. of Persius. His collection of letters and verses give one an excellent picture of monastic life ca. 1000. Poem—*In Crucifixo.* (Waddell, Manitius)

Frutolf of Michelsberg: d. 1103. Wrote a world history, one of the most important of the Middle Ages, according to Manitius. Usual sources: Jerome, Isidore, Orosius, Bede (qq.v.). It was continued by one Ekkehard.

Fuficius: Author of a (lost) treatise on architecture mentioned by Vitruvius (q.v.).

Fulbert of Chartres: 975-1029. One of the great teachers and humanists of the 10-11th centuries. Studied under Gerbert (q.v.). Fulbert was in great measure responsible for the renown of the Cathedral School at Chartres. A philosopher, bishop, poet, musician, and educator, he left a large body of miscellaneous works, including letters, biographies, tracts and sermons, and poetry. Called "Socrates noster" (our Socrates) by a whole generation of pupils. Waddell says he was "the first of the almost unbroken succession of humanists and Platonists whose memory still makes Chartres a holy place." His poem on the nightingale is worthy of special comment. Among Fulbert's pupils were: Rainaldus, Berengarius, Hildebert, Franco of Cologne, et al. (Waddell, Manitius)

Fulcher of Chartres: b. 1059. Wrote a *Historia Iherosolymitana* (on the First Crusade). Most of the chapters end with verses.

Fulco: Minor French poet of the 12th century. Wrote an historical epic on the First Crusade (*Historia Gestorum Viae Nostri Temporis Hierosolymitanae*).

Fulda: Famous French monastery. See Hrabanus Maurus.

Fulgentius (1) Fabius Planciades: ca. 480-550. African poet of the 5th-6th centuries. Surviving works are: *Mitologiarum libri iii* (a dialogue between the author and Calliope, whose purpose is to discover the real meaning of old myths);

Expositio Vergilianae (q.v.), dealing with the *Aeneid* alone; *De Aetatibus Mundi et Hominis,* probably his best work, based largely on Bible history, but also dealing with general world history; *Expositio Sermonum Antiquorum,* a study of rare Latin words. His work is generally marked by rhetorical affectation, artificial mannerisms (see under "lipogrammatic"), carelessness, and sometimes downright foolishness. Fulgentius has been identified with Fulgentius (2) of Ruspe (q.v.), but this is by no means certain. (Rand, Raby, OCD)

Fulgentius (2): Bishop of Ruspe, 468-532. Theologian and follower of St. Augustine. Author of numerous works on theology, as: *Contra Arianos, De Trinitate, De Veritate,* etc. See under Fulgentius (1) for possible identification with the poet-grammarian Fulgentius.

Fullo: Two works of this title existed, both lost. One is an Atellan farce (see Fabula Atellana), the other a mime by Laberius (q.v.).

Fundanius: Augustan writer of comedies, mentioned by Horace. A member of the literary circle of Maecenas. None of his work has survived.

Furius, A.: Writer of an historical epic, "Annales" in the Ennian style. Furius, who lived ca. 100 B.C., is one of the links between Ennius and Virgil.

Furius Bibaculus, M.: 1. Wrote an epic on Caesar's Gallic War.

2. Wrote lampoons, mentioned by Catullus.

There is a possibility that there were two different authors of this name, which certain age-discrepancies would tend to corroborate, but this is not at all certain.

Furius Philus, L.: An important member of the Scipionic Circle of the second century B.C. Cicero commends his Latin style, both in speaking and in writing.

Furnius: An able orator of the Augustan Age.

Fuscus, Arellius: Augustan rhetor and teacher. The elder Seneca and Ovid were among his pupils.

Fuscus, M. Aristius: Poet and grammarian of the Augustan Age. His works are lost, and his chief claim to fame today is the joke he played on Horace (Sat. i, 9), where he refused to rescue the poet from the clutches of the "Bore."

Gaetulicus, Lentulus: Historian (?) and erotic poet put to death by Caligula for his part in a conspiracy against the emperor's life.

Gaius (1): (Emperor) See Caligula.

Gaius (2): Famous jurist of the second century. Member of the Sabinian School of jurisprudence. Author of numerous books on law, including: *Ad Edictum Provinciale, Ad Edictum Praetoris Urbani, Ad Legem xii Tabularum,* etc. His chief work, however, was the great *Institutionum Commentarii, iv.* His language is always clear and concise, and his explanations plain and readable.

Galatea: (Mythology) A sea-nymph, beloved by the Cyclops Polyphemus, who killed her lover Acis. A favorite subject with pastoral writers, the myth appears in Ovid, Virgil, Theocritus, etc. Handel wrote one of his most delightful operas on the subject, to a libretto by John Gay.

The name Galatea is also associated with the ivory maiden fashioned by Pygmalion, though not in Ovid or in the OCD. The name means "milk-white." H. J. Rose (Handbook of Greek Mythology) says that it is one of the lesser mysteries of mythology how the name Galatea came to be associated with this statue. None of the ancient authors makes this association.

Galen: 129-199. Greek physician in Rome. Wrote voluminously on medicine, logic, metaphysics, etc. A staunch believer in monotheism, he seems to have foreshadowed the Middle Ages. Although he wrote in Greek, his influence on later generations is comparable only to that of Aristotle, hence his inclusion here.

Galerius Trachalus: Mentioned by Quintilian as one of the recent orators. The emperor Otho used him to compose speeches. See "Ghost-writers."

Gallio, Junius: Rhetor mentioned by the elder Seneca (q.v.) one of whose sons he adopted. His declamations were famous in Jerome's time.

Gallus (1), Aquilius: Jurist of the first century B.C. Teacher of S. Sulpicius Rufus (q.v. 6).

Gallus (2), Asinius: Son of Pollio (q.v.). An orator under Tiberius.

Gallus (3), C. Sulpicius: Author of a work on astronomy in the second century B.C.

Gallus (4), Cornelius: 70-27 B.C. First in the canon of the Augustan elegiac poets (see Ovid, Tibullus, Propertius). His life was tragic, ending with his disgrace and suicide. His four books of elegies on "Lycoris" have not survived.

Gandersheim: Famous convent. See Hroswitha.

Ganymeda et Helena, de: Medieval debate or "Streitgedicht" (q.v.) in goliardic verse.

Gargilius Martialis, Q.: 3rd century author of a treatise on gardens (*De Hortis*). For possible identifications, see Gargilius (2).

Gargilius (2): Three other persons of this name are known to us. Any or all of them may be identical with Gargilius Martialis, but there are no certain grounds for believing or disbelieving this. They are:

1. Author of a treatise on diseases of oxen.
2. Historian who wrote about Alexander Severus.
3. Statesman mentioned on inscriptions.

Since they all lived at about the same time, it is highly probable that the first of the above is identical with Gargilius Martialis. In this case, the work on gardens and that on the diseases of oxen may have been parts of a larger work on agriculture. (OCD)

Garland, John: See John of Garland.

Gaufred Malaterra: Wrote a history of the Normans, from Rollo to 1099. Deals largely with Italy and the islands.

Gaunilo: 11th century author of *Liber pro Insipienti* (Book for a Fool).

Gautbert: (Gozbert ?) 10th century grammarian, author of a *Grammaticorum Diadoche*.

Gautier de Châtillon: See Walter of Châtillon.

Gavius Bassus: Grammarian of the first century B.C. Wrote *De Origine Verborum et Vocabulorum.*

Gavius Silo: Orator of the Augustan Age.

Gebhard of Salzburg: Wrote a letter to Hermann of Metz in which he said that the blame for the struggle between Church and State in the 11th century rested with the State (i.e., Henry IV).

Gellius (1), Aulus: ca. 123-ca. 165. Author of "Attic Nights," a miscellany of anecdotes, grammatical information, law, philosophy, antiquities, history and biography, literary criticism, etc. Duff calls it "an ancient museum of curiosities." Gellius preserves extracts from nearly 300 Greek and Roman authors whose works are otherwise completely or almost completely lost.

Gellius (2), Gnaeus: Annalist of the second century B.C.

Genealogiae: (Fabulae) See Hyginus (3).

Genethliacon: A birthday poem. We possess examples by Tibullus, Horace, Propertius, Ovid, Persius, Statius (see *Gen. Lucani*), Martial, and Ausonius. A new interpretation was given to the *Genethliacon* by Christian authors such as Sidonius and Ennodius, who deal with death as a sort of birthday, but in a classical vein.

Genethliacon Lucani: Poem by Statius (q.v.) to the widow of Lucan. It combines elements of the true *genethliacon*, the funeral praise or panegyric, and the *consolatio.*

Gennadius Scholasticus: Christian-Latin author of the 5th century. Wrote many anti-heretical works which have not survived. The only extant work is a *Liber de Dogmatibus Ecclesiasticis.*

Gente Populi Romani, de: Lost historical work by Varro (1).

Geoffrey of Monmouth: (Galfred or Gruffud) 1100?-1154. Wrote a *Historia Regum Britanniae* and a *Vita Merlini.* The latter is a life of the wizard Merlin, in hexameters.

Geoffrey of Vendôme: b. 1070. Abbot of monastery of Vendôme. Wrote many popular hymns.

Geoffrey of Vinsauf: Early 13th century. Wrote *Poetria*

Nova, a work on the Art of Poetry which was important in the new curriculum (see *Laborintus*). This work was in verse, and he wrote another, in prose (*Documentum de Modo et Arte Dictandi et Versificandi*).

Geography: See Pomponius Mela, *Stadiasmus Maris Magni, Itineraries.* Writers who include geographical information are: Caesar, Bede, Pliny the Elder, Curtius Rufus, Tacitus, and others, as well as many of the medieval writers on the Crusades, and Aethicus Cosmographus.

Georgica: Long religious pastoral poem of the 12th century (?), which has been attributed, although with little foundation, to Walter of Châtillon. Much confusion and controversy has arisen over the work. (Raby)

Georgics: (Virgil) The greatest piece of didactic poetry in the Latin language, save only for that of Lucretius (q.v.). The four books deal with crops, trees and vines, cattle, and bees. A blend of practical and scientific lore with poetry, legend, mythology. A great love for nature and for Italy permeates the whole work. The national feeling is never absent. Not all the parts are of uniform excellence, some being rather dull, but many sections are truly worthy of the author of the Aeneid; indeed, some critics think the Georgics to be Virgil's greatest work. It took the poet seven years to complete this work.

Geraldus of St. Gall: Dedicated the *Waltharius* (q.v.) to Bishop Erchambald of Strasbourg.

Gerard of Czanad: 11th century. Called by Manitius one of the most peculiar authors of the 11th century. Wrote works on number-symbolism, on the Divine Paternity, in Praise of the Virgin Mary, and various exegetical works, which are not true commentaries or explanations, however, but a random series of comments on words, etymologies, etc. Uses Isidore frequently, but never by name. Puts questions into the mouth of Isengrim (his dedicatee) and then proceeds to answer them. (Manitius)

Gerbert: (Pope Sylvester II) 10th century. "The most astute scholar and statesman of the medieval popes."—Waddell. Teacher, scholar, poet, a man of many and varied talents, a monk at Fleury, scholasticus at Reims, finally elevated to the Holy See. (Waddell, Manitius)

Gerhard of Augsburg: Tenth century author of *Life of Udalric* (Bishop of Augsburg), which he says he wrote "by popular request." One of the most revealing and important biographical works of the 10th century. (Manitius)

Gerhard, Johann: Lutheran dogmatist, author of *Loci Theologi, Confessio Catholica, Meditationes Sacrae.*

Gerhard of Seeon: Wrote a poem in 54 hexameters to King Henry II.

Gerhard of Soissons: Middle of the 10th century. Wrote a *Vita Sancti Romani.*

Gerhoh of Reichersberg: b. 1094? A very prolific writer. Wrote a *Liber de Edificio Dei* (an allegorical and mystical picture of the Church), an *Epistola ad Innocentium Quid Distet Inter Clericos Seculares et Regulares* (in dialogue form, on the difference between regular and secular clergymen), and many others of theological and exegetical nature. (Manitius)

Germania: Ethnological essay by Tacitus on Germany, its geography, climate, peoples, government, warfare, religious practices, economy, etc. Much information of historical and anthropological importance, such as food and clothing, customs and superstitions, gambling, war-councils, etc. of the Germans. Much speculation has taken place on the true reason for the work. Was it a political pamphlet, to warn Rome by contrasting the vigor and virility of these barbarians with the effete life of the city; or a plea for better patrolling of the frontier? Both are plausible guesses. In any case, the work is a veritable mine of information.

Germanicus, Julius Caesar: Son of Drusus, adopted in A.D. 4 by Tiberius. An able orator, he also wrote comedies in Greek, epigrams, translated the *Phaenomena* of Aratus, and wrote a work called *Prognostica.* Had nine children, including the emperor Gaius (Caligula) and Agrippina, the mother of Nero. Died mysteriously, possibly of poison, in A.D. 19.

Gerson, Jean de: 1363-1429. French ecclesiastical author; Chancellor of the University of Paris. Wrote tracts *De Unitate Ecclesiastica, De Auferibilitate Papae ab Ecclesia.* A nominalist and mystic.

Gervase of Melkley: Author of a treatise on Poetics, ca. 1200.

Gesta: "Deeds"—appears in the titles of innumerable chronicles, historical epics, etc. in the Middle Ages.

Gesta Alberonis Trevirensis: Two works by this name, dealing with the life and deeds of the archbishop Albero. One is by Balderich, the other, in leonine hexameters, is by an unknown author.

Gesta Apollonii: Tenth century versification of a Greek romance by Apollonius of Tyre. Probably written at the monastery of Tegernsee.

Gesta Berengarii: A medieval epic by an unknown author.

Gesta Cnutonis regis: The Deeds of the Danish King Knut, written ca. 1041 by an unknown monk of St. Omer and St. Bertin, and dedicated to Queen Emma. The work shows study of Roman historians and Virgilian expressions, which sound rather strange in the description of a Scandinavian king. The author fails to appreciate Knut's true importance.

Gesta Danorum: Historical work by Saxo Grammaticus (q.v.).

Gesta Episcoporum Cameracensium: History of the bishops of Cambrai, written about the middle of the 11th century, by an unknown monk of Cambrai.

Gesta Episcoporum Virdunensium: A long chronicle of the bishops of Verdun, begun in 893 by Dudo, continued by Bertar, Laurentius of Liége, and others.

Gesta Francorum et Aliorum Hierosolymitanorum: History of the Crusades by an unknown author, possibly an Italian Norman.

Gesta Friderici: Prose history of Frederic Barbarossa, also one in verse. See Otto of Freising, Rahewin, Godfrey of Viterbo, and *Ligurinus.*

Gesta Hammaburgensis Ecclesiae Pontificum: See Adam of Bremen.

Gesta Karoli: Collection of legends of Charlemagne by Notker the Stammerer (Notker Balbulus).

Gesta Romanorum: Medieval compilation of anecdotes, accounts of lawsuits, etc., partly culled from the *Controversiae* of Seneca the Elder (q.v.).

Gesta Willelmi Conquestoris: See William of Poitiers.

Gestis Langobardorum, de: History of the Lombards by Paulus Diaconus (q.v.).

Geta: A medieval comedy, probably by Vitalis of Blois. Also called *"Amphitryo"* (q.v.).

Geta, Hosidius: African poet of the 3rd century. Wrote a tragedy *Medea* composed entirely of Virgilian quotations (see Cento).

Gezo of Tortona: Second half of 10th century. Author of a long work on the blood and the body of Christ (*De Corpore et Sanguine Domini*). Mostly consists of quotations from such Church Fathers as Hilary, Cyprian, Ambrose, Augustine, Gregory, Isidore, Jerome, Bede, et al. (Manitius)

"Ghost-writers": The practice of writing speeches to be delivered by someone else was fairly frequent in ancient times. The Greek orator Lysias was noted for his ability to project himself into the part of the subject of his speeches. In Roman times, Seneca wrote speeches for Nero, Galerius Trochalus for Otho, Licinius Sura for Trajan, etc.

Gibbon, Edward: Author of the masterly *Decline and Fall of the Roman Empire*, which begins with the Antonine Age.

Gibuin of Langres: Archbishop of Lyons 1077. Minor French poet of the 11th century. Author of a famous poem on the joys of Paradise.

Gilbert: German or Belgian poet of the 12th century, author of two "goliardic" poems: *De Superfluitate Clericorum*, and *Quispiam ad Quandam Virginem.*

Gilbert de la Porrée: See Guibert de la Porrée.

Gildas: Anglo-Saxon priest and historian of the 6th century.

Wrote letters, *Lamentations* (a jeremiad on the state of England in his day). Perhaps the author of *Lorica*. Bede admired his works excessively and used them frequently.

Giles of Corbeil: Thirteenth century. Wrote a poem of 6000 lines on pharmacy.

Giles of Rome: ca. 1246-1316. Theologian and philosopher. Wrote a work *On Ecclesiastical Power.*

Gilles of Paris: Wrote a poem *Carolinus* on Charles the Great, ca. 1200.

Gilo: Minor French poet of the 12th century. Wrote of the Crusades.

Giovanni del Virgilio: Contemporary and friend of Dante, with whom he exchanged Latin letters, and on whose death he wrote a Latin epitaph.

Giovannino of Mantua: Dominican friar, ca. 1300, known for his controversy with Mussato (q.v.).

Giraldus Cambrensis: 1147-1223. Scholar and humanist of the 12th-13th centuries. Wrote many varied works, including one on the geography of Ireland, one on the Creation of the world, others on logic, grammar, theology, education, poetry, and the well-known *Gemma Ecclesiastica* and *Speculum Ecclesiae.* (Manitius)

Gislebert of St. Amand: Minor French poet of the 11th century. Wrote a poem on the destruction of his monastery in 1066.

Giustiniani, Leonardo: 1388?-1446. Italian humanist and poet. Translated Plutarch into Latin.

Glabrio, Acilius: See Acilius Glabrio.

Gladiolus: Lost comedy by Livius Andronicus, based on a Greek model. A plausible theory is that this play was the ancestor of the *Miles Gloriosus* (q.v.) of Plautus.

Glanvill, Ranulf de: d. 1190. Possibly the author of a *Tractatus de Legibus et Consuetudinibus Regni Angliae,* a treatise on English common law.

Glaucus: Epyllion by Cornificius (q.v.).

Gloria, de: Lost work in two books by Cicero.

Gloria, Laus: See Theodulf.

Glossa: Marginal note—interpretation of a difficult passage or an obscure word. Collections of these (Glossaries) were made in the monasteries (e.g., St. Gall) from the 6th century, and arranged in a roughly alphabetical order. The *Liber Glossarum* (*Glossarium*) *Ansileubi* is a 9th century compilation which includes long passages from Ambrose, Jerome, Gregory, Isidore, etc. These glossaries are of considerable philological and even literary value.

Glossa Ordinaria: Abridgement of patristic commentaries made by Walafrid Strabo (q.v.).

Gnipho, M. Antonius: Roman scholar and teacher of the first century B.C. Teacher of Cicero. Wrote on the Latin language. Edited, with commentary, the *Annales* of Ennius.

Godfrey (1) of Breteuil: (also known as Godfrey of St. Victor) Author of *Fons Philosophiae*, a philosophical poem, and of *Microcosmus.*

Godfrey (2) of Cambrai: Prior of St. Swithin's. Wrote two books of epigrams in feeble imitation of Martial.

Godfrey (3) of Fontaines: ca. 1260-1320. Bishop of Tournai. Wrote fourteen *Quodlibeta* in defense of the doctrines of Aquinas.

Godfrey (4) of Reims: French poet of the mid-11th century; wrote poetry in the form of letters.

Godfrey of St. Victor: See Godfrey (1) of Breteuil.

Godfrey (5) of Viterbo: Late 12th century poet. Wrote *Speculum Regum* (Mirror of Kings); *Pantheon; Liber Memorialis,* and an epic on Frederic Barbarossa (*Gesta Friderici*).

Golden Age: Applied to Latin literature, the term embraces the period from 70 B.C. to 14 A.D., i.e., the Ciceronian and Augustan Ages. The Latin language, during this period, attained to a perfection of form and depth of concept which it never again equalled. Typical authors of the Golden Age are: Catullus, Lucretius, Cicero, Caesar, Sallust, Virgil, Horace, Livy, Ovid, Tibullus, and Propertius.

Golden Ass: Another name for the *Metamorphoses* of Apuleius (q.v.).

Golden Bough: In Virgil's *Aeneid,* the passport to the Underworld.

Golden Fleece: In mythology, the fabulous object of Jason's quest. For the most complete treatment in Latin, see the *Argonautica* of Valerius Flaccus.

Golden Legend: Collection of the Lives of the Saints. The trend, which begins with Jerome, goes on to the time of Jacopo da Voragine in the 13th century.

Golden Sequence: The sequence *Veni, Sancte Spiritus,* attributed to Langton, Archbishop of Canterbury. See Sequence.

Golding, Arthur: English translator of Ovid's *Metamorphoses* (1565-1575).

Goliard: A wandering clerk of the 12th-13th centuries. Member of the burlesque *Ordo Vagorum.* Hence "goliardic verse." Golias (Goliath) was their patron saint. They wrote poems of love, satire, revelry, invective, etc. See Vagantenlieder, Carmina Burana, Goliardic verse, etc.

Goliardic Verse: The secular Latin lyric of the 12th-13th centuries. Mostly in rhymed quatrains, the verse was by turns satiric and tender, full of romance and invective. It has been called "the last flowering of the Latin language." See Archpoet, Hugh Primas of Orleans, Vagantenlieder. (Waddell, Manitius)

"Golias": A legendary clerk or "wandering scholar," founder of the Goliardic order (see *Ordo Vagorum*)—the prototype of all the ribald clerks, goliards, scholars, and loose-living prelates. The name seems to be identified with the giant Goliath, although it may be derived from "gula" (glutton). It was also used as a nickname for Abelard (q.v.). The best treatment of the lyrics, goliardic poems, etc. in English, is that of Helen Waddell. Manitius and Raby are also standard.

Gonzo, Abbot of Florennes: Wrote on the Miracles of St. Gengulf, ca. 1050.

Gorgonius, St., Miracles of: By an unknown author in the middle of the 10th century. Used by John of Arnulf. (Manitius)

Gottschalk (1) of Fulda: ca. 805-870. Ninth century priest, poet, and heretic. Friend of Walafrid Strabo. Wrote treatises on predestination. His old teacher, Hrabanus Maurus (q.v.), had him convicted of heresy. The famous John Eriugena was brought to refute Gottschalk, who was condemned to solitary confinement and died without receiving the sacrament. His poetry is rather fine, and seems to be a harbinger of the lyric of the twelfth and thirteenth centuries. It has an intricate metrical and rhyme scheme. It has been suggested that Gottschalk is the author of the *Theodulus Eclogue* (q.v.). (Waddell, Raby, Manitius)

Gottschalk (2) of Limburg: ca. 1010-1098. 11th century poet, author of Sequences (q.v.).

Gower, John: Minor English poet of the 13th century.

Gozwin of Mainz: b. ca. 1000. Wrote a *Passion of St. Alban.* Probably identical with one *Gozechin,* who wrote a long and famous letter to Walther. (Manitius)

Gracchi: Tiberius and Gaius Sempronius Gracchus, both tribunes in the second century B.C. (Tiberius, trib. 133; Gaius, trib. 123). Both were orators of great ability, and Gaius is known to have been an extremely flamboyant speaker. Both were killed during uprisings in which the bitter party-strife of the following century was foreshadowed.

Gracchus: Tragic playwright of the Augustan Age. Little more than his name survives.

Graecinus, Julius: See Julius Graecinus.

Graffiti: Scribblings found on Roman walls, e.g., at Pompeii. They are a good example of the "sermo plebeius" or everyday speech.

Grammar and Grammarians: (See under individual names) Greek influence evident from the earliest stages. The works of Lucilius (q.v.) reveal interest in grammar. The first Roman grammarian of any importance is Aelius Stilo (q.v.). In the first century B.C. Gnipho, Nigidius Figulus, Opilius, Ateius were the most noted grammarians, except for Varro, whose lost work on the Disciplines and whose *De Lingua Latina* recognized four parts of speech: nouns (incl. adjectives and pronouns), verbs, participles, and particles (incl. adverbs).

In the first century B.C. the analogy-anomaly dispute raged (q.v.). In the first century A.D. the *Ars* of Remmius Palaemon was an important work. Here eight parts of speech were differentiated. In the second century, the *De Orthographia* of Velius Longus and the work of Terentius Scaurus are to be mentioned; and in the third century, Julius Romanus and Sacerdos, the oldest extant Latin grammar. In the 4th century the names of Donatus, Servius, Dositheus, Cominianus, and Marius Victorinus are prominent; in the 5th, several unimportant works (e.g., those of Asmonius, Phocas, Rufinus, Cledonius, et al.) were produced. The monumental work of Priscian was published in the 6th century, and was a standard work for the Middle Ages, until supplanted, in the 12th-13th centuries, by the work of Alexander of Villedieu and Eberhard of Béthune. Works on grammar included sections on orthography, meters, syntax, accidence, idioms, and other allied fields.

Grammatici: The teachers of secondary education (cf. the present term "grammar school"). The subject matter was not confined to formal grammar, however. The grammatici taught reading and writing, and even the study of literary works in Latin and Greek. See Education.

Grammaticis, de: (Suetonius) Part of this author's larger work *De Viris Illustribus*. Deals with literary teachers and grammarians.

Grandio: See Seneca (3).

Granius Licinianus: Second century historian. His history is annalistic in conception. The remains are from a London palimpsest.

Gratian: Jurist and humanist of the 12th century. Compiled a *Concordia Discordantium Canonum* which was the foundation for the *Corpus Juris Canonici* (q.v.).

Gratiarum Actio: See Panegyric.

Grattius: Augustan didactic poet, author of *Cynegetica,* a work on dogs and hunting. The separate parts of the poem deal with the equipment, such as nets, traps and weapons; dogs, care, breeding, diseases, etc.; horses; the work contains many interesting digressions.

gravitas: Gravity or seriousness. One of the most important aspects of the Roman character.

Grecismus: Grammatical work by Eberhard of Béthune (q.v.). Together with the *Doctrinale* of Alexander of Ville-dieu it gradually supplanted the standard Priscian in the later Middle Ages.

Greek, influence of: The Hellenic influences on Roman literature, thought, mythology, are incalculable. Nearly all the Roman literary forms are borrowed from the Greeks. Meters (e.g., hexameter, iambics, etc.) are a notorious example. The educated Roman spoke Greek just as the educated English-men of today speak French.

Gregorian Chant: A musical composition of monodic na-ture, sung either solo or in unison, usually to Biblical texts. The official liturgical music of the Roman Catholic Church. The earliest collection was that of Ambrose, but it was revised and edited under the supervision of Pope Gregory the Great (hence the name).

Gregory I "the Great": Pope 590-604. One of the four Doctors of the Church. A man of tremendous erudition and energy, he was interested in theology, liturgy, music, and missionary work. Works: *Dialogues, Letters, Regula Pastoralis,* and the *Moralia on the Book of Job.* Most of his theology is based on that of Augustine of Hippo.

Gregory VII, Pope: 1073-1085. One of the greatest of medieval popes. Reformed the clergy and redefined the rela-tionship between secular and ecclesiastical powers. Excom-municated the Emperor Henry IV.

Gregory of Rimini: 14th century teacher at Bologna, Padua, Perugia and Paris. A nominalist, he was the author of a book on usury.

Gregory of Tours: 538-593. Wrote *Annals* in ten books (a chronicle of the Church to the year 591): *Lives of the Saints; History of the Franks.* The last-named is his most important work.

Gretser, Jakob: 1562-1625. German Jesuit and dramatist; author of *Udo* and other plays.

Grillius: 5th century grammarian. Wrote a Commentary on Cicero's *De Inventione,* which has survived in part.

Gromatics: The science of surveying, and books on the subject. See Frontinus, Hyginus (2), Aggenius Urbicus, Junius Nipsius, Siculus Flaccus, and Innocentius.

Groote, Gerard: 1340-1380. Dutch theologian and philosopher. Modern ecclesiastical scholars say that he (*not* Thomas a Kempis) is the author of the famous *Imitation of Christ,* and that Kempis merely edited the work.

Grosseteste (Grossetête), Robert: d. 1253. Oxford scholar and mathematician. Teacher of Roger Bacon (q.v.).

Grotius, Hugo: 1583-1645. Dutch Renaissance scholar and jurist. Edited Martianus Capella. His *De Jure Belli et Pacis* is one of the great landmarks of international law. Known for the "governmental theory" of atonement; political theory, etc.

Grunius Corocotta: The name of the pig in the satirical *Testamentum Porcelli* (q.v.).

Gryphius: Author of *Vergiliocentones Continentes Vitam Salvatoris Nostri Domini Jesu Christi* (i.e., Virgilian centos on the life of Our Lord Jesus Christ).

Guaiferius: Lombard monk and humanist of the 11th century. Associated with the monastery of Monte Cassino. Author of religious poetry.

Gualdo or Waldo: Middle of 11th century. Monk at Corbie, deacon of Hamburg. Wrote a poem on the life of St. Anskar.

Guarino: Renaissance humanist who translated into Latin the treatise of Pseudo-Plutarch on Education.

Gubernatione Dei, de: See Salvianus.

Guiard: Chancellor of the University of Paris in 1238. Author of *Sermons.*

Guibert de Nogent: (or Gilbert or Wibert) 1053-1121. Abbot of Nogent, Platonist and poet. Wrote an autobiography (*De Vita Sua*) in the manner of Augustine of Hippo; other works include *Gesta Dei per Francos, Moralium in Genesim, de Laude S. Mariae, De Virginitate, De Pignoribus Sanctorum,* etc.

Guibert de la Porrée: (or Gilbert) Twelfth century scholar and theologian. Bishop of Poitiers. Probably the only man ever to have been accused unsuccessfully of heresy by St. Bernard. Wrote commentary on the Bible and on Boethius' *opuscula sacra; Liber 6 Principiorum in Philosophiam,* and other works. (Manitius)

Guido (1) of Arezzo: The inventor of the names do- re- mi, etc. for the diatonic scale, wrote prolifically on music (modes, scale, rhythm, musical education, etc.). Also wrote a famous letter in 1031 to Heribert against the practice of simony. (Manitius)

Guido (2) (Guy) of Bazoches: ca. 1146-1203. Humanist of the 12th century. Took part in the Second Crusade and the siege of Acre. Works: *Apologia in Maledicos,* letters, poetry.

Guido (3) of Pisa: Wrote *Historiae,* the first part of which is purely geographical, the second part historical-legendary.

Gumpold: Bishop of Mantua in 967. Author of a work describing the martyrdom of Wenceslaus (murdered in 935). Shows influence of Sallust. Long digressions: the prologue concerns human activities and achievements, and touches on such widely different subjects as: astronomy, mathematics, poetry, music, etc.

Gundissalinus, Dominicus: Spanish scholar of the 12th century who translated Avicenna (q.v.) into Latin.

Gunther: Possibly the author of *Ligurinus* (q.v.), a long narrative poem on the deeds of Frederic Barbarossa.

Gunzo of Novara: Scholar of the 10th century, appointed by the Emperor Otto II to institute learned studies in Germany.

Guy of Amiens: See Wido of Amiens.

Guy de Bazoches: See Guido of B.

Gyraldus, Julius Gregorius: Author of *Dialogus de Poetarum Historia,* 1545.

Hadoard: 9th century author of *Sententiae Philosophorum;* mostly excerpted from Cicero.

Hadrian (1), Emperor: 76-138. Patron of arts and literature; author of a (lost) collection of poetry called *Catachannae,* and of one very famous little poem "to his soul" which was probably worth all the rest. For his role in the history of education, see under Education.

Hadrian (2): Abbot of SS. Peter and Paul. Originally from Africa. Teacher of Aldhelm (q.v.).

Hagiography: "Sacred writings"—the term is most frequently used to denote the lives and passions of saints, martyrs, etc.

Haimar: Archbishop of Caesarea. Author of a long narrative poem on the 3rd Crusade, entitled *Liber de Recuperatione Ptolemaidae.*

Hales, Alexander of: See Alexander of Hales.

Halieutica: (Ovid) A fragment in hexameters, dealing with the fishes of the Black Sea. Written by Ovid towards the end of his life, when he was in exile.

Hamartigenia: Poem on the origin of sin (*De Origine Peccatorum*) by Prudentius (q.v.).

Handbuch der klassischen Altertumswissenschaft: This massive "handbook" is in nine parts, each with several subdivisions and sections, and deals with the entire field of Greek and Roman literature, and many related fields. The volumes on Roman literature are by Schanz, Hosius and Krüger; those on Greek literature, by Schmid-Stahlin, and those on medieval Latin literature by Max Manitius. The series was begun by Iwan von Müller, and is now edited by Walter Otto.

Hanville, John of: See John of Hanville.

Hariolus: A lost play by Naevius, in which he is supposed to have made his apologies for the abuse of certain officials that caused him to be incarcerated. It is said that this play, together with the *Leo* (q.v.), procured his release.

Hariulf of St. Riquier: b. ca. 1060. Wrote (A) *Chronicon Centulense,* a history of his own monastery (which was called Centulum, as well as St. Riquier), (B) *Vita Arnulfi Episcopi Suessionensis;* and other works.

Hartman: Minor poet of the monastery of St. Gall in the 10th century.

Haruspicum Responsis, de: Speech by Cicero, replying to

the allegation of Clodius (q.v.) in the Senate that he, Cicero, had offended the gods.

Hastingae Proelio, de: Historical epic on the Battle of Hastings by Wido of Amiens.

Haterius, Q.: Celebrated orator of the Augustan Age. Seneca (1) speaks of the rapidity of his speech, and tells us that Augustus said that Haterius needed brakes!

Hawk and the Peacock, the: Allegorical poem of the Carolingian Renaissance. Latin title is *De Accipitre et Pavone*. The peacock symbolizes Christ.

Heautontimoroumenos: "The Self-Tormentor"—a comedy by Terence which concerns a father who punishes himself (like Mr. Darling in *Peter Pan*) for having driven his son abroad.

Hebdomades: Gallery of 700 famous Greeks and Romans, by Varro (1). Said to be the first illustrated book ever written in Europe.

Hector Proficiscens: Lost play by Naevius (q.v.) on the Trojan War.

Hecuba: Lost plays of this title by (1) Ennius, (2) Scaeva Memor.

Hecyra: ("the Mother-in Law") Comedy by Terence. A young bride quits the house because of a previous misfortune, only to find out that it is her own husband who was responsible. The character of the courtesan is especially finely drawn. Actually, there is nothing comic about this play, but a great deal of sentimentality.

Hedyphagetica: (Lost) "Manual of Good Eating" by Ennius (q.v.).

Heimo of Michelsberg: First half of the 12th century. Wrote a work, *De Decursu Temporum*. In seven parts. The first four treat the history of the world from the Creation to Heimo's day. The fifth deals with the Popes and Emperors, the sixth with man's slavery since the fall from grace, and the seventh with the brotherhood of man through Christ's blood and resurrection. Not a work of true historical understanding, but contains much valuable material nevertheless. (Manitius)

Heinsius, Daniel: Dutch scholar. See Scholarship, Classical.

Heiric of Auxerre: Wrote, in the 9th century, a life of St. Germanus, composed with great numerical exactitude, and discussion of the mystical significance of numbers. The verse is a mixture of Latin and Greek.

Heisterbach, Caesarius von: See Caesarius von Heisterbach.

Helgaud: (Helgald?) Monk at Fleury, middle of the 11th century. Wrote a life of King Robert. Not really a biography at all, but a collection of unrelated anecdotes. (Manitius)

Helia et Ieiunio, de: See Ambrose of Milan.

Helinand: Monk, scholar and troubador of the early 13th century.

Hellenism, effects on Rome: The effects of the Hellenic civilization on Rome were widespread, varied, and of long duration. They left virtually no phase of Roman life untouched: art, philosophy, literature, books, education, religion and mythology, architecture and medicine, etc. The attitude of Romans to this influence varied. Sometimes it was welcome, sometimes (cf. Juvenal's xenophobia) far from welcome.

Helmhold: Monk and priest of Saxony, b. 1125. Wrote a *Chronica Slavorum,* one of our most important sources for the early history of the Slavs. (Manitius)

Heloise: Beloved of Abelard (q.v.), heroine of one of the most famous and tragic romances of history. Her letters to Abelard reveal her as an extremely intelligent woman.

Helperic of Auxerre: 9th century author of a *Computus.*

Helvia: Wife of Seneca (1), mother of Seneca (2).

Helviam Matrem, ad, de Consolatione: See *Consolatio.*

Helvidius Priscus: Famed orator of the Neronian period.

Hemina, Cassius: See Cassius Hemina.

Hemingburgh, Walter de: fl. 1300. English chronicler (*Chronicon de Rebus Gestis Regum Angliae*).

Hemmingsen, Niels: 1513-1600. Danish theological writer (*De Methodis, De Lege Naturae,* etc.).

Hendecasyllables: A favorite meter of Catullus, equally appropriate to expressions of joy, sorrow, jest and earnest.

Henry of Augsburg: A canon at Augsburg, middle of the 11th century. Wrote a long poem, the *Planctus Evae* (Eve's Lament), which has survived only in part. See Biblical epic.

Henry of Avranches: fl. 1230-1260. Grammarian and poet. Very fond of etymological interpretation of names.

Henry of Ghent: Scholastic and theologian of the 13th century (d. 1293). Wrote *Quodlibeta* and an incomplete *Summa Theologica*.

Henry of Huntingdon: 1084-1155. Author of an English History (*Historia Anglorum*) to which is appended a book of satires and epigrams.

Henry of Langenstein: ca. 1340-1397. Professor at the Universities of Paris and Vienna. Wrote *Epistola Concilii Pacis* calling for unity of the Church.

Henry of Pisa: 12th century Italian poet, who wrote an epic on the Crusades.

Henry of Settimello: Italian poet of the late 12th century. Author of a famous elegy *De Diversitate Fortunae et Philosophiae Consolatione* (On the Diversity of Fortune and the Consolation of Philosophy). Cf. Boethius.

Heptateuchon: See Thierry of Chartres.

Heptateuchos: Versified edition of the Old Testament, from Genesis to Judges, by Cyprian (q.v.).

Hercules: The Greek hero Herakles. Worshipped early at Rome, especially by merchants. "Mehercule" or "By Hercules" is a common oath in Plautus.

Hercules: Lost play by Scaeva Memor (q.v.).

Hercules Furens: (The Mad Hercules) Play by Seneca (2). Although the play is based on the Greek model of Euripides, it is very different. For example, it has the slaughter of H.'s wife and children *on the stage*, which the Greeks would never have tolerated.

Hercules Oetaeus: Play by Seneca (2), based on the *Trachiniae* of Sophocles, but far inferior to that play. It deals with Deianira, the wife of Hercules, who is here represented as a jealous termagent, instead of the sympathetic matron of the Sophocles tragedy.

Herennium, ad: See *Rhetorica ad Herennium.*

Herennius Senecio: Stoic of the first century who wrote a eulogy of Helvidius Priscus which cost him his life.

Heribert: Bishop of Eichstädt in the 11th century. Author of several hymns.

Heriger of Lauboch: Latter part of the 10th century. Author of works in the fields of history (*Gesta Episcopum Leodensium*), biography (*Lives of the Saints*), music, mathematics, chronology, etc. Wrote hymns and antiphons.

Herimannus Contractus: 1013-1054. (Also known as Hermann of Reichenau) Monk of Reichenau. Man of universal learning. Taught mathematics, music, astronomy, etc. Wrote Sequences, antiphons, on the Astrolabe, on mathematics, a world-chronicle, poetry (On the eight chief vices, Debate between the Sheep and the Flax—see Streitgedicht. Various works on music, and theological works (*De Sancta Cruce, De Sanctissima Trinitate,* etc.). Hermann was a cripple, hence the name Contractus.

Hermann of Cologne: A converted Jew who wrote an autobiography in the first half of the 12th century.

Hermann of Tournai: First half of the 12th century. Wrote (a) *De Restauratione Monasterii S. Martini Tornacensis,* (b) *De Miraculis S. Mariae Laudunensis,* and (c) *de Incarnatione Christi.* The first of these deals with various subjects besides the restoration of the above-named monastery.

Hermaphroditus: Poem attributed to Matthew of Vendôme (q.v.).

Hermione: Mythology. The daughter of Menelaus and Helen. Two Roman plays, both lost, with this title, one by Livius Andronicus, one by Pacuvius (qq.v.).

Heroïdes: (Ovid) (or, *Heroidum Epistulae*) Letters to and from the most famous heroines of Greek literature and mythology. In elegiac verse. Among the heroines are: Sappho, Penelope, Hermione, Phaedra, Briseis, Dido, Deianira, Medea, and Hero. All are sad because of their lovers' absence. The moods vary a good deal. Some have much pathos. The characterizations are, for the most part, vivid, but the Latin is too rhetorical.

Herrad of Landsberg: Abbess of Hohenberg in the 12th century (d. ca. 1195). Wrote *Hortus Deliciarum* and other poetry.

Herrmann of Dalmatia: 12th century humanist (fl. 1143). Translated the *Planisphere* of Ptolemy into Latin.

Hessus, Helius: 1488-1530. German humanist; translated the *Iliad* and Psalms into Latin hexameters.

Hexaemeron: 1. Lost epic on Creation by Prudentius (q.v.).

2. Series of sermons, also on Creation, by Ambrose (q.v.).

3. Poem by Sunesen (q.v.).

Hexameter, Dactylic: The standard meter of epic in Latin, as well as Greek. The first Roman author to use the meter was Ennius (q.v.). If one compares the rude lines of Ennius with the perfection of Virgil, one can see the polish and mastery of the latter. All Latin epics (see Epic) were composed in this meter. The English language is singularly ill-adapted to the dactylic hexameter, as Longfellow proved with such lines as:

"This is the forest primeval, the murmuring pines and the hemlocks."

Hiemale tempus vale: Medieval lyric found in a 12th century Zurich MS.

Hieronymus: See Jerome, St.

Hilary (1) Bishop of Poitiers: ca. 300-ca. 367. One of the earliest, if not the earliest writer of Latin hymns. Retold the Gospel in trochaic tetrameters. Author of exegetical works on the Psalms; *De Trinitate*, etc.

Hilary (2), the Englishman: Early 12th century. One of the Wandering Scholars. Attended Abelard's lectures. Wrote poems which represent an interesting mixture of piety and secularity—love-lyrics to nuns, etc. (Waddell)

Hildebert of Le Mans: (or H. of Lavardin) 1056-1133. Scholar, teacher, and poet of great genius and versatility. Wrote: *Moralis Philosophia,* Satires, Letters, Sermons, *Conflict*

of Body and Soul (see Streitgedicht), Hagiographical works
(Lives of Saints), and much poetry (Biblical, liturgical, moral,
hagiographic, historical); also works on mathematics. Most
famous, perhaps, are his lines on Rome, which impress us
with the beauty, rather than the sanctity of that city. Hildebert's mastery of rhyme and rhythm was proverbial. (Manitius,
Waddell)

Hildebrand: See Pope Gregory VII.

Hildegar, Bishop of Meaux: d. 875. Author of a life of
St. Faro of Meaux (d. 672), in which he "quotes" lines from
a Latin epic on King Clotaire's victory over the Saxons. This
was thought to be concrete evidence for the existence of
Merovingian heroic poetry. But the story has been proved to
be a forgery by Hildegar. See Forgeries. (Curtius)

Hildegard of Bingen: 12th century nun who wrote prolifically in various fields: theology, medicine, physics, hagiography, and poetry.

Hildesheim, Annals of: Chronicle written at Hildesheim at
different periods. Mostly dates from the first half of the 11th
century. It begins with Isidore's account of Creation, has a
catalogue of the Popes, a history of the Franks, etc. (Manitius)

Hincmar: Archbishop of Reims, 845-882. Author of a poem
of 100 lines to the Virgin Mary—an example of numerical
composition (Ten Commandments multiplied by ten).

Hirsau: Famous Benedictine monastery in the Black Forest.

Hirtius, Aulus: Author of Book VIII of Caesar's *De Bello
Gallico,* and possibly also of the *Bellum Alexandrinum* (qq.v.).

Hisperica Famina: "Western Sayings"—a collection of texts
on various subjects. The Latinity is terrible. Probably from
England and Ireland, 6th or 7th century.

Historia Apollonii Regis Tyrii: An anonymous romance,
based on a Greek original, and dating from the 5th or 6th
century. It was exceedingly popular in the Middle Ages.

Historia Augusta: A collection of the lives of 30 Emperors
from Hadrian to Numerian. The authors are: Aelius Spartianus,
Julius Capitolinus, Vulcacius Gallicanus, Aelius Lampridius,

Trebellius Pollio, and Flavius Vospiscus. The *Historia* is modeled on the *Lives of the Caesars* of Suetonius (q.v.) and is replete with court anecdotes, etc.

Historia Britonum: An anonymous historical work (rather, a collection of small historical works) dealing with the history of the Britons. Made in the 7th-8th century. (Manitius)

Historia Compostellana: History, by an unknown author, of the church in Spain. Written in the 12th century. Style is almost Biblical.

Historia Francorum: History of the Frankish nation, by Gregory of Tours (q.v.).

Historia Gothorum: History of the Goths, by Isidore of Seville (q.v.).

Historia Hierosolymitana: Crusade-history by Robert of St. Remi (q.v.).

Historia Normannorum: See Amatus of Monte Cassino.

Historia Regum Britanniae: History of the kings of England, by Geoffrey of Monmouth (q.v.).

Historia Rerum Anglicarum: See William of Newborough.

Historia Roderici: Latin prose story of the Cid, ca. 1100.

Historiae: See Sallust.

Historiae Philippicae: See Trogus, Justinus.

Historical Drama: See Praetexta, *Octavia.*

Historical Epic: (See under individual authors and works) The first Roman historical epic was the *Bellum Punicum,* of Naevius, in the Saturnian meter. Ennius was the first to use the dactylic hexameter, which became the standard epic meter of Roman epic, as it had been in Greek since the time of Homer. Pre-Virgilian epic authors include Hostius (*Bellum Histricum*), Varro of Atax (*Bellum Sequanicum*), and Furius Bibaculus. Virgil's *Aeneid,* a fusing of history, legend, and myth, belongs perhaps in a separate category, except that any discussion of the epic that omits Virgil would be unthinkable. He gave the form a perfection and polish which was never surpassed, and seldom even rivaled. In the Augustan Age, Varius Rufus (*De Morte Caesaris*) and Cornelius Severus (*Bellum Siculum*) also wrote historical epics as did Albinovanus Pedo. In the first century of the Empire or Principate, Lucan (*Pharsalia*) and Silius Italicus (*Punica*) are to be distinguished. In late antiquity, Claudian (epic on Stilicho), Sidonius, Corippus are writers of the genre. It is at this time that the historical epic begins to be eclipsed by the Biblical epic (q.v.).

In the Middle Ages, outstanding examples of historical epic are: Wido (*Battle of Hastings*), the *Carmen de Bello Saxonico*, *Gesta Berengarii*, *Historia Roderici* (prose and poetry), the *Alexandreis* of Walter of Châtillon, the *Waltharius* (semihistorical), *Solimarius*, and *Ligurinus*. For other forms of epic, see Epic, Biblical epic, Mythological epic, and Epyllion.

Histories: (Tacitus) Covers the period 69-96 A.D. Chronologically, after the *Annales* (q.v.) but written before. Includes the Year of the Four Emperors (69 A.D.: Galba, Otho, Vitellius, Vespasian), and the Flavian dynasty (Vespasian, Titus and Domitian). The *Histories* reveals the same depth of perspective, brilliant insight into character, understanding of cause and effect, and gift of compression that characterize the *Annales*. The text is mutilated.

History: (See under individual authors) Earliest period: Fabius Pictor, Acilius, Cincius Alimentus, Albinus. These were the first annalists. In the next period, Cato, Hemina, Piso Frugi, who wrote mostly in the annalistic manner. Contemporary with Sulla, Claudius Quadrigarius and Valerius Antias continued in the same tradition. Important names of the Ciceronian Age are Caesar, Sallust, Nepos, Nigidius Figulus, and Varro.

Augustan Age: Livy, Pollio, Trogus, Fenestella, et al. In the first century: Velleius Paterculus, Curtius Rufus, Pliny the Elder. Tacitus is in a class by himself. Suetonius wrote imperial biographies which were continued by the writers of the Historia Augusta. Florus, Aurelius Victor, Eutropius and Festus, Granius Licinianus and others continue in later Imperial times. The epitome (q.v.) becomes a popular and necessary form. Ammianus Marcellinus is the only later historian worth mentioning alongside of Tacitus and Livy, and even he falls far short of the genius of earlier historians. Jerome, Orosius, Isidore of Seville, and Cassiodorus are early Christian historians. In the Middle Ages, besides the innumerable chronicles and histories of monasteries, bishoprics, etc., mention must be made of the histories of: Bede, Adam of Bremen, Gregory of Tours, Robert of Reims, Geoffrey of Monmouth, William of Newborough, William of Malmesbury, Baronius, and Paulus Diaconus. Einhard's Life of Charlemagne, although it belongs more properly to the realm of biography, should also be mentioned here. Modern historians include Gibbon, Mommsen, Niebuhr, Rostovtzeff, Tenney Frank, etc.

History of the Franks: See Gregory of Tours.

Hoger of Werden: 9th century author (?) of the *Musica Enchiriadis.*

Hohenheim, Theophrastus von: See Paracelsus.

Holkot, Robert: Taught theology at Cambridge in the 14th century (d. 1349). Insisted on a separation between the logic of faith and the logic of Aristotle.

Holland, Philemon: Translator of Pliny the Elder's *Natural History,* and of Suetonius.

Hollonius, Ludwig: ca. 1600. Wrote an allegorical play, *Somnium Vitae Humanae,* about a peasant who dreams he is king for a day.

Homerus Latinus: See *Ilias Latina.*

Honoratus, M. Servius: See Servius.

Honorius Augostodunensis: Late 11th, early 12th cent. Wrote a work *Offendiculum* on clerical marriages. Other works: *Summa Gloria, Elucidarium* (theological), *Euchar-istion, Scala Caeli,* and many other theological, homiletic, exegetical (*Super Psalterium, Hexaemeron*), historical (*Imago Mundi, Summa Totius*), and philosophical works (*Speculum Ecclesiae*).

Horace: (Quintus Horatius Flaccus) 65-8 B.C. Rome's greatest lyric poet. We know a great deal about his life from his own works. His father was a freedman, a fact of which the poet was inordinately proud, and sent his son to Rome for a good education. Horace studied with the famed teacher Orbilius (q.v.) and also at Athens. He was a tribune under Brutus. After the Civil Wars, he became a member of the literary circle of Maecenas. He was offered a secretaryship by Augustus himself, but declined, preferring a life of leisure.

Works (qq.v.): *Odes* and *Epodes, Satires* (*Sermones*), *Epistles, Ars Poetica.*

Perhaps Horace's greatest literary attribute is his extraordinary gift for compressed, almost lapidary expressions; in the words of Pope: "what oft was thought, but ne'er so well expressed." Many of his phrases have become the common property of European civilization: carpe diem, in medias res, aurea mediocritas, non omnis moriar (see under Quotations). His character was mellow, genial, tolerant and urbane. His satires have none of the bitterness of Juvenal, Swift and Voltaire, but are mellow comments on the foibles of mankind. His philosophy was truly eclectic, borrowing now from Plato, now from Aristotle, now from the Stoics and Epicureans, with possibly a slight preference for the last-named school. But he created his own personal philosophy, one of moderation, enjoyment of life, of adherence to duty, of sunny Epicureanism. Horace, more than Virgil, is typical of his age. He has great frankness, charm, and his conceit is easier to swallow than that of Cicero. The chief reasons for his fame are: (i) his self-revelation, (ii) the picture he gives us of his times; (iii) his universality, expressing the best of Greek and Roman philosophy in never-to-be-forgotten phrases; (iv) the beauty of his poetry. In spite of Goethe's harsh criticism, Horace was a master of every form he touched. Quintilian speaks of him as "felicissime audax" (most happily daring), Petronius mentions his "curiosa felicitas" (painstaking felicity of expression). And withal, he was possessed of a great love of his country, and of life. Where Virgil is respected and admired, Horace is loved. (Duff, OCD)

Horatius Cocles: Legendary Roman hero whose gallant stand against the Etruscans (Horatius at the Bridge) is familiar to every schoolboy. The story appears in Livy.

Horman, William: 1450-1535. Author of *Vulgaria* and *Anti-bossicon;* vice-provost of Eton.

Hortensius: Lost philosophical work by Cicero.

Hortensius Hortalus, Q.: Second only to Cicero among orators of his day. He was defeated by Cicero in the trial of Verres. In addition to his speeches, he wrote love-poetry, annals, and a work on rhetoric.

Hortulus (or, **De Cultura Hortorum**): See Walafrid Strabo.

Hosidius Geta: See Geta, Hosidius.

Hostia: See "Cynthia."

Hostius: Author of a *Bellum Histricum* (1st cent. B.C.)

Housman, A. E.: 1859-1936. One of the greatest of modern English classical scholars; professor at Cambridge. In addition to his well-known English poetry ("Shropshire Lad"), he edited Manilius and Juvenal.

Hoveden, John of; Roger of: See John of Hoveden. Roger of Hoveden.

Hrabanus Maurus: Abbot of Fulda, Archbishop of Mainz. One of the chief figures of the Carolingian Renaissance (q.v.). A pupil of Alcuin. Wrote a learned commentary of encyclopedic breadth, also poetry. He is the reputed author of the famous hymn "Veni Creator Spiritus." Also wrote on grammar, on mathematics, on the Clergy, on language. Hrabanus also wrote works in the vernacular.

Hroswitha: (or Hrothswitha) A nun of the convent of Gandersheim, who wrote six comedies, in order to provide a more wholesome substitute for the un-Christian comedies of Terence, which, however, she also annotated. See *Dulcitius, Callimachus and Drusiana, Abraham.* She also wrote a series of Christian legends in leonine hexameters.

Hucbald: 9th cent. Author of *Eclogue on Baldness* (*Ecloga de Calvis*) dedicated to Charles the Bald (so Curtius; Raby and Manitius say to Archbishop Hatto). The poem is a reductio ad absurdum of alliteration. It consists of 146 lines, and every word begins with the letter "c." Cf. Swinburne's Parody on himself, and see Pangrammatic writing. H. also wrote *Lives of the Saints.*

Hugh of Orleans: (Hugh Primas) 12th century. One of

the "Wandering Scholars." The "Primate" of the *Ordo Vago-rum*. Wrote Latin lyrics with skillful use of rhyme. See Primas, Goliardic poetry, *Ordo Vagorum*.

Hugh of St. Victor: 12th century author, d. 1141. Wrote on philosophy (*Epitoma in Philosophiam*), grammar, geometry, and history.

Hugh of Trimberg: Wrote a *Registrum Multorum Auctorum*, listing 80 curriculum authors (1280).

Hugo: The otherwise unknown author of a poem against Manegold (q.v.). Presumably Hugo was a high church official. The poem is in partly leonine, and partly end-rhymed hexameters. (Manitius)

Hugo of Flavigny: b. ca. 1065. Travelled widely, had access to the archives of Lyon, Dijon, Verdun, etc. Wrote a Chronicle of the diocese of Verdun and the monastery of Flavigny. Useful, in spite of its subjective and ecclesiastical nature, because of the vast number of otherwise unknown sources used. (Manitius)

Hugo of Fleury: Wrote a work *De Regia Potestate et Sacerdotali Dignitate* on the rights and duties of kings and clergymen. Takes a moderate viewpoint. The work is dedicated to Henry I of England. A more important work is the *Historia Ecclesiastica* (1109). Other works: *Modernorum Regum Francorum Liber, Lives of the Saints*, etc. (Manitius)

Hugo of Folieto: 12th century. Wrote many mystical-allegorical works on the soul; on famous marriages; on birds; and other works.

Hugutio: 12th century grammarian, author of a *Liber Derivationum*, a work *de Dubio Accentu*, and a *Rosarium*, of which only a fragment or an abridgement has been found.

Humanist, humanism: In its broad sense, humanism may be defined as a love for classical and liberal arts. Rand's definition of a humanist is: "one who has a love of things human, one whose regard is centred on the world about him and the best that man has done, one who cares more for art and letters—particularly the art and letters of Greece and Rome, than for the dry light of reason or the mystic's flight into the unknown; one who distrusts allegory; one who adores critical editions . . . one who has a passion for manuscripts . . . one who has an eloquent tongue. . . ." Rand then mentions Jerome, Cicero, John of Salisbury, Poggio, Budaeus and Casaubon, Erasmus and Heinsius, and others, omitting only to mention E. K. Rand! Great periods of humanism are: the 12th century revival at Chartres, the 14-15th century in Italy, the Transalpine Renaissance (ca. 1500), etc. But such men as Cicero and St. Jerome have every right to the title of humanist.

Humbert, Cardinal: Middle of the 11th century. Wrote a work on the subject of simony (*Libri iii Adversos Simoniacos*).

Humbert de Montmoret: d. 1525. French Neo-Latin poet. Wrote patriotic epics (*Bellum Ravenne*).

Humor, Roman: The humor in Plautus is perhaps the most diverse, including puns, slapstick, farce, ribaldry, mistaken identity, and so forth. Terence's humor is a gentler sort, portraying manners (cf. Meredith's *Essay on Comedy*). Horace has a genial, kindly humor that is very different from the sardonic, biting type of Juvenal, which does not deserve to be mentioned under the rubric of humor. Cicero has charm and wit, but little humor. Nor is there much humor in the satire of Seneca and the epigrams of Martial. Petronius comes closer to true humor with his *Satyricon*. All in all, humor is a Greek rather than a Roman characteristic. Wit and satire are not the same as humor.

Hussovius, Mikolaj: d. ca. 1533. Polish-Latin poet, wrote on the Polish countryside.

Hutten, Ulrich von: See *Epistolae Obscurorum Virorum.*

Hyginus (1), G. Julius: Freedman and librarian of Augustus —author and antiquarian. Wrote commentaries on Cinna and Virgil, also works on theology, agriculture, bee-keeping, history, geography. Probably came from Spain.

Hyginus (2) "Gromaticus": ca. 100 A.D. Wrote a gromatic treatise *De Limitibus* (on boundaries). Various other works on gromatics (i.e., land-surveying) attributed to him are probably of later date.

Hyginus (3) and (4?): There are two extant works by a Hyginus (or two Hygini) who cannot be identified with either Hyginus (1) or (2). They are as follows: *Genealogiae,* a mythological handbook; and a manual of astronomy and astrology. These two works may be by the same author, but this is by no means certain.

Hymns: The most important contribution of the Church to Latin poetry. Earliest are by Hilary of Poitiers. Ambrose and Prudentius (qq.v.) wrote hymns, as did Fortunatus, Wigo, Adam of St. Victor, Thomas of Celano, Jacopone da Todi, and many others. See also Sequence.

Hypognosticon: See Laurence of Durham.

Iaculatione Equestri, de: Book on cavalry javelins by Pliny the Elder.

Iambic Senarii: The meter of Roman comedy and tragedy. A six-footed iambic line (as if one said: "To be or not to be, that is the question *now.*") Phaedrus (q.v.) also used the meter for his *Fables.*

Ibis: Elegiac invective by Ovid, in imitation of Callimachus (q.v.).

Idlefonsus: Spanish bishop in the 7th century. Wrote poetry.

Idolatria, de: Work by Tertullian (q.v.), in idolatry.

Iguvinian Tables: Bronze tablets, dealing with priestly ritual. Our chief source for the Umbrian language. See *Dialects, Italic.*

Iliacon: Lost work by Lucan on the Trojan War.

Ilias Latina: A crude Latin paraphrase and condensation of the *Iliad.* Probably written in Neronian times, possibly by one Baebius Italicus. An acrostic at the beginning and end names "Italicus" as the author but this can scarcely be Silius Italicus. The verse is careful, but wholly uninspired.

Imaginum Libri: (Varro) See *Hebdomades.*

Imitation of Christ (*Imitatio Christi*) Famous book of devotion and meditation of the Roman Catholic Church. Usually ascribed to Thomas a Kempis, though recent ecclesiastical scholars say that he merely edited the work, which was written by Groote (q.v.).

In: Titles beginning with this word will be found listed under the following word. E.g., *Catilinam, in.*

Incarnatione Verbi, de: A cento (q.v.) falsely attributed to Sedulius.

Incendio Urbis, de: Lost work on the great fire of Rome, by Lucan.

Indecency: A feature of much Roman comedy, as also of the Greek. Origins probably in the primitive Atellan and Fescennine literature. Catullus, Petronius, and Martial are noted for the indecency in their works. A well-known example in late antiquity is the *Cento Nuptialis* of Ausonius. Cicero discusses the subject in the "amo verecundiam" letter (Fam. 9.22) to Paetus.

Index Librorum Prohibitorum: List of books forbidden by the Catholic Church. The censorship of literature for moral purposes is not a new concept, going back at least as far as Plato.

Index Rerum Gestarum: (*Monumentum Ancyranum*) Found on a bronze tablet in a mosque in Ancyra, previously a temple of Augustus. In addition to a list of the "honores" and expenditures, the Index contains the *Res Gestae* (i.e., the deeds, campaigns, victories, etc.) of Augustus.

Indigitamenta: Ancient archives of priestly colleges, instructions for worship, etc. Some of the oldest Latin is found in these archives, but their importance is historical and linguistical, rather than literary.

Indignatio: Work by Valerius Cato (q.v.).

In Dulci Jubilo: Famous Christmas hymn, chiefly notable for its mixture of Latin with the (German) vernacular:

"In dulci jubilo
Nun singet und sei froh.'"

Ingulf: English monk and abbot, 11th century. Wrote history of his monastery (Croyland).

Innocent III, Pope: 1198-1216. One of the most eloquent

and learned of the medieval popes. Wrote sermons, missals, decretals. An authority on canonical law.

Innocentius: A writer on gromatics, or land-surveying.

Ino: Plays with this title were written by Livius and Laevius.

Institutio Oratoria: (Quintilian) The *magnum opus* of Quintilian, equally illuminating for the fields of law, oratory, education, literary criticism, and grammar. He traces the education of a child from infancy, embodying many practices that are recognized as sound today. The best parts of the work are: the description of early education (book I), the list of authors, with brief but memorable bits of criticism (Book X), and the picture of the Compleat Orator (Book XII). Quintilian stresses the importance of broad cultural, rather than narrow vocational training. In many ways, he anticipates John Dewey and the Progressive movement in education. The book represents the fruit of 20 years as an educator. It is replete with common sense and wisdom.

Institutiones Divinarum ac Saecularium Litterarum: See Cassiodorus.

Institutiones Grammaticae: See Priscian.

Institutionum Comentarii: See Gaius.

Instructiones: Among the first Christian-Latin poetry. By Commodianus (q.v.).

Interpretatio Romana: The identification of foreign gods with Roman divinities, or, more properly, the use of Latin names for other gods (e.g., Jupiter for Zeus, Neptune for Poseidon, etc.).

Invectiva in Ciceronem: See Pseudo-Sallust.

Inventio: One of the five branches of rhetoric (q.v.). Inventio is the finding of subject-matter.

Inventione, de: Rhetorical work by Cicero.

Inventione Dialectica, de: Treatise on rhetoric by Rudolph Agricola (q.v.).

Io: See Calvus.

Iphigenia: In mythology, the daughter of Agamemnon, sacrificed by him to secure a favorable wind. Plays of this title were written by Ennius and Naevius (qq.v.).

Ira, de: (Seneca-2) Dialogue by Seneca in three books on anger—its nature, uselessness, remedies, etc. The viewpoint is typically Stoic throughout. Date must be post-Caligula, because of the criticism of that emperor. The dialogue is addressed to Seneca's brother Novatus. See also Martin of Bracara.

Ireland: Great seat of monastic learning in the 6th century and afterward. See Columba, Columbanus. Irish monks founded some of the most important monasteries in Europe (e.g., Bobbio, St. Gall).

Irenaeus: Bishop of Lyons in the second century. Wrote a book *Adversus Haereses,* ca. 180, in Greek, which was almost immediately translated into Latin.

Irnerius of Bologna: ca. 1050-1130. Jurist and scholar. Began the work which Gratian (q.v.) finished.

Isagoge: Greek "introduction." A work by Porphyry, chiefly important for his adaptation of Aristotelian logic to Neo-Platonic philosophy. Translated by Boethius into Latin, and of considerable importance in the Middle Ages.

Isagogic literature: Any work that gives the reader an "introduction" to a subject, science, or skill. Examples: Cato, Varro, Columella on agriculture; Cicero and Quintilian on oratory; Horace on poetry; Vitruvius on architecture; Celsus on medicine; Vegetius on military science; and many others. See Technical prose.

Ischyrius: (Sterck, Van Vrijaldenhoven) Dutch Neo-Latin poet, author of *Hortulus Animae* and other works.

Isidore of Seville: 560?-636. One of the chief figures of Christian learning in the early Middle Ages, and, with Boethius, one of the most important links between antiquity and the Middle Ages. His works are varied: *Chronica,* a general history to his own day; *Historia Gothorum,* a history of the Goths; *De Natura Rerum; Differentiae; Quaestiones in Vetus Testamentum;* and the great *Etymologiae* or *Origines.* The latter was his most important work. It is a treasury of encyclopedic learning, embracing the liberal arts, medicine, geography, law, and various other topics. It was one of the basic books of the Middle Ages. Isidore, unlike other Christian authors, regarded pagan literature as worth knowing. Waddell calls the work the "Encyclopaedia Britannica of the Middle Ages." (OCD, Waddell, Manitius)

Italicus, Silius: See Silius Italicus.

Iter: (*The Journey*) A lost work by Julius Caesar.

Itinerarium Aetheriae Abbatissae: A letter by a 4th century abbess to her nuns, describing her pilgrimage to the Holy Land. See *Peregrinatio Aetheriae.*

Itinerarium Mentis Dei: Work by St. Bonaventure (q.v.).

Itinerarius: See Rutilius Namatianus.

Itineraries: Road maps or descriptions of journeys. The *Antonine Itinerary* from the third century is one of the best examples. There was also an *Itinerarium Maritimum* giving distances by sea in the Mediterranean, the *Jerusalem Itinerary,* etc.

Iudicium Paridis: A virgilian cento (q.v.) by Mavortius. Probably dates from the 6th century.

Iure Civili, de: Lost work by Varro (1) on law and jurisprudence.

Iustitia: The Roman personification of Justice, equivalent to the Greek Dike.

Ivo of Chartres: 1040-1116. Bishop of Chartres. Wrote letters, sermons, made a collection of Papal Decrees and canon law.

Jacopo da Voragine: 1230-98. Archbishop of Genoa. His *Legendae Sanctorum* or *Legenda Aurea* (Golden Legend), a collection of the legends of the saints, arranged according to the calendar, was one of the most popular books of the later Middle Ages. (Ferm, Encycl. of Religion)

Jacopone da Todi: 13th century Franciscan friar. Probable author of the majestic and beautiful *Stabat Mater,* one of the loveliest of the Sequences. (See Sequence.) Also wrote a *De Contemptu Mundi.*

Jacques de Vitry: 1180-1240. Bishop of Acre; author of *Historia Orientalis et Occidentalis.*

Janicius (Janicki) Klemens: 16th century Polish-Latin poet. Imitated Ovid (*Tristium Liber I, Variarum Elegiarum Liber I, Carmina,* etc.). Probably the greatest of the Polish Neo-Latin poets.

Januarius Nepotianus: Epitomizer of Valerius Maximus (q.v.).

Janus: Roman god of doors and beginnings. The first month of the calendar was named after him. Represented as a two-faced god.

Jason: Hero of the Argonauts legend. See Valerius Flaccus. Varro of Atax.

Javolenus Priscus: Noted Roman jurist, ca. 100 A.D. Teacher of the great Salvius Julianus. His *Epistulae* were used by Justinian and his compilers.

Jerome (Hieronymus) St.: 340-420. The most learned of the Church Fathers. Pupil of Donatus. Works: Translated and continued the *Chronicle of Eusebius* (q.v.); *De Viris Illustribus; Dialogues; Letters; Lives of Eremites;* the *Vulgate,* etc. The *Vulgate* is Jerome's translation of the Bible, and has become the standard text of the Church. He was a man of tremendous erudition and phenomenal energy. His greatest importance is his study of Scriptural texts. Lived as an ascetic in the desert for many years. Founded a school where he taught the monks to copy manuscripts. The story of his dream is famous. He was chastised by God for being "a Ciceronian, not a Christian." Jerome is one of the original four Doctors of the Church (q.v.). (Rand, Labriolle)

Jerusalem Itinerary: See Itineraries.

Jesu dulcis memoria: Famous hymn, probably by Bernard of Clairvaux (q.v.).

Joachim of Fiore: (or Floris) Theologian and scholar of the 12th century (1145-1202). Most important works: *Concordia Novi et Veteris Testamenti, Expositio in Apocalypsin Psalterium Decem Chordarum, De Unitate Trinitatis.* His writings were condemned by Aquinas and the Council of Arles.

Jocundus: of unknown origin and date. Wrote a *Vita et Translatio S. Servatii.*

Johannes Canaparius: Author of a Life of Adalbert, one of the best biographies of its time (ca. 1000). He was a monk in the Roman Aventine monastery.

Johannes Diakonus: Author of a *Chronicon Venetum,* one of several Venetian chronicles produced in the 10th and 11th centuries.

Johannes Magnus: 1488-1544. Swedish clergyman and historian (*Historia Metropolitanae Ecclesiae Upsalensis, Historia de Omnibus Gothorum Sveonumque Regibus*).

Johannes Monachus: (John the Monk) 11th century monk. Wrote *Liber de Miraculis.* Mentions the four Pillars of the Church (Ambrose, Augustine, Jerome and Gregory).

Johannis: Epic by Corippus (q.v.).

John of Amalfi: Second half of the 10th century. Wrote the *Life of St. Irene,* a book of Miracles, and an account of the death of St. Nicholas.

John of Arderne: 1307-1380. English physician and author of medical treatises in Latin.

John of Beauvais: 12th century author of a didactic poem entitled *De Declinatione Nominis et Verbi.*

John Duns Scotus: See Duns Scotus.

John Eriugena: (John Scotus) 815-877. Greatest scholar of the ninth century. Not to be confused with Duns Scotus (q.v.). A Platonist, he translated the Pseudo-Dionysian works into Latin and reconciled Christian theology with Neo-Platonic doctrine, and thus is one of the first Scholastics. Most important work: *De Naturae Divisione,* a highly mystical work.

John of Garland: 13th century humanist. Wrote *Poetria, De Triumphis Ecclesiae,* etc. Complained about the withering away of the Latin language.

John of Hanville: 12th century poet, author of the allegorical satire *Architrenius* (q.v.).

John of Haute-Seille: Wrote, towards the end of the 12th century, a work *Dolopathos,* about a Sicilian king during the Age of Augustus, his son Lucinius, and the Seven Wise Men. The work is full of references to the Greek philosophers, mixed with ancient tales from Herodotus and elsewhere, and Christian lore. Needless to say, Lucinius is converted to Christianity at the end. In an epilogue the author begs the reader not to take him to task for writing about such improbable events.

John of Hoveden: 13th century English poet. Author of *Philomela,* an epic-lyric representation of the life and passion of Christ; the Fifteen Joys of Mary (*Quindecim Gaudia Virginis Gloriosae*).

John of Jandum: Teacher at University of Paris in the 14th century. Wrote *De Laudibus Parisiis,* and (with Marsilius of Padua q.v.) *Defensor Pacis.* Also commentaries on Aristotle.

John of Mirecourt: 14th century theologian and philosopher, follower of the Ockhamist movement (See Ockham).

John Quidort of Paris: Dominican friar and teacher. Wrote *De Potestate Regia et Papali, De Modo Existendi Corporis Christi in Sacramento Altaris.*

John of St. Arnulf: Tenth century author of biographies. (*Vita Johannis Gorziensis* and *Vita et Miracula St. Glodesindis*) The last-named belongs, properly, to the realm of hagiography.

John of St. Vincent: Wrote a history of the monastery of St. Vincent at Volturno from its founding in 703 to the election of Alexander II in 1061.

John of Salisbury: 1115?-1180. One of the greatest humanists of the Middle Ages. Bishop of Chartres, secretary to Thomas a Becket. Wrote letters, historical, biographical, philosophical, hagiographical, political, and legal works. Used the Roman jurists as well as the Church Fathers, and had great respect and love for the pagan authors. His Latinity was very elegant. Most important works: *Policraticus* (with the famous doctrine of the Two Swords—on temporal and church powers), and *Metalogicon,* a treatise on the value and use of logic.

John Scotus: See John Eriugena.

John of Tilbury: 12th century. Wrote a *Summa Dictaminis.* Teacher of theology at Oxford.

John of Wurzburg: Made a pilgrimage to Jerusalem 1160-1170, which he then described (*Descriptio Terrae Sanctae*).

Johnson, Samuel: 1709-84. Wrote Latin verse; translated and paraphrased Juvenal (e.g. *Vanity of Human Wishes*).

Johnston, Arthur: Scottish scholar. Extremely proficient in Latin verse.

Jonas of Orleans: b. ca. 780. Wrote sermons, poetry, biography, and a book for kings and one for laymen (*Institutio Regia, Inst. Laicalis*). (Manitius)

Jordan of Osnabrück: 13th century German poet. Wrote a satire on the Papacy (*On the Peacock*).

Jordanes: Author of a *Gothic History* which preserves the (lost) one of Cassiodorus, and which was used by Liutprand of Cremona, Hermann of Reichenau, et al. Also wrote a *Summa Temporum*.

Joseph of Exeter: (Josephus Iscanus) English monk and poet. fl. ca. 1200. Wrote an epic *De Bello Troiano*, based on Dares Phrygius (q.v.), and an epic on the Crusades (*Antiocheis*).

Josephus Scottus: 8th century Irish poet, contemporary of Charlemagne, to whom he addressed poetry.

Jotsald of Cluny: 11th century monk who wrote a famous lament on the death of Odilo of Cluny.

Journey to Brundisium: One of the best-known of Horace's satires (Sat. 1.5), probably based on a similar satire by Lucilius (q.v.).

Jove: See Jupiter.

Jovinian: A pre-Augustinian monk (fl. ca. 390) who maintained the equal merit of marriage and celibacy.

Juba II: King of Mauretania. A man of great learning, he wrote (in Greek) on history, geography, botany, grammar. A source for Pliny the Elder.

Jugurtha (Sallust): See *Bellum Jugurthinum*.

Julian, Bishop of Toledo: 7th century clergyman and poet. Also wrote on grammar and biography.

Julian "the Apostate": Roman Emperor 361-3. Sought to abolish Christianity and return to paganism, but with no lasting results after his death.

Julio-Claudian period: Under the emperors (Augustus), Tiberius, Caligula, Claudius and Nero. The first half of the Silver Age. Normally, the term does not include the reign of Augustus.

Julius Africanus (1): A rhetor highly praised by Quintilian.

Julius Africanus (2): Christian philosopher, historian and chronicler. Used as a source by Eusebius.

Julius Atticus: Writer on vineyards and wine-culture, in the time of Tiberius.

Julius Avitus: Contemporary of the younger Pliny (ca. 100). An extremely prolific writer who died prematurely.

Julius Caesar: See Caesar.

Julius Canus: See Julius Kanus.

Julius Capitolinus: One of the six authors of the *Historia Augusta* (q.v.).

Julius Cerealis: Minor epic and pastoral poet of the Flavian period.

Julius Exsuperantius: Wrote on the war between Marius and Sulla, probably in the 4th or 5th century. Included in a MS. of Sallust.

Julius Florus: See Florus.

Julius Gabinianus, S.: Prominent Gallic rhetor in the Flavian period. Mentioned by Suetonius.

Julius Graecinus: Writer on wine-culture under Tiberius.

Julius Kanus: (or Canus) Philosopher sentenced to death by Caligula for his reproaches of the emperor.

Julius Modestus: Grammarian of the first century. Freedman of Hyginus (1).

Julius Obsequens: Historian, probably of the 4th century. Drew on Livy's epitomizers.

Julius Paris: 4th century (?) epitomizer of Valerius Maximus.

Julius Romanus: See Romanus.

Julius Secundus: An orator mentioned by Quintilian. One of the interlocutors in the *Dialogus de Oratoribus* of Tacitus. Wrote biography of Julius Africanus (1).

Julius Solinus: See Solinus.

Julius Tiro: Rhetor of the first century.

Julius Valerius: Author of *Itinerarium Alexandri*. Fourth century.

Julius Victor, C.: 4th century rhetor. Wrote an *Ars Rhetorica* based on Quintilian (q.v.).

Junius Congus: A friend of the satirist Lucilius. Wrote legal and historical works.

Junius, Franciscus: 1589-1677. Dutch scholar and philologist. Wrote a glossary of Gothic, edited the Caedmon MS., etc.

Junius Gracchanus, M.: Wrote historical works ca. 130. Nothing survives of his work.

Junius, Hadrianus: 1511-75. Dutch humanist, poet, historian, and scholar; wrote works on philosophy, medicine, history, etc.

Junius Nipsus: 2nd century author of works on gromatics (surveying).

Junius Otho: Augustan rhetor. Teacher and friend of the ill-fated Sejanus. Wrote four books of "colores."

Juno: In Roman mythology, the queen of the gods. Sister and wife of Jupiter. Equivalent to the Greek Hera.

Jupiter: (Diu-pater) King of the gods. Equivalent of the Greek Zeus and the Norse Thor. God of the thunderbolt. Also known as Jove.

Jurisprudence: One field in which the Romans far surpassed the Greeks. Names from the earliest period include Rutilius Rufus, Balbus, and Q. Mucius Scaevola, who wrote the first systematic treatise on law. Contemporary with Cicero, his friend S. Sulpicius Rufus was a leading jurist. Varro wrote on law. In the time of Augustus, a great legal library was founded, and the rival schools of the Sabinians and Proculians (qq.v.) began. Other important names are: Javolenus Priscus, Gaius, Salvius Julianus, Ulpian, Papinian, Paulus. See under these names, see also Justinian, Tribonian, Digest, *Ius Civile*. For Church law, see Canon law, Gratian, *Corpus Juris Canonici*, etc.

Justinian, Emperor of the East: 527-567. Compiled the

Digest, Institutiones, and *Novellae* (q.v.), the most comprehensive collections of Roman law ever made. See also Trebonianus, jurisprudence.

Justin Martyr: 100-165. Author of *Apology, Second Apology,* etc.

Justinus (Justin): Made an epitome of Pompeius Trogus' history, probably in the third century.

Juvenal: (D. Junius Juvenalis) ca. 60—ca. 140. There is very little known about the life of the greatest of Roman satirists. His dates are a matter of conjecture. He is said to have been exiled, but why, whither and by whom, are unknown. His satires are marked by vitriolic bitterness, graphic detail and realism, grim humor, and quotable phrases. Indeed, he is second only to Horace for his felicity in phrase-turning. One calls to mind the well-known "mens sana in corpore sano" (sound mind in a sound body), "quis custodiet ipsos custodes" (who'll watch the watchmen?) "panem et circenses" (bread and circuses), "nemo repente fuit turpissimus" (nobody ever became wicked overnight), and many others. See under *Satires*: Juvenal, *Rome, Vanity of Human Wishes,* for details of satires. (Duff, OCD)

Juvencus: The earliest of Christian epic poets. Wrote, ca. 330, *Evangelorum libri LV,* a biblical epic which imitated Virgil, was highly praised by Jerome, and became popular in the Middle Ages.

Juventius: A writer of "palliata" comedies. Only his name survives.

Juventius Celsus: There seem to have been two Roman jurists of this name, one under Vespasian, the other under Trajan.

Kaddroae abbatis, Vita: Anonymous biography of the Irish abbot Kaddroe, written about 1000 A.D.

Kanus, Julius: See Julius Kanus.

Karoli, Vita: (Life of Charlemagne) See Einhard.

Karolus Magnus et Leo Papa: Epic fragment from the Carolingian Renaissance, commonly ascribed, though with little validity, to Angilbert.

Keil, H.: Edited the *Grammatici Latini.*

Kempis, Thomas a: See Thomas a Kempis.

Kochanowski, Jan: 1530-84. Polish-Latin poet and playwright. Wrote love poems, elegies, epigrams.

Konrad von Ammenhausen: 14th century Swiss monk, author of a famous chess allegory (*De Moribus Hominum et De Officiis Nobilium Super Ludo Scaccorum*).

Kromer, Marcin: 16th century Polish chronicler. Wrote a Latin history of Poland (*De Origine et Rebus Gestis Polonorum Libri XXX*), also theological works.

Kunstprosa: German: "Artistic prose." The first of the ancients to write artistic prose was the Greek Gorgias of Leontini. Plato and Thucydides were among the greatest Greek prose writers, Cicero and Tacitus and Livy were outstanding in Rome.

Labeo (1), M. Antistius: ca. 54 B.C.-17 A.D. Jurisconsult, head of the legal sect known as the Sabinians. Orator, lawyer, and writer on philosophy and linguistics. A man of tremendous erudition and energy, he is said to have written 400 volumes.

Labeo (2), Attius: Translated the Iliad and Odyssey into Latin hexameters in the first century A.D.

Laberius, D.: ca. 100-45 B.C. Writer of mimes, of which 43 titles and 155 lines have survived. Difficult to form an estimate of his style.

Labienus, T.: Orator of the early Empire. Called "Rabienus" because of his furious invectives. His books were burned by decree of the Senate.

Laborintus: A didactic poem by Eberhard the German (13th century). Important for its complete listing of "curriculum authors" studied in his day. The authors include (qq.v.): Cato (i.e., the *Disticha Catonis*), Theodulus, Avianus, Aesop, Maximianus, the *Geta* by Vitalis of Blois, Statius, Ovid, Horace (Satires only), Juvenal, Persius, the *Architrenius* by John of Hanville, Virgil, Lucan, Walter of Châtillon's *Alexandreis*, Claudian, "Dares Phrygius," *Ilias Latina*, Sidonius, the *Solimarius*, Marbod of Rennes on jewelry, Sedulius, Peter Riga

(*Aurora*), Arator, Prudentius, the *Anticlaudianus* of Alan of
Lille, the *Doctrinale* of Alexander of Villedieu and the *Grecismus* of Eberhard of Béthune, the *Poetria Nova* of Geoffrey of
Vinsauf, Martianus Capella, Boethius, Bernard Silvestris,
Matthew of Vendôme, and other authors. The list shows the
fact that the grammars of Donatus and Priscian have been
supplanted by the works of Alexander of Villedieu and Eberhard of Béthune.

Labyrinthus: Work by Paracelsus (q.v.).

Lachmann, C.: Great German scholar and textual critic of
the mid-19th century. Especially important for his work on
the text of Lucretius.

Lactantius: b. 250. The "Christian Cicero." One of the
early Apologists. Works: *De Opifico Dei* (on the body and
soul of man); *Divinae Institutiones,* an anti-pagan polemic;
De Ira Dei (On the Wrath of God), and others. We are indebted to Lactantius for his preservation of fragments of
such early writers as Ennius and Lucilius. Unlike other Church
fathers, L. did not reject pagan literature per se. He kept much
of what was great in antiquity. L. is believed to be the author
of *The Phoenix,* an allegorical poem. His greatest work is the
Divinae Institutiones, which "laid the foundations for Christian humanism." (E. K. Rand)

Lactantius Placidus: 7th (?) century author of a prose
abridgement of Ovid's *Metamorphoses* (q.v.).

Lacuna: A gap in a MS. as, for instance, in the Satyricon
of Petronius.

Laelius: See *Amicitia, de* (Cicero).

Laelius Archelaus: Friend of the satirist Lucilius (q.v.).
Lectured and commented on the latter's satires.

Laevius: Roman poet, ca. 100 B.C. There is much confusion
and obscurity concerning him: he has been confused with
both Naevius and Livius (Andronicus). Laevius wrote a work
called *Erotopaegnia.* This consisted of six books of love poems
in various lyric meters.

Lambert (1) of Ardre: Wrote (ca. 1194) the history of the family of the Counts of Ghisnes, presumably to regain lost favor. The work is of much historical value. (Manitius)

Lambert (2) of St. Omer: Wrote, ca. 1100 a *Liber Floridus,* a compilation of useful information in the fields of history, geography, astronomy, theology, chronology, etc. Shows an exceedingly wide knowledge of classical and medieval authors.

Lambert (3) of Pouthières: 12th century monk and grammarian. Wrote a letter to one Alberich, dealing with accent, compound words, and even some Greek words (which, however, he writes incorrectly).

Lambinus: Early (16th century) editor of texts, such as Lucretius, Nepos, etc.

Lamentations: See Gildas.

Lampadio, G. Octavius: Grammarian of the second century B.C. Arranged the *Bellum Punicum* of Naevius in seven books.

Lampert of Hersfeld: 11th century historian and biographer. Wrote *Annales,* the biography of Bishop Lul, and the history of his own monastery.

Lampoon: Grew out of the Versus Fescennini (q.v.). Naevius was imprisoned for his lampoons against the Metelli. Catullus and Bibaculus, and the emperor Augustus himself wrote lampoons. Martial's epigrams often fall into this category.

Landino, Cristoforo: 1424-1492. Italian humanist; wrote Neo-Platonic dialogues, and commentaries on Virgil, Dante, etc.

Lando, Ortensio: 1512-1553. Italian humanist; author of various scholarly and satirical works in Italian and Latin.

Landulf of Mailand: b. ca. 1025. Wrote a history of his times to the year 1085.

Lanfranc: 1003-98. Italian scholar of the 11th century. Was brought to Canterbury by William the Conqueror. Wrote letters to popes, kings and others. Famous for his controversy with Berengar of Tours.

Langton, Stephen: Archbishop of Canterbury in the 12th century. Perhaps author of the "Golden Sequence" (Veni, Sancte Spiritus). Co-author of Magna Charta.

Lantbert of Deutz: Wrote a *Vita Heriberti,* middle of 11th century, which contains even more than the usual complement of visions, miracles, etc. (Manitius)

Lapo de Castiglionchio: 15th century Italian humanist, noted for Latin translations of Greek authors.

Lappa Rubrenus: Roman tragedian of uncertain date who wrote an *Atreus.*

Lares: Spirits of the dead. See Penates, Religion.

Lascivos Sodales, ad: Satirical poem by Arnulf of Lisieux (q.v.).

Latin Iliad: See *Ilias Latina.*

Latin Language: The language of literature was not the same as the everyday language of speech. See Sermo plebeius, rusticus, cotidianus. The Latin of Italy differed from that of Gaul, Spain, Africa. See also Petronius, elocutio novella.

Latin literature: May conveniently be divided into the following periods: 1. Earliest Latin (500-240 B.C.). 2. Republican Lit. (240-70 B.C.) incl. epic, comedy, tragedy. 3. The "Golden Age" (70 B.C.-14 A.D.). The Ciceronian and Augustan ages. 4. The "Silver Age" (14-180 A.D.), marked by increasing artificiality, rhetoric, etc. 5. Late Antiquity (180-500). Beginnings of Christian-Latin literature, Apologists. 6. "The Dark Ages" (500-800) Monasticism, Patristic literature, etc. 7. Carolingian Revival (q.v.) Monastic libraries, poetry, learning. 8. High Middle Ages (Schools of Chartres, etc., Scholastics). 9. Late Middle Ages (Latin lyrics, etc., of the 12th-13th centuries). 10. The Renaissance (Latin begins to be replaced by the vernaculars). 11. Post-Renaissance or Neo-Latin.

Latin lyric, medieval: The "Last Flowering of the Latin Language." 12th-13th centuries brought a new kind of poetry, poems of love and sadness, of spring, of conviviality, of satire. See Goliardic poets, Vagantenlieder, etc.

Latin, Vulgar: See Vulgar Latin.

Latinitate, de: See Caper, Flavius.

Latinus: Eponymous (q.v.) hero of Latium. He appears in Virgil, Naevius, et al.

Latomus, Bartholomeus: 1485-1570. Latinist and Ciceronian. Professor of Latin at the College Royal of Francis I.

Latro, M. Porcius: Orator and teacher in the Augustan Age. Ovid was his pupil. Seneca (1) speaks highly of his ability.

Laudatio Pisonis: Poem in praise of Piso, the Neronian conspirator, by an unknown author. It has been attributed to various people, such as Lucan, Calpurnius Siculus, etc.

Laudationes Funebres: Eulogies of the dead.

Laude Virginitatis, de: Poem in praise of chastity by Avitus (q.v.).

Laudem Justini, in: Poem by Corippus (q.v.) in praise of the emperor Justin II.

Laudes Neronis: Panegyric of Nero by Lucan (q.v.).

Laudibus Dei, de: Poem by Dracontius (q.v.).

Laudibus Divinae Sapientiae, de: Poem in praise of Divine Wisdom by Alexander Neckham (q.v.).

Laurence of Durham: English monastic poet of the 12th century. Wrote a *Hypognosticon* (versification of material from the Bible), tales of saints and martyrs, Dialogues, hagiographic works, and a *Consolatio*.

Laurentius of Monte Cassino: Monk, later bishop. Wrote numerous works: a *Life of St. Maurus*, a *Passion of Wenceslaus* (much better than that of Gumpold q.v.), a versified *Passion of Bishop Castrensis of Volturno*.

Laureolus: See Catullus (2).

Lavardin, Hildebert of: See Hildebert of Le Mans.

Law: See Jurisprudence, Justinian, Canon Law, etc.

Learning, miscellaneous: See Cato, Varro, Aelius Stilo, Nigidius Figulus, Pollio, Hyginus, Pliny (2), Quintilian, Cicero, Boethius, Isidore, Martianus Capella, Alcuin, Hrabanus Maurus, Bernard Sylvestris, Conrad of Hirsau, Aimeric. See also Education, Grammar and grammarians, curriculum authors, technical works.

Lefèvre d'Étaples: French humanist of the Renaissance (ca. 1500). His chief work is the Quintuplex psalter: 5 versions of the Psalms side by side. Also wrote commentaries on the Epistles of Paul, edited Nicolas of Cusa, etc.

Lege Manilia, pro: Cicero's speech advocating that command of the Mithridatic War be given to Pompey. It is full of glowing eulogy, without becoming sycophantic or fulsome.

Legenda Sanctorum: See *Golden Legend*, Jacopo da Voragine.

Legibus, de: Cicero's (incomplete) treatise on Law. Largely based on Stoic philosophy.

Lemma: See Scholia.

Lemnius, Margadant, Simon: 1511-1550. Raeto-Romansch poet and humanist. Wrote *Amores*, epigrams and an epic (*Raeteis*), describing the wars for Swiss independence and the victory over the Austrians.

Leo: Play by Naevius.

Leo I (the Great), Pope: 440-461. Doctor of the Church. Author of many sermons, letters, etc.

Leo of Monte Cassino: Wrote a history of his monastery up to the year 1057. This was continued by Peter the Deacon, also of Monte Cassino.

Leo of Naples: Translated Pseudo-Callisthenes' story of Alexander into Latin.

Leo of Vercelli: Friend of Gerbert (q.v.). fl. ca. 1000, Wrote elegies on the deaths of Otto III and Peter of Vercelli.

Leonine rhyme: Internal rhyme, usually of more than one syllable. Very popular in the Middle Ages. An English example:

"When you're lying awake with a dismal headache
    And repose is tabooed by anxiety
 I conceive you may use any language you choose
    To indulge in without impropriety." (W. S. Gilbert)

Lerins, Vincent of: See Vincent of Lerins.

Lesbia: See Catullus (1).

Letald of Micy: 10th century. Wrote a Life of St. Julian, and an account of the Miracles of St. Maximinus.

Letters: A truly Roman genre. In general there are three sorts: the true letter, written to a friend as we should write a letter today—the best example of this type is to be found in the letters of Cicero (q.v.)—they are chatty, informal, and use the *sermo cotidianus,* although one might note a difference between the letters to Atticus and those to a casual acquaintance. The second type is the literary epistle, written with a view to publication. Pliny's letters (q.v.) illustrate this type. They are more polished, more self-conscious than those of Cicero. But they are still letters, meant to be sent as well as published. The third type includes the philosophical epistle (e.g., Seneca's), the poetical epistle (e.g., Horace's *Epistles, Ars Poetica*; Ovid's *Heroides*). These "letters" are a literary device, and are not really letters at all, in the usual sense of the word. Seneca's "Letters" are philosophical essays thinly disguised. For other examples, see Fronto, Symmachus, Gregory I, Gregory VII, Leo I, Baudri de Bourgeuil, Jerome, Augustine, Ambrose, Sidonius, Salvian, Paulinus of Nola, Walo of St. Arnulf, Tertullian, Marcus Aurelius, Macrobius, Cassiodorus, Claudianus Mamertus, Marbod of Rennes, Notker Balbulus, Paula, Peter the Venerable, the *Epistulae Obscurorum Virorum,* and elsewhere, *passim.*

Letters of Cicero: There are four collections: those to Atticus, to Brutus, to his brother Quintus, and to various friends (ad Familiares). The collections include letters from, as well as to, some of the recipients. Those to Atticus are the most informal and self-revealing. Cicero's letters were not as popular as his other works, and were only discovered in the 14th century by Petrarch. They are extremely valuable for the picture they give us of Cicero's times.

Letters of Pliny the Younger: It is rather ironic that Pliny's letters, which he thought far inferior to his speeches and poetry, have alone survived as his one claim to immortality. We have nine books of letters, and one of his official correspondence with the emperor Trajan. These belong to the second type of letter (see *Letters*)—the literary epistle. Composed with an eye towards eventual publication, they are polished, self-conscious, and thus very different from the letters of Cicero. They are brilliant in the description of events, moods, and characters which they furnish us. Among the more familiar subjects are: the eruption of Vesuvius, a ghost story, the boy and the dolphin, a day in the country, sketches of various disagreeable characters. Others deal with literary criticism, the question of the Christians, and numerous other topics. All are readable, most are charming. We can infer much about Pliny's own character from the letters: his vanity, his love of fame, his charm, wit, friendliness, piety, etc. Pliny was the true type of a Roman gentleman. The literary epistle is one of Rome's most important legacies to modern literature. Other authors of this type of letter: Tertullian, Macrobius, Symmachus, Cassiodorus. The letters of Mme. de Sévigné are a modern example. (Duff, Silver Age)

Leucadia: Lost comedy by Sextus Turpilius (q.v.). Only fragments remain. It seems to have been a burlesque of the story of Sappho.

Lex Duodecim Tabularum: See Twelve Tables.

Liber: Another name for the god Bacchus.

Liber de Caesaribus: A work by Aurelius Victor (q.v.), giving an account of the lives of the emperors from Augustus to Constantine.

Liber de Dogmatibus Ecclesiastici: See Gennadius Scholasticus.

Liber de Gemmis: See *Liber Lapidum*.

Liber de Miraculis: "Book of Miracles." See Johannes Monachus.

Liber de Orthographia: See Scaurus.

Liber de Poetis: See Sedigitus.

Liber de Recuperatione Ptolemaidae: Poem on the Third Crusade, attributed to Haimar (q.v.).

Liber Glossarum Ansileubi: See Glossa.

Liber Gomorrhianus: See Damiani, Peter.

Liber Historiae Francorum: An anonymous 8th century history of the Franks.

Liber Lapidum (or *Liber de Gemmis*): Poem on jewels by Marbod of Rennes, containing all the fantastic theories of the ancient and medieval world concerning the magical properties of precious stones. The work was extremely popular in the Middle Ages. See under Laborintus for its inclusion on lists of "curriculum authors."

Liber Memorialis: See Ampelius.

Liber Monstrorum De Diversis Generibus: Anonymous work, probably of the 7th century, dealing, as the name implies, with monsters of all sorts. (Manitius)

Liber Pontificalis: The official biographies of the popes by various authors. The first collection ends with the life of Stephen V (885-891). Duchesne's edition brings the biographies to the year 1431.

Liber Spectaculorum: 33 poems by Martial (q.v.) written for the opening of the Colosseum.

Liberal Arts: See Education, Artes Liberales, Martianus Capella.

Libertas: Personification of Liberty. She had a temple at Rome, dating from the third century B.C.

Libraries: The first private library was that of Aemilius Paulus in the second century B.C. (167). In 39 B.C. Asinius Pollio founded the first public library, which was followed within a dozen years by the great Palatine Library of Augustus. By the end of the 4th century, there were 28 at Rome. Seneca says that a library is as much an essential for a home as a bath. One excellent specimen has been found in the ruins of Herculaneum. In the Middle Ages, the only libraries were in the monasteries (e.g., St. Gall, Cluny, Bobbio, etc.). See under Jerome, Cassiodorus, etc. In the later medieval period, the centers of education, and with them, the libraries, shifted to the Cathedral Schools and the Universities.

Libri Carolini: Books written at the request of Charlemagne, ca. 800, to denounce the heresy of the Greeks.

Libri duo de Natura Corporis et Animi: See William of Thierry.

Libri Iuris Notarum: See Probus.

Libri Lintei: The famous "linen books"—early Roman archives preserving the *Libri Magistratuum*. They were kept in the Capitol.

Libri Musarum: See Opilius.

Libri Navales: Lost book on navigation or seafaring by Varro (1).

Licentius: Friend or relation of St. Augustine, who wrote a poem highly praised by the latter. The poem is preserved in Augustine's letters, and hardly seems to merit such extravagant praise.

Licinius (1) Imbrex: Early writer of comedies (palliatae) mentioned by Gellius.

Licinius (2) Mucianus: A general and historian; source for Pliny the Elder, especially on art in Asia.

Licinius (3) Sura: Spanish rhetor who wrote speeches for Trajan. See under "ghost-writers."

Licinus Largius or Larcius: Author of *Ciceromastix*, a lost work criticizing Cicero.

Liége: (Lüttich) One of the great medieval cathedral schools. See Egbert, Ratherius, Balderich, etc.

Ligario, pro: Speech by Cicero. One of the "Caesarianae" (q.v.).

Ligurinus: Epic poem, attributed to one Gunther, on the deeds of Frederick Barbarossa. See also *Gesta Friderici.*

Limitibus, de: Treatise on gromatics (surveying) by Hyginus (2).

Limon: Lost work by Cicero, dealing with literary criticism.

Lingua Latina, de: Work on the Latin Language by Varro, which survives in part. The portion we have deals mostly with etymology and syntax. Varro's etymologies are often quite fanciful, not to say ludicrous, but occasionally they are sound. In the Analogy-Anomaly controversy (q.v.) Varro was an analogist, but he admitted that anomaly is justified by custom.

Lios [Elias?] Monocus: See Minor Carolingian Poetry.

Lipogrammatic writing: A highly artificial style in which one letter of the alphabet is omitted from each line (e.g.,

"a" in the first, "b" in the second, and so on). See Fulgentius
(1).

Lipsius, J.: French humanist and classical scholar of the
16th century. Edited Tacitus (1574), and Seneca, and wrote
a Menippean Satire (q.v.) in imitation of Seneca's *Apocolocyntosis.*

Literary Circles: Early circles include that of Scipio (to
which Terence belonged), and that of Q. Lutatius Catulus
(including Archias, Antipater, etc.). In the Augustan Age
there were three such circles, that of Maecenas, that of
Asinius Pollio, and that of Messalla (qq.v.). For medieval
examples, see Desiderius of Monte Cassino, and the Carolingian Renaissance.

Literary Criticism: In the Scipionic circle, and in the works
of Lucilius, the beginnings of literary criticism are to be
found. The lines of Sedigitus on the poets give another early
example. Cicero was a profound literary critic, and wrote of
poetry, oratory, etc. In the Augustan Age, Horace's *Satires,
Epistles,* and *Ars Poetica* come immediately into mind. The
elder Seneca, Persius, Petronius, Martial, Pliny, Tacitus, and
especially Quintilian reflect Silver-Age literary criticism. Later,
Gellius and the grammarians (e.g., Donatus, Servius, Priscian,
etc.) are to be cited. For the Middle Ages, see Alcuin, Bede,
John of Salisbury, Geoffrey of Vinsauf, Alexander of Villedieu,
Eberhard of Béthune, etc.

Litterator: Teacher of elementary education—the "three
R's." See Education.

Liturgy, Christian: See Mass, Gregorian chant, and Ferm,
Encyclopedia of Religion (s.v.)

Liutprand of Cremona: A Lombard, bishop of Cremona.
Sent on an embassy to Constantinople in 946, he wrote of his
mission, portraying the court of the Byzantine Emperor in the
most opprobrious terms ("the city which was once so rich
and flourishing is now famished, perjured, deceitful, rapacious,
greedy, vainglorious"). The work is entitled *Relatio de Legatione Constantinopolitane.* He also wrote a *Liber de Rebus
Gestis Ottonis.*

Lives of the Caesars: (Suetonius) Biographies of the Caesars from Julius to Domitian. The first few chapters of *Julius* are missing, but the rest is intact. The work is readable, chatty, full of miscellaneous information, like the Diary of Pepys. Gives the reader a good idea of the physical appearance and character of the emperors. Its faults are: a tendency to scandal-mongering and gossip, monotony, lack of historical perspective and faulty chronology. The pictures of Nero and Caligula are especially good.

Livius Andronicus: ca. 284-204 B.C. The father of Roman literature. The first to translate Greek literature into Latin (Homer's Odyssey). He is the ancestor of Virgil in epic, of Plautus in comedy, of Accius in tragedy (we possess nine titles), and of Horace in lyric poetry. The surviving fragments are few and far between, so that it is impossible to form any good estimate of Livius' style. The epic fragments are crude; the meter is Saturnian (q.v.). The dramatic fragments, on the whole, are better. (Duff, OCD)

Livius de Frulovisiis, Titus: b. ca. 1400. Humanist and Latin playwright. Wrote satirical comedies, and a *Vita Henrici Quinti.*

Livy (Titus Livius): 59 B.C.(?)-A.D. 17. Greatest of Augustan prose writers, and second only to Tacitus among Roman historians. His history is entitled *Ab Urbe Condita* (*Libri*) (q.v. for a discussion of the work). His prose is vivid and graphic, but he does not sift and weigh his sources. Uses all the old annalists, Greek and Latin, as sources. Pollio derided him for his "Patavinity," but Quintilian speaks warmly of his "lactea ubertas" (milky richness of style). The history, which appeared in installments, made Livy famous.

Loci communes: (or communes loci) Commonplaces, or clichés of rhetoric.

Loci Communes: Title of a treatise by Melanchthon (1521). The first Protestant theological work to be published.

Logistorici: Lost essays or dialogues on ethical subjects by Varro (1). Titles include: *Orestes de Insania, Marius de Fortuna,* etc.

Lombard, Peter: See Peter Lombard.

Longchamps, Nigel de: See Nigel Wireker.

Longus, Velius: See Velius Longus.

Lorica: Poem ascribed to Gildas (q.v.).

Lotichius Secundus, Petrus: 1528-60. German Neo-Latin poet, author of elegies, in imitation of Ovid and Virgil.

Love-Poetry, Latin: Isolated examples in Plautus and Terence. The *Erotopaegnia* of Laevius seems to belong to the category. In the first century B.C. Calvus, Ticidas, Cinna, Cato, Varro of Atax, and others are said to have written love-poetry, but the name that immediately stands out is that of Catullus (q.v.), whose Lesbia poems describe the whole cycle of love, ambivalence, despair, scorn, etc. Horace's love-poems are more like literary exercises. The Augustan elegiac poets: Ovid, Tibullus, and Propertius, brought love-poetry to its peak of perfection. Virgil did not write love-poetry per se, but some is to be found in the *Aeneid*. The *Pervigilium Veneris* is a fine example of later love-poetry. See also Goliardic poems, Carmina Burana, etc.

Loyola, Ignacio de: 1491?-1556. Founder of Society of Jesus (Jesuits). Wrote: *Exercitia Spiritualia,* in Spanish, later translated into Latin.

Lucan: (M. Annaeus Lucanus—39-65 A.D.) Roman epic poet of the Neronian period. Died very young, having written epic, drama, miscellaneous verse, letters, speeches, etc. Only the *Pharsalia* (q.v.) has survived. Lucan was a member of the Pisonian conspiracy, and was compelled to commit suicide. Grandson of Seneca (1), nephew of Seneca (2). His lost works include *Laudes Neronis,* epigrams, a work on the Fire (*De Incendio Urbis*), a *Medea,* and many other works. Lucan inclined toward the Stoic philosophy. In spite of certain inaccuracies, artificialities, etc., his epic is a vivid and moving poem. It was a rather daring undertaking to write an epic on the Civil War in Nero's day. Lucan was extremely popular in the Middle Ages.

Lucilius (1), C.: ca. 180-ca. 102 B.C. First Roman author of satire *qua* satire. Wrote 30 books, of which we have some

1300 lines of fragments. L. made hexameter the meter of satire, as Ennius had done for the epic. Horace (q.v.) imitates Lucilius in his satires. L. was a highly individualistic poet, and made vehement attacks on personalities. He wrote of travels, literary criticism, social life, politics, etc. Lucilius was inferior as a poet, as Horace remarks, but he was greatly esteemed by Cicero, Juvenal, Tacitus, and Quintilian. Had a profound influence on later poets.

Lucilius (2): "Junior." Friend and correspondent of Seneca (2). Thought by some to be the author of the *Aetna* (q.v.).

Lucretius: (T. Lucretius Carus) 99?-55? B.C. Great epic poet of Nature and Epicureanism. Almost nothing known of his life. Jerome's story about his madness and suicide, due to a love-potion, is without other corroboration, and sounds highly unlikely. Cicero is said to have "emended" the *De Rerum Natura* (q.v. for fuller discussion of the work). Lucretius was a friend of the notorious Memmius, to whom he addressed his work, the chief purpose of which was to free mankind from the fear of death which arises from ignorance and superstition. This he does by expounding the atomist theory of the Epicureans in "sugar-coated" verse. Pleasure, i.e., freedom from pain, and peace of mind, says L., are life's greatest blessings. He continually mentions the difficulty of dealing with a subject so new that he has to invent many words. The poem is full of little hymns in praise of Epicurus, in which Lucretius reaches a real spiritual ecstasy. Lucretius must be judged under three separate headings: as a philosopher, a scientist, and a poet. It has taken the world a long time fully to appreciate L., but he seems now to have come into his own, i.e., to an appreciation in all three categories. There is much beauty, as well as some crudeness, in his poetry. He had a keen eye for beauty and detail. The poem was lost for about 1000 years, and rediscovered by Poggio (q.v.) in the Renaissance. His influence in modern times is great (Tennyson, Goethe, Elizabeth Barrett Browning: "He denied divinely the divine . . ."). (Duff, OCD)

Lucullus: See Cicero, Academica.

Ludi Scenici: "scenic games"—festivals devoted to dramatic representations.

Ludolf of Saxony: A Carthusian monk (14th century), author of a *Life of Christ* which was very popular in the later Middle Ages.

Ludus de Antichristo: A religious drama of the 12th century. (See Religious Drama.)

Ludus super Anticlaudianum: See Adam of La Bassée.

Lul: Anglo-Saxon poet ca. 700. Wrote rhythmical verse in the Irish manner.

Lull, Raymond: 13th century Franciscan friar and martyr. A great scholar, who was instrumental in securing chairs in Oriental languages at the universities of Oxford, Paris and elsewhere.

Lupercalia: Ancient Roman festival, whose purpose was presumably to insure fertility of land, livestock and people. The festival was held on February 15. Two youths ran around the Palatine, dressed in goatskins. (Cf. Shakespeare, Julius Caesar.)

Lupus of Ferrières: See Servatus Lupus.

Lupus, Rutilius: Early first century rhetor, who abridged and translated a work on rhetoric by Gorgias (not the Sophist of that name).

Luscinius, Ottmar: 1481-1537. Author of *Joci et Sales Miri Festivi.*

Luscius Lanuvinus: Roman writer of comedies; rival of Terence (q.v.) who wrote retorts to him in most of his prologues.

Luxorius: 5th century African author. Wrote a Virgilian cento entitled *Epithalamium Fridi;* imitated Martial.

Lycanthropy: Stories of werewolves occur in Plato, Virgil, Pliny. Most famous is that of Petronius (Sat. 61.2). Ovid tells the story of Lycaon, who was changed into a wolf for sacrificing a child on the altar of Zeus Lycaeus.

"Lycoris": The person to whom Gallus (q.v.) dedicated his four books of elegies. Probably identical with Cytheris, a notorious mime-actress.

Lycurgus: Lost tragedy by Naevius (q.v.).

Lydia **(1):** A poem of the Appendix Virgiliana, formerly incorporated with the *Dirae* (q.v.). Some have thought Valerius Cato (q.v.) to be the author. It shows a fine feeling for nature, and the influence of Virgil and the Alexandrines.

Lydia **(2):** A 12th century "comoedia" or versified tale by an unknown author, probably French. Boccaccio later used the story.

Lydius: (?) Comedy by Livius Andronicus. Only slight fragments remain.

"Lygdamus": Author of six poems in the *Corpus Tibullianum.* A member of Messalla's circle. Various people have attempted to identify Lygdamus with Propertius, Ovid, Ovid's brother, etc., but to no avail. The poems are addressed to a lady named Neaera.

Lynceus: Friend of Propertius, member of Messalla's circle. Said to have written tragedies.

Lyra, Nicholas de: 1270-1340. Franciscan friar. Author of *Postillae,* a Biblical commentary. Lyra was a professor at the Sorbonne.

Lyric Poetry, Medieval: See Cambridge Songs, Goliardic poets, Carmina Burana, Vagantenlieder, Archpoet, Hugh Primas, Hymns, Sequences, etc.

Lyric Poetry, Roman: See Laevius, Catullus, Horace, Annianus, Statius, Ausonius, *Pervigilium Veneris.*

Mabillon, J.: 17th century scholar, the father of modern palaeography.

Macaronic Verse: A burlesque form, mixing Latin with vernacular words, often of several languages. See *Baldus,* Folengo. A modern macaronic work is *Finnegans Wake.*

Maccus: One of the stock figures of the Atellan Farce. Such titles exist as: *Maccus Copo, Maccus Miles, Maccus Virgo,* etc.

Macer, (1) Aemilius: Minor didactic poet of the Augustan age. Wrote on birds (*Ornithogonia*), snakes (*Theriaca*), and plants (*de Herbis*).

Macer, (2) Iliacus: Augustan poet who wrote on the Trojan War.

Macer (3): Poet, friend of Tibullus, possibly identical with one of the preceding poets.

Macer, (4) Licinius: Orator and historian. Wrote history from a democratic viewpoint. Claimed to have seen the famous libri lintei (q.v.). The father of the poet Calvus (q.v.).

Mackail, J. W.: English scholar and classicist. Wrote on Latin poetry, especially Virgil and the *Appendix Virgiliana*.

Macrobius, Ambrosius Theodosius: ca. 400. One of the chief philosophical and grammatical authorities for the Middle Ages. His *Saturnalia* is a compendium of poetics, philosophy, antiquarian lore, Virgilian criticism, etc. His *Commentarii in Somnium Scipionis* is replete with Neo-Platonic philosophy, and was popular with the medieval Platonists. It is not known whether he was a Christian.

Macropedius, Georgius: 1475-1558. Dutch neo-Latin poet and playwright; wrote Biblical plays, comedies, and an adaptation of *Everyman* (*Hecastus*).

Maecenas, C.: Friend of Augustus, patron of the most powerful literary circle of the Augustan Age, he numbered Virgil and Horace among his protégés.

Maecenatem, Elegiae in: See *Elegy*.

Maecianus, L. Volusius: Prominent jurist of the 2nd century, teacher of the emperor Marcus Aurelius; author of several treatises on law.

Magdeburg Centuries: A history of the Church, conceived by Matthias Flacius Illyricus in the 16th century—a protest against Protestantism.

Magnus of Reichersberg: Author of a *Chronicle,* and of *Annals,* listing the popes and emperors in parallel columns.

Mago: Carthaginian author of a work on agriculture, which was translated into Latin by order of the Senate.

Mai, Cardinal: Discovered the famous Ambrosian palimpsest (q.v.) in 1815; and, in 1822, another palimpsest containing one-third of the lost *Republic* of Cicero.

Mailduib (or Maildubh): Irish monk of the 7th century,

founder of the monastery of Malmesbury; teacher of Aldhelm (q.v.).

Maiolus of Cluny: 10th century monk, librarian, later abbot of Cluny. Not a humanist, Maiolus had no use for Virgil and the classics.

Mair (Major), John: 1470-1550. Scottish historian (*De Historia Gentis Scotorum Libri VI*).

Mallius Theodorus: Wrote, ca. 400, works on philosophy, astronomy, and prosody (*De Metris*). Only the last has survived.

Malsachanus: (Mac-Salchan) Irish grammarian of the 8th-9th centuries.

Mamertus, Claudianus: See Claudianus Mamertus.

Manegold of Lautenbach: Author of a work on the struggle between Church and State, in which he takes the side of the Pope, saying that all followers of the king should be killed and that to deny the authority of the Pope is to rebel against God. (Manitius)

Manes: In Roman religion, spirits of the dead, Di Manes. The usual inscription on tombstones was D.M.S. (Dis Manibus Sacrum).

Manetti, Gianozzo: 15th century Florentine humanist; studied rhetoric, theology, logic, science. Proficient in Greek and Hebrew; translated Aristotle into Latin.

Manfredi, Eustachio: 1674-1739. Italian scientist; wrote letters, technical works, etc., in Latin and Italian.

Manfred of Magdeburg: 11th century German poet; wrote verses based on Bede's *De Temporibus et de Ratione Temporis*.

Manilian Law: See *Lege Manilia, pro* (speech by Cicero).

Manilius, (1) Manius: Jurist of the second century B.C., member of the Scipionic Circle (q.v.). He appears as one of the speakers in Cicero's *De Republica*.

Manilius, (2) Marcus: Didactic poet of the late Augustan Age. Wrote the *Astronomica*, of which we have five books. His hexameters are good, but they show small literary ability. Describes the Creation, the arrangement of the stars, the signs of the zodiac, astrology, etc. A. E. Housman, one of the greatest of modern Latinists, edited Manilius.

Manitius, Max: Author of the most comprehensive account of medieval Latin Literature (*Geschichte der lateinischen Literatur des Mittelalters*).

Manlius Torquatus: Semi-legendary Roman hero, illustrating the ancient Roman virtues. Said to have killed a giant Celt and removed the latter's collar (torques). This is an etiological myth invented to explain the name Torquatus. He sentenced his own son to death for disobeying orders.

Mannerisms, literary: Among the various sorts of literary mannerisms which are found when the strain of genius begins to thin out, are the lipogrammatic, pangrammatic, figure-poems, palindromes, rhopalic verse, monosyllabic lines (qq.v.); see also Hucbald, Optatianus, Ausonius, Sidonius Apollinaris.

Mantuan, Baptista: Italian scholar, humanist, and Latin poet of the Renaissance. He wrote pastoral poetry, and was called by Erasmus "the Christian Maro."

Map, Walter (or **Mapes**): 1140?-1209?. "The English Anacreon." 11th century English poet, author of *De Nugis Curalium*, and other poetry. The *Metamorphosis Goliae* has been attributed to him.

Marbod of Rennes: 1035-1123. Bishop of Rennes, friend of Hildebert. Wrote letters, *Lives of the Saints*, *De Apto Genere Scribendi*, and the famous book on jewels (*Liber Lapidum*, q.v.). Also miscellaneous poetry on nature, love, etc.

Marcellinus, Ammianus: See Ammianus Marcellinus.

Marcello, pro: Speech by Cicero, one of the three *Caesarianae* (q.v.). Fulsome in its praise of Caesar. The elegance of the style is marred by the flagrancy of the hypocrisy.

Marcellus (1), M.: Orator, contemporary of Cicero, mentioned in the latter's *Brutus*.

Marcellus (2), Nonius: See Nonius Marcellus.

Marcellus (3), Pomponius: See Pomponius.

Marcellus (4) Ulpius: Roman jurist of the second century.

His main work is the *Digesta* in 31 books, which was extensively used by later writers on law, notably Ulpian.

Marciam, ad, de Consolatione: See *Consolations.*

Marcius: Legendary Roman seer, reputed author of several oracular sayings (e.g., "postremus loquaris, primus taceas."); supposed to have prophesied the defeat at Cannae.

Marcius Philippus, L.: Orator and statesman, ca. 100 B.C.

Marcus Aurelius: 121-80. Roman emperor. His *Meditations* on Stoic philosophy do not properly belong here, as they were written in Greek.

Marcus of Monte Cassino: A monk of Monte Cassino who, shortly after the death of St. Benedict, wrote an elegiac poem of 33 distichs in praise of that saint.

Mare, William de la: See William de la Mare.

Mariale: Long poem of praise to the Virgin Mary, by Bernard of Morlaix (q.v.).

Mariana, Juan de: 1535?-1624: Spanish historian. Wrote a treatise on monarchy, and a history of Spain in 30 books, in Latin.

Marianus Scotus: 1028-1082. Irish monk (name originally Moelbrigte). Founded monastery of St. Peter in Ratisbon. Wrote a *Chronicle* of world history.

Marineo, Luca: 1444-1533. Italian humanist and historian (*De Rebus Hispaniae Memorabilibus*).

Marius: Lost poetical work by Cicero, written in his youth: a tribute to the great general. One passage survives. It is a good imitation of Homer; Virgil later imitated it.

Marouzeau, J.: French classical scholar, compiler of *Dix Années,* and of *L'Année Philologique,* the most comprehensive modern bibliography of classical subjects.

Mars: Roman war-god. Together with Venus, the mythological ancestor of the Roman people. Second in importance only to Jupiter. Equivalent of the Greek Ares. In addition to his attributes as a god of war, Mars appears to have had some agricultural functions.

Marsilius of Padua: Rector of the University of Paris in the 14th century. Lectured on political theory. Wrote (with

John of Jandum q.v.) *Defensor Pacis*. Marsilius follows Aristotle's concepts of the state.

Marsus, Domitius: Minor Augustan poet. Wrote epigrams, elegies, an epic (*Amazonis*), and a lament on the death of Tibullus.

Martial: (M. Valerius Martialis) ca. 40-104 (?). The most important of the writers of epigrams, he made the form (q.v.) into a literary instrument capable of expressing wit, satire, tenderness, literary criticism, and invective. Martial has an eye for the ugly as well as the beautiful. He paints a witty and realistic picture of the society of his day, poking fun at types rather than individuals. His chief faults are his servility and his obscenity. Works: *Liber Spectaculorum, Xenia, Apophoreta, Epigrams*. He developed the sting in the tail of the epigram. He gives us a vivid, three-dimensional picture of himself, his tenderness, enthusiasm, joy, sorrow, his love of the city and the country. Martial had considerable influence on later writers.

Martialis Gargilius: See Gargilius.

Martianus Capella: fl. 410-430. 5th century encyclopedist whose work (*De Nuptiis Philologiae et Mercurii*) was one of the chief authorities for the liberal arts in the Middle Ages. The work is an allegorical description of the Arts, in the form of an Apuleian romance. The seven bridesmaids are: Grammar, Logic, Rhetoric, Geometry, Arithmetic, Astronomy, and Music (see Education, trivium, quadrivium, Liberal Arts, etc.). The whole is in the form of a Menippean Satire (q.v.). This peculiar combination of erudition and allegory was much beloved in the Middle Ages.

Martin of Bracara: Monk from Pannonia; d. 580. Wrote various philosophical works: *Formula Vitae Honestae, De Ira* (cf. Seneca), *De Paupertate, Liber de Moribus, De Superbia*, etc.

Martyr, Peter: 1459-1526. Italian humanist; wrote a history of Spanish America.

Marulic, Marko: 1450-1524. Dalmatian poet; wrote Latin poetry, moral sermons, etc.

Marullo, Michele: 1453-1500. Italian poet and soldier; wrote love-poems and *Hymni Naturales.*

Marullus: Had a school of rhetoric at Rome. Seneca (1) and Latro (qq.v.) were among his pupils.

Mass: The chief liturgy of the Roman Catholic Church. Probably so named from the words "Ite Missa Est." The divisions are: *Introit, Kyrie, Gloria, Credo, Offertory, Sanctus, Canon, Agnus Dei, Communion.* Low mass is spoken, high mass is sung. Originally, the music followed the type of early plainsong, then became polyphonic, inspiring such composers as Palestrina, Machault, Bach, Haydn, Schubert, Beethoven, etc. to some of their greatest masterpieces. These works soon outgrew the scope of the Church; in fact, they are not permitted to be sung there, being thought too operatic. See Gregorian chant, liturgy.

Masurius Sabinus: See Sabinus.

Maternus, Curiatus: See Curiatus.

Maternus, Firmicus: See Firmicus.

Mathematicus: A story in verse, variously ascribed to Hildebert of Le Mans, Bernard Sylvestris (qq.v.) and others.

Mathesis: See Firmicus Maternus.

Matius (1), C.: Friend of Augustus, who published a work on gastronomy.

Matius (2), Gn.: Contemporary of Sulla; translated the *Iliad* into Latin hexameters, wrote mimes, and introduced scazons into Latin verse.

Matthew Paris: See Paris, Matthew.

Matthew of Vendôme: fl. 1150. Twelfth century poet. author of an *Ars Versificatoria* (q.v.), *Tobias,* a Biblical poem in elegiacs, letters, *Pyramus,* comedies, and other miscellaneous poetry.

Mavors: See Mars.

Mavortius: 5th or 6th century author of 2 Virgilian centos: *De Ecclesia* and *Iudicium Paridis.*

Maximianus: 6th century Latin author, one of the last of the non-Christian Roman poets. Wrote elegies after the manner of Ovid. Much used as a textbook in the Middle Ages, imitated by Henry of Settimello (q.v.).

Maximus (1): Roman author, contemporary of Pliny.

Maximus (2), Fabius: Wrote on Stoicism in the time of Augustus.

Maximus (3), Marius: Historian and biographer, ca. 200 A.D. His works are lost.

Maximus (4), the Confessor: Theologian of the early 7th century. Wrote on the doctrine of Incarnation.

Maximus (5) of Turin: Author of many sermons, theological tractates, letters, homilies, etc. Lived in the 4th-5th centuries.

Maximus (6), Valerius: See Valerius Maximus.

May, Thomas: 17th century scholar who translated the *Pharsalia* (q.v.) of Lucan, and wrote a Latin *Supplementum* to the death of Caesar. See Neo-Latin.

Medea: Heroine of Greek mythology, the subject of several Roman tragedies, as well as of the one by Euripides. Plays were written about Medea by Ennius, Accius, Ovid, Lucan, Curiatus Maternus, Seneca, and a Virgilian cento on the subject by Hosidius Geta.

Medea: (Seneca) This play could not have been intended for performance. It shows marked differences from the play by Euripides, such as having the children murdered "onstage." It is thought that Seneca imitated Ovid's *Medea*.

Medicamina Faciei Feminae: A fragment by Ovid on female use of cosmetics.

Medicina, de: Treatise on medicine by Celsus (q.v.).

Medicina Plinii: A 4th century abridgement of part of the Elder Pliny's *Natural History* (q.v.).

Medicina, Praecepta de: Didactic poem by Serenus Sammonicus (q.v.).

Medieval Comedy: See Vitalis of Blois, Matthew of Vendôme, William of Blois, Hroswitha, *Lydia, Pamphilus, Baucis, Babio,* etc. Other comedies or "comoediae" which should be mentioned here: *De Tribus Puellis* (the Three Girls), *De Nuntio Sagaci* (The Wise Messenger), *Pamphilus de Amore, De Tribus Sociis, De Clericis et Rustico, De Mercatore, De Lumaca et Lombardo, Paulinus et Polla.*

Medieval Literature: See Biblical epic, Lyric poetry,

medieval; history, letters, comedy, allegory, and under the various other genres. A favorite type of literature was that dealing with the lives and passions of the saints (hagiography). See *Laborintus* for listing of medieval "curriculum authors." See also scholastics, philosophy, etc.

Mediolano Civitate, de: 8th century poem on the city of Milan.

Megacosmus et Microcosmus: Alternate title of the *De Mundi Universitate* of Bernard Silvestris (q.v.).

Meinzo of Constance: 11th century mathematician, pupil of Hermann of Reichenau with whom he exchanged letters on mathematical subjects.

Mela (1), M. Annaeus: Son of Seneca (1), who rated his talents more highly than those of his eminent brother Seneca (2); father of the poet Lucan. Cf. the Mendelssohn who was famous only for being the son of his father and the father of his son.

Mela (2), Pomponius: See Pomponius Mela.

Melanchthon: (Schwarzert or Schwarzerd) German humanist and scholar of the Renaissance. His pseudonym is a literal translation into Greek of his name.

Melanippa: Lost tragedy by Ennius.

Meleager: Play by Accius (q.v.) famous for its pathos.

Melissus: Freedman of Augustus, who is said to have invented the *fabula trabeata* (q.v.).

Melmoth, William: Translator of Pliny's letters into English; 1746.

Memmius, C.: Praetor of 58 B.C. A dissolute character, to whom Lucretius addressed his *De Rerum Natura*. Memmius wrote erotic verse, none of which has survived.

Memoirs: See *Autobiography*.

Memoria Seculorum: Prosimetron by Godfrey of Viterbo.

Menander: Foremost Greek playwright of the New Comedy; imitated by Plautus and Terence (qq.v.). In a famous line, Caesar called Terence "O dimidiate Menander." (Menander halved.)

Menaechmi: (Plautus) One of Plautus' best comedies. The plot revolves around the mistaken identity-theme, long-lost brothers, etc. Some of the scenes are hilarious. Shakespeare imitated it with his *Comedy of Errors,* but the play of Plautus is more believable, since it only forces *one* set of identical twins on our credulity.

Menippean Satire: (or prosimetron) A form of literature with alternating prose and verse. Varro wrote Menippean satires (the title comes from Menippus of Gadara). Examples in Roman literature: Seneca's *Apocolocyntosis,* Petronius' *Satyricon.* In later literature: the *Consolatio* of Boethius and the *Wedding of Philology and Mercury* of Martianus Capella. In the Middle Ages, the form is represented by Alan of Lille, Bernard Silvestris, Godfrey of Viterbo (qq.v.) and many others. In French literature, the Satyre Ménipée continues the tradition.

Mensura Orbis Terrae: See Dicuil.

Mercator: (Plautus) One of the better comedies of Plautus. The figures are typical of the palliata: the girl purchased by the young man, the irate father, the slave, the shrewish wife, etc.

Mercury: In Roman mythology, the messenger of the gods, god of trade, thieves, etc. An inveterate trickster, he appears in Plautus' *Amphitruo.* For his role in later writings, see Martianus Capella's *Wedding of Philology and Mercury.* Mercury is the equivalent of the Greek Hermes.

Merobaudes, Flavius: Spanish poet of the 5th century. Wrote hexameters in praise of Christ; eulogized Aetius; imitations of Statius, etc.

Mesostich: An acrostic (q.v.) occurring in the middle of the line. See also telestich.

Messalla: (M. Valerius M. Corvinus) Statesman, orator, and poet, patron of the literary circle including Tibullus, "Lygdamus," etc. None of his own poetry has survived.

Messallinus: Son of Messalla, an orator in the early Empire.

Messiad: An epic on the Messiah by Eupolemius.

Messianic Eclogue: The *Fourth Eclogue* of Virgil (qq.v.), supposed to have foretold the birth of Christ.

Metalogicon: A treatise on the value and use of logic, by the great 12th century humanist John of Salisbury. He derides pedantic logicians.

Metamorphoses: (Apuleius) Apuleius' (q.v.) greatest work, also called the *Golden Ass.* Almost the only extant example of the Roman novel, a fascinating blend of romance, magic, adventure and humor, containing the famous story of *Cupid and Psyche.*

Metamorphoses: (Ovid) Ovid's greatest work. A vast tapestry covering practically the entire field of Greek Mythology. The verse is always facile, sometimes inspired. Some of the finer portions include: Deucalion and Pyrrha, Phaeton, Echo and Narcissus, Medea, Pyramus and Thisbe, Venus and Adonis, Polyphemus and Galatea, Orpheus and Eurydice, etc. One of the chief sources for mythology in the Renaissance, its influence in literature and art was profound, as also on music. The last three stories named above inspired operas by Blow, Handel and Gluck, respectively. Shakespeare drew heavily on the *Metamorphoses.* Never profound, it is often moving and beautiful. (Duff)

Metellus, Q. Caecilius (1): The consul of 206 B.C. A famous orator, he delivered a funeral oration on his father.

Metellus (2), Numidicus: Orator and statesman, consul of 109 B.C. Author of a famous speech on compulsory wedlock.

Metellus (3): German monk of Tegernsee, who wrote "Horatian" odes, eclogues, and miscellaneous poetry.

Meteorology: See Manilius, Lucretius, Seneca (*Nat. Quaest.*), *Aetna,* Aratus.

Meter: Nearly all Roman meters were borrowed from the Greek. The notable exception is the Saturnian meter (q.v.). Earliest verse was probably accentual rather than quantitative. The epic meter was the dactylic hexameter, also used for satire. The elegiac (q.v.) is a development of the hexameter. Iambic meters were used for comedy and tragedy, as in Greek literature. The iambic senarius was the chief iambic meter, and it was used by Phaedrus as well. Trochaic meters are also found in comedy, and are a common form of meter, especially the trochaic tetrameter, used in the *Pervigilium*

Veneris, in Hilary's version of the Bible, etc. The hendeca-
syllable was a favorite form of Catullus and other Alexandrian
poets. Other lyric meters include glyconics, Sapphic and
Alcaic strophes, asclepiads, pherecrateans, etc. Anapests were
used, e.g. in comedy, for quick-moving tempi. The scazon or
limping iambic, was another form imported from the Greeks.
In late antiquity, the trend was back to accentual verse again,
and the introduction of rhyme (e.g., in the hymns) began a
whole new type of verse. The hymns and sequences of the
Middle Ages are mostly in rhymed accentual quatrains, and
the rhyme is often leonine. The goliardic lyrics used a rhymed
quatrain.

Metris, de: See Mallius Theodorus.

Metris Fabularum Terentii, de: Work by Priscian on
meters in Terence (qq.v.).

Metris Horatii, de: See Servius.

Mettius Pompusianus: Made a volume of excerpts from
Livy, consisting of speeches of kings, generals, etc., for which
he paid with his life, by order of the tyrant Domitius.

Mevius: Poet, enemy of Horace and Virgil. See Bavius.

Meyer, Wilhelm: German scholar and medievalist. His
chief work was the editing of medieval Latin lyrics, e.g., Hugh
Primas of Orleans.

Michael of Cornwall: Chiefly known from his invective
against Henry of Avranches. fl. ca. 1250.

Michael Scottus: One of the translators of Averroes (q.v.).

Mico of St. Riquier: Teacher, author of parodies, elegies,
epigrams. Early 9th century.

Microcosmus: See Godfrey of St. Victor.

Midas: Legendary Phrygian king, well known for the story
of the "Golden Touch"—which is undoubtedly an etiological
myth invented to explain the presence of gold in the river
Pactolus. The story is found in Ovid's *Metamorphoses* (q.v.).

Migne, J. P.: 19th century scholar, editor and publisher of
the PL (Patrologia Latina), a gigantic corpus of theological
and patristic writings.

Miles Gloriosus (1): Comedy by Plautus. The Boastful

Soldier is a stock figure of Greek and Roman comedy, and so is the meretrix Acroteleutium.

Miles Gloriosus (2): An anonymous 12th century "comoedia" or versified tale. It has nothing to do with the Plautine comedy.

Milesian Tales: Romantic stories, originally from Miletus in Asia Minor. Usually of a rather coarse nature. Sisenna (q.v.) translated a group of them into Latin. The story of the *Widow of Ephesus* in Petronius is a good example.

Milic, John: 14th century Czech reformer. Wrote a *Libellus de Antichristo*. He was condemned as a heretic.

Milo: 12th century French poet, author of *De Mundi Philosophia*.

Milo: Comoedia (versified tale) by Matthew of Vendôme (q.v.).

Milo of St. Amand: Middle of 9th century. Author of an ethical didactic poem *De Sobrietate,* carmina figurata, and *Lives of Saints.*

Milone, pro: Speech by Cicero, in defense of Milo, the murderer of Clodius. The speech we have was not delivered, but was subsequently published.

Milton, John: A skillful Latinist, Milton wrote many of his pamphlets in Latin. He was Oliver Cromwell's Latin secretary.

Mime: Of Greek origin, the mime became very popular in Rome, eventually replacing almost all other forms of drama. Noted for its coarseness, it used female performers, which other forms of drama did not. The mime was called "fabula riciniata" from the short cloak or "ricinium" worn by the actors. Literary mimes were written by Publilius Syrus and Laberius (qq.v.).

Minerva: Roman goddess of wisdom, strategy and handicraft; identified with the Greek Athena.

Minor Augustan Poets: In the latter part of the Golden Age, literally scores of poets flourished. Some are known to us only by name. See Turrianus, Gracchus, *Priapea, Appendix Virgiliana,* Bassus, Sextilius Ena, Albinovanus, Pedo, Sabinus, Severus, Rabirius, etc.

Minor Carolingian Poetry: Mention should be made of a *Carmen de Timone Comite*; a *Carmen de Exordio Gentis Francorum*; a moral epic by one *Lios* (Elias?) *Monocus*; and a certain *Audradus Modicus*.

Minucius Felix: Early apologist, probably a native of Africa. His one surviving work is the *Octavius,* a dialogue of high literary quality, written in defense of Christianity. Minucius lived ca. 200 A.D.

minuscule: A type of writing found in manuscripts of the Carolingian Revival. Also called cursive.

Mirabilia Romae: There are several works with this or similar titles. They are all descriptions of the wonders of Rome, one by Gregorius Magister Anglicus, one anonymous, etc.

Miracle Plays: See religious drama.

Misogynos: Lost comedy by Atilius (q.v.).

Missa: See Mass.

Missale Gothicum: One of the most ancient documents of the Church, it contains the Eucharistic liturgy (see liturgy, mass).

Mitologiarum libri III: Dialogue by Fulgentius (1) between the author and the muse Calliope, dealing with mythology.

Mock epic: An early form of literature. The Greek *Battle of the Frogs and Mice* is one of the first examples. The *Culex* in the Appendix Virgiliana, Catullus' *Coma Berenices,* are examples. In the Renaissance the form became popular again. See Baldus, macaronic epic, and cf. Pope's *Rape of the Lock.*

Modoin of Antun: Poet of the Carolingian Revival. Wrote an eclogue to Charlemagne.

Mohammed, life of: See Embricho of Mainz.

Molo, Apollonius, of Rhodes: Famous teacher of rhetoric. Cicero was his pupil.

Mommsen, T.: 1817-1903. One of the greatest of modern Roman historians. His *Römische Geschichte* and *Römische Staatsrecht* are masterpieces of penetrating analysis, and his work on the *Corpus Inscriptionum Latinorum* should also be mentioned.

Monarchio, de: Political treatise in Latin by Dante Alighieri.

Monasteries: The great centers of learning in the Middle Ages. Famous monasteries are: Monte Cassino, Fulda, Cluny, Reichenau, Tegernsee, Jarrow and Wearmouth, St. Gall, Bobbio, St. Victor, Clairvaux, etc.

Monasticism: See Cassian, Jerome, Cassiodorus, Benedict, Gregory the Great.

Montaigne, Michel de: 1533-1592. The great French humanist and essayist writes on the importance of the classics in education. He tells that he himself learned to speak Latin before he learned French.

Montanists: See Tertullian.

Montfaucon: One of the founders of paleography, q.v.

Monte Cassino: Famous Italian monastery.

Monumentum Ancyranum: (*Res gestae divi Augusti*) See Index Rerum Gestarum.

Moral Epistles: See *Epistulae Morales*.

Moralia: See Gregory I.

Moralis Philosophia: See Hildebert of Le Mans.

More, Thomas: Chancellor under Henry VIII. Author of many fine Latin epigrams, as well as the famous *Utopia*.

Moretum (1): "The Salad"—poem in the *Appendix Virgiliana*, dubiously attributed to Virgil, though much of it is good enough to be his. The poem, which is in 123 hexameters, depicts a series of scenes: the peasant rising in the morning, lighting the fire, grinding grain, gathering herbs for the salad, etc.

Moretum (2): Another poem of this name appears to have been written by one Sueius (q.v.).

Morhof: 17th century author who wrote a treatise *De Patavinitate Liviana,* in which he retorted to Asinius Pollio's imputation of "Patavinity" to Livy, by writing of the "Asinity" of Pollio.

Moriae Encomium: See *Praise of Folly* (Erasmus).

Morte Caesaris, de: Lost epic on the death of Caesar by Varius Rufus, the dean of Augustan poets.

Mortibus Boum, de: Christian eclogue probably by Endelechius (q.v.).

Mortibus Persecutorum, de: A work dealing with the Diocletian persecution, attributed to Lactantius (q.v.), but of doubtful authenticity.

Mosella: (Ausonius) One of the last great works of antiquity. A charming description of a journey on the Moselle, in 483 hexameters. Ausonius (q.v.) describes the buildings along the banks, the fish in the river, the vineyards, etc.

Moses of Bergamo: Italian poet of the 12th century who wrote a hexameter poem on his native city.

Mostellaria: (Plautus) "The Haunted House"—The plot of this comedy concerns an old man who must be kept from entering the house where his son is entertaining a party of rather disreputable people, and the efforts of the slave, Tranio, to accomplish this. Has many very funny scenes. The wily slave is a stock figure of Roman comedy.

Mozarabic Hymnary: Collection of Spanish religious poetry, dating from the period of Moorish domination.

Mucianus, Licinius: See Licinius.

Müller: Four German scholars of this name are to be cited:
1. C. F. W. Müller, who studied the prosody of Plautus.
2. K. O. Müller, who edited Varro's *De Lingua Latina*.
3. L. Müller, who worked on the early poets, e.g., Ennius, Lucilius, etc.
4. Iwan von Müller, who began the editing of the "Handbuch der klassischen Altertumswissenschaft" (q.v.).

Mulomedicina Chironis: A Latin translation of a Greek work on veterinary medicine.

Mundi Universitate, De: One of the greatest books of the Middle Ages. A work in alternating prose and verse (Prosimetron, or Menippean Satire), by Bernard Silvestris of Tours (q.v.), on the Universe, God, the Creation, etc. The work is partially based on Plato's *Timaeus* and the comment of Chalcidius. The intellect of God is represented by *Nous* (Greek: mind).

Mundo, de: Apuleius' translation of a work by Pseudo-Aristotle.

Munitionibus Castrorum, de: A work on fortifications ascribed to Hyginus (3), but probably of later date.

Munro, H. A.: English scholar of the 19th century. A proficient Latinist, he translated Gray's Elegy into Latin verse (see Neo-Latin). His important work in the field of classical literature was concerned with Lucretius, Catullus, and Lucilius, and with the *Aetna*.

Murena, pro: Speech by Cicero in defense of Murena, who was charged with bribery. In it, Cicero makes fun of lawyers, and of the Stoicism of Cato.

Murmellius, Johannes: 1480-1517. German scholar; author of *Pappa Puerorum*, a first Latin reader.

Murredius: A rhetor mentioned by Seneca (1) for his silliness.

Musa: A rhetor criticized by Seneca for his excessive artificiality.

Musa, Antonius: Physician of the Augustan Age. It is now generally believed that the medical treatise attributed to him belongs to a much later period.

Music, works on: Works on music were written by Augustine, Boethius, and Bede. The treatise by Bede was still being used at Oxford in the 18th century. Other writers who dealt with the Liberal Arts (e.g., Martianus Capella, Varro, etc.) necessarily treated the subject of music. Hermann of Reichenau, Guido of Arezzo, William of Hirschau, are other authors in the Middle Ages who wrote on music. See Sequence, Gregorian chant.

Mussato, Alberto: 1251-1329. Italian statesman, humanist, and Latin poet. He wrote a Latin tragedy, the *Ecerinis*.

Mystery Plays: See Religious Drama. (The term has nothing whatever to do with "mystery"—it is a corruption of French *mestier*, or trade.)

Mythographus Vaticanus II: A collection of Greek myths, based on an earlier Mythographus Vaticanus I, which abounds in allegorical interpretations and fanciful etymologies.

Mythological Epic: See Livius Andronicus, Virgil, Calvus, Valerius Flaccus, Statius, and Claudian. The 3 most frequent types of epic in antiquity were the didactic, historical and the mythological. Virgil's *Aeneid* is a blending of the last two. In the Middle Ages, the Biblical or allegorical epic was also very popular.

Mythology, Roman: Consists mostly of Greek myths adapted, and with the gods being given the names of the Roman equivalents (e.g., Jupiter and Venus for Zeus and Aphrodite), or Latinized spellings for the names of the Greek heroes (e.g., Ulysses, Ajax, Hercules for Odysseus, Aias, Herakles). In addition, however, there is a small, but important body of native Latin myths and legends, such as the Romulus-Remus story, Coriolanus, Horatius, Decius Mus, etc. The development of the Aeneas legend seems to be a mixture of Greek and Roman elements. Homer mentions Aeneas, but early Roman authors like Naevius developed the legend.

Naevio Arpiniano, pro: Speech by Quintilian.

Naevius, Cn.: (ca. 270-199 B.C.) One of the earliest Latin poets of whom we have any fragments, and possibly the earliest native Latin poet. Served in the First Punic War. Imprisoned for his abuse of officials, but recanted, and was liberated. Finally, N. was exiled and died at Utica. Works: Naevius is said to have invented the fabula praetexta, or historical drama, and we have two titles: *Romulus* and *Clastidium*. His tragedies seem mostly to have been drawn from the Trojan Cycle: *Hesione, Andromache, Danaë, Equos Troianus, Hector, Iphigenia.* He wrote 34 comedies, although here there is much confusion because of the similarity of the names Naevius, Laevius and Livius. We have one sizable fragment from his comedy *Tarentilla*. But it was in the field of the epic that Naevius had the greatest influence on Roman literature. His *Bellum Punicum* is the first Roman epic that we know of. N. may have introduced the Dido episode into the Aeneas legend, but this is not certain. His style is uneven and crude, but he was a great innovator, and deserves to share with Livius Andronicus the title of "Father of Roman Literature." His epitaph, quoted by Gellius, says: "If immortals may weep for mortals, the Muses weep for the poet Naevius; after his death, they forgot how to speak Latin at Rome."

Namatianus, Rutilius: See Rutilius.

Names, Roman: Entries will usually be found under the *nomen gentilicium* or family name, except where the common English form is the cognomen. Thus, M. Tullius *CICERO*, C. Julius *CAESAR*, but Q. *HORATIUS* Flaccus, P. *OVIDIUS* Naso, see under Anglicized forms Horace and Ovid.

Nationes, ad: See Tertullian.

Natura Deorum, de: (Cicero) A philosophical, or theological treatise, which summarizes the prevailing systems of thought in Rome in the first century B.C.: Stoic, Epicurean, Academic. The work was dedicated to Brutus the tyrannicide.

Natura Rerum, de: A treatise on Nature by Isidore of Seville (q.v.), also one by Alexander Neckham.

Natura Rerum juxta Propria Principia: Treatise by Telesio (q.v.).

Naturae Divisione, de: See John Eriugena.

Naturalis Historia: (Pliny the Elder) A great work, in 37 books, by the Elder Pliny, which deals with cosmography, geography, ethnology, human and animal physiology, botany, horticulture, medicine, metallurgy, mineralogy, art, etc. There is a sort of logical arrangement to this gigantic work, which was said to contain 120,000 facts, based on 2000 volumes by 100 authors. Pliny often quotes his sources (e.g., Aristotle, Theophrastus, Cato, Varro, Virgil, Vitruvius, Mela, Celsus, Columella, etc.). The work may be said to sum up, as had Varro, all the learning of Pliny's time. In spite of errors, omissions, and other faults, the work contains much that is of importance and interest, and many good stories, anecdotes, superstitions. It is often very readable. The philosophy is basically Stoic, and human interest prevails throughout.

Neaera: The lady-love of "Lygdamus" (q.v.).

Neckham (or Neckam), Alexander: 1157-1217. English scholar who taught in Paris. His works include a poem on Divine Wisdom, a *De Natura Rerum,* which is a handbook of popular science, and a collection of fables (*Novus Aesopus,* see Fable, medieval), *Corrogaciones Promethei,* and numerous other works dealing with theology, hagiography, history, grammar, medicine, the life of Christ, commentaries, hymns, sermons, metrics, the Wonders of the World, etc.

Nemesianus, M. Aurelius Olympius: Carthaginian poet of the 3rd century, author of four eclogues previously incorporated with those of Calpurnius Siculus (q.v.), and also of a poem on hunting (*Cynegetica*). The eclogues imitate those of Calpurnius. Two fragments on bird-catching (*De Aucupio*) are also attributed to him.

"Nemesis": See Tibullus.

Nenia: A funeral dirge combining lamentation and eulogy of the deceased person. We have no examples, except for a parody in the *Apocolocyntosis* of Seneca. Nenia is also a goddess of death or dying.

Neo-Latin: Since the Renaissance, Latin has virtually ceased to be a living language, and compositions in the language consist mostly of erudite tours de force, of translations from the vernacular (e.g., Munro's translation of Gray's *Elegy,* or, to pick more ludicrous examples, translations of Busch's *Max und Moritz,* and even of *Alice in Wonderland*). These works do not properly belong to the study of Latin Literature. The seventeenth century saw the end of Latin as an original language of philosophy and science. Prefaces, notes, etc. in scholarly editions and articles are still in Latin, as are many dissertations, and papal communications.

Neo-Platonism: Mystical school of the 4th-5th centuries, based on Plato's philosophy, in part. It became the basis for much of the philosophical speculation in the Middle Ages (see John Eriugena, Pseudo-Dionysius).

Neo-Stoicism: Roman school of philosophy involving asceticism, self-examination. Taught by the Sextii, Fabianus, and others, this school had a great influence on the younger Seneca's writings, if not on his life. More tolerant and humanitarian than the Stoicism of Zeno. Neo-Stoicism was modified by Roman common sense.

Neoterics: This term was used for the *Cantores Euphorionis* (q.v.), and also for the new poets of the age of Hadrian.

Nepos, Cornelius: ca. 100-25 B.C. An Insubrian Gaul, whose *Lives* (*De Viris Illustribus*) in 16 books, comparing Greeks and Romans, is only partly extant. We possess the biographies of Hannibal, Atticus, and several Greek generals (e.g., Miltiades, Epaminondas, etc.). In spite of certain inaccuracies, the work is readable and interesting, the style simple and clear, if devoid of artistry. Nepos also wrote a universal history, a Life of Cato, *Exempla* (anecdotes) in five books, a geographical treatise, and love poetry. All these works are lost. (Duff, OCD)

Neptune: Roman god of the sea, identified with the Greek Poseidon. Neptune was the brother of Jupiter.

Neratius Priscus: A jurist of the Flavian-Trajan periods.

Nero: This emperor appears to have been a poet of more than mediocre ability. He sang his own verses on the burning of Troy during the Fire at Rome (N.B. He did *not* fiddle!). It is said that he was contemplating an epic in 400 books, and that Cornutus was banished for daring to say that this was too long.

Nerva, M. Cocceius: A renowned jurist, and grandfather of the emperor Nerva. His son Nerva was also a jurist.

Nettleship, H.: Classical scholar who wrote on Suetonius, Phaedrus, Horace, Virgil, and many other authors and aspects of Latin literature and philology.

Neville, Alexander: 1544-1614. English scholar and Latinist. Good writer of Latin prose and verse.

Newborough, William of: See William of Newborough.

New Comedy: Greek comedy of manners. Chief authors were Menander, Diphilus and Philemon. Stock figures include irate fathers, despairing young lovers, parasites, soldiers, cooks, wily slaves, rascally panderers, courtesans, etc. Plots often hinged on abandoned infants, shipwrecks, slave-girls later found to be freeborn. Nearly all dealt with some aspect of romantic love. These comedies were imitated (but not combined) by Plautus and Terence in the *fabulae palliatae.*

Newton, Isaac: Some of the scientific and philosophical works of this great 17th century mathematician and physicist were written in Latin (*Philosophiae Naturalis, Principia Mathematica*) showing that at this time, Latin was still the universal language of science. Newton also wrote Latin poetry.

Nicander, Saevius: See Saevius.

Niccoli, Niccolo de: Humanist of the Italian Renaissance.

Niceta of Remesiana: ca. 400 A.D. Missionary, friend of Paulinus of Nola (q.v.). Wrote *De Psalmodiae Bono, De Vigiliis*, and the great hymn *Te Deum Laudamus*.

Nicholas of Autrecourt: Philosopher of the 14th century. An anti-realist, he criticized the traditional arguments of the realists (q.v.).

Nicholas of Cusa: 1401-1464. Represents the transition from the Middle Ages to the Renaissance. A theologian and philosopher, influenced by John Eriugena and the Neo-Platonists. Rejected the idea of fixed points in the universe. His mottos were "learned ignorance" and "identity of opposites." (Runes, Dictionary of Philosophy)

Nicholas de Orbellis: Franciscan monk of the 15th century. Responsible for the well-known mnemonic distich:

GRAM loquitur, DIA vera docet, RHET verba colorat,

MUS canit, AR numerat, GE ponderat, AST colit astra.

These lines enumerated the subjects of the trivium (q.v.): Grammar, Dialectic, Rhetoric, and of the quadrivium (q.v.): Music, Arithmetic, Geometry, Astronomy.

Nicolaus Maniacutius: Italian poet of the 12th century who versified catalogues of the Popes.

Niebuhr's Theory: This theory, long since exploded, stated that Rome must have possessed a great body of popular epic (cf. Macaulay's *Lays of Ancient Rome*), which was subsequently lost. Although the theory is no longer believed (Taine was the first to reject it), it nevertheless has a certain value. Some heroic ballads of Roman legend must have been in existence. It is necessary to differentiate between epic *material* and epic *creation*. In America, for example, the Paul Bunyan, John

Henry, and Pecos Bill stories are instances of epic material, but no epic poems on these figures exist.

Nigel Wireker: English author of the 12th century (ca. 1130-1200). Wrote *Speculum Stultorum* (Mirror of Fools), a satire on the monastic orders. The central figure is Brunellus, a donkey who is dissatisfied with his short tail. Also wrote a *Tractatus contra Curiales et Officiales Clericos,* and other works.

Nigellus Ermoldus: See Ermoldus Nigellus.

Niger, Sextius: See Sextius Niger.

Nigidius Figulus: See Figulus, Nigidius.

Ninnius Crassus: Translated the *Iliad* into Latin. Date unknown.

Niptra: Play by Pacuvius (q.v.) about Ulysses.

Nithard: The grandson of Charlemagne, author of chronicles.

Nivard of Ghent: Author of the beast-epic *Ysengrimus* (q.v.).

Noctes Atticae: See Gellius, Aulus.

Nominalism: Medieval school of philosophy represented by William of Ockham (q.v.). A denial of the doctrine of *Realism* (q.v.). Roscelin, one of the founders of the system, held that universals are a mere word (flatus vocis), and that only individuals exist outside the mind. The nominalist school (fr. nomen, name) was characterized by an analytical and empirical approach and a critical attitude toward metaphysical arguments. One important result of the school was to effect a separation between theology and philosophy, leaving traditional metaphysics to the former, while the latter tended to become more occupied with logic and analysis. See Roscelin, Abelard, Universals, William of Champeaux. (Runes, Dictionary of Philosophy)

Nomine et Verbo, de: See Consentius.

Nonianus, Servilius: See Servilius Nonianus.

Nonius Marcellus: Lexicographer and grammarian of the early 4th century. His work *De Compendiosa Doctrina,* in roughly alphabetical order, is especially useful for the many quotations from the early authors of the Republic, such as Lucilius, and for the poetry of Varro.

Notae Tironianae: See shorthand.

Notker Balbulus: (or Notker the Stammerer) Late 9th century author of a *Gesta Karoli,* or collection of legends about Charlemagne, of letters, and supposed to have invented the Sequence (q.v.). Notker also wrote much miscellaneous poetry, and made a collection of riddles.

Notker Labeo: (or Notker the German) 11th century monk of St. Gall, teacher, philosopher, and theologian.

Notker of Liége: Bishop of Liége, d. 1008. A sound scholar, he wrote a commentary on Boethius, and hagiographic works.

Novalese, Chronicles of: Written about 1000 A.D. Five books of chronicles. An interesting and informative work, despite errors of chronology, poor historical and critical sense.

Novatian: Anti-pope of 251 who founded a dissident sect. Wrote several theological works, including *De Trinitate, De Cibis Iudaiicis,* etc. His style was exceedingly good.

Novatus: Elder brother of Seneca (2), son of Seneca (1). The former dedicated his *De Ira* and *De Vita Beata* to Novatus. Took the name of Gallio, who adopted him.

Novel, Latin: The first Roman author of a novel was, as far as we know, Petronius. His *Satyricon* is fragmentary, contains elements of the Milesian Tales (q.v.). Apuleius' *Metamorphoses* is the only complete Latin novel we possess. It, too, contains Milesian tales. The anonymous *Historia Apollonii,* is a later example. In the Middle Ages, the *Dolopathos* by John of Haute-Seille may be cited.

Novella, Novellae Constitutiones: See Justinian, Jurisprudence.

Novius: A popular author of Literary Atellan Farces. We possess 40 titles.

Novum Instrumentum: Erasmus' great work of Biblical scholarship. It consists of the New Testament in Greek, together with Erasmus' own Latin translation.

Novum Organum: Bacon's *magnum opus* in the field of logic and the scientific method (see Bacon, Francis).

Novus Aesopus: See Neckham, Fable (medieval).

Novus Avianus: Another collection of fables by Neckham.

Numan, Philip: 1550-1617. Dutch poet; wrote poetry in Latin as well as in the vernacular.

Numitorius: Author of the *Antibucolica*, a parody of Virgil's *Eclogues*.

Nuptiis Philologiae et Mercurii, de: (*Wedding of Philology and Mercury*) See Martianus Capella.

Nux: (Ovid) Poem about a nut-tree. Its authenticity has frequently been challenged, but now seems to be satisfactorily established, although there is not universal agreement on the point.

O Roma Nobilis: A famous poem by an unknown poet, probably of the 10th century.

Obscuris Catonis, de: Lost work by Verrius Flaccus (q.v.).

Occupatio: A philosophical poem by Odo of Cluny (q.v.), dealing with the Creation, the origin of sin, etc.

Ockham, William of: ca. 1280-1349. Franciscan friar; taught at Oxford. Ockham was one of the important members of the *Nominalist* cf. *Nominalism* school. He was an empiricist who rejected the idea of universal realities. *Ockham's Razor* (q.v.) is his famous principle of economy. He insisted on the primacy of intuition. Some things, however, he felt must be decided by faith rather than by logic. So his ethics were conditioned by theology, not by logic, i.e., "it is wrong because God says so." (Runes, Dictionary of Philosophy)

Ockham's Razor: The principle of economy, i.e., that one should not postulate more factors when fewer will do. Actually, Ockham did not invent the principle, though it is associated with him.

Octavia: The one existing example of a *praetexta* or historical drama. Attributed to Seneca, but almost certainly not by him. It must be post-Neronian. Plot deals with Octavia, the neglected empress, and Nero's new wife Poppaea. The play is full of repetition and frigid mythology.

Octavianus: Poet of the African Anthology, ca. 500 A.D.

Octavius: Dialogue by Minucius Felix, called "one of the first monuments of Christian Latin literature." The dialogue, in Ciceronian form, is between Octavius, a Christian, and Caecilius, a pagan, with Minucius the arbiter. It is based on Cicero's *De Natura Deorum* to some extent. Minucius cites many ancient authors, e.g., Virgil, Plato, Ennius, Homer. The work is an argument against paganism, especially Epicureanism. (Rand)

Octavius Rufus: Minor writer of epic poetry, ca. 100 A.D.

Octo Partibus Orationis, de: Anonymous 9th century work on the 8 parts of speech.

Ode to a Nightingale: See Fulbert of Chartres, Paulus Albarus.

Odes: (Horace) Horace says that he was the first to write native poetry in Greek meters. While this is not precisely true, it can certainly be said that he achieved a perfection of expression that no poet before or after him equaled, in a great variety of Greek meters. The Odes represent the fullest development of Horace's genius, and the ripest expression of his personal philosophy. The poems are chiefly modeled on those of the Greek poets, Sappho and Alcaeus. The subjects are many and varied: love, wine, the duties of a Roman, Horace's bid for immortality (exegi monumentum), the Golden Mean (auream mediocritatem), the "Gather ye rosebuds" theme (carpe diem), the fleeting years (Eheu fugaces . . .), the delight at the return of spring, the Stoic conception of the upright man (integer vitae), and many others. His philosophy is an eclectic blend of Epicureanism, Stoicism, with a liberal mixture of his own personal way of life. His "lapidary precision," his beauty of metrical expression, his choice of subject, his frank self-revelation, his warm humor, all these have contributed to make Horace the most beloved and the most often-quoted of all Roman poets. Quintilian says that he is, in fact, the only Roman lyric poet worth reading. (Duff, OCD)

Odo of Cheriton: 13th century Cistercian monk (d. 1247), author of sermons.

Odo of Cluny: 10th century. Wrote hymns, long poems

(*Occupatio*, etc.). Best remembered for his famous dream about Virgil, in which he saw a beautiful vase with snakes creeping out of it, and heard a voice telling him that this was the poetry of Virgil. From this time on, Odo was an anti-classicist. (Waddell)

Odo of Meung: Clergyman and physician in the first half of the 11th century. Wrote a poem *De Viribus Herbarum* (on the powers of herbs). (Manitius)

Odyssey: See Livius Andronicus.

Oeconomicus: Translation by Cicero (now lost) of a work by Xenophon.

Oedipus: This well-known story of incest and parricide, from the Greek plays of Sophocles, was treated, in Latin, by Caesar, Nero, and Seneca (2).

Oedipus: Seneca. It is difficult to imagine anything more different from the great play of Sophocles than this frigid piece. Jocasta kills herself on the stage, a circumstance which would have been most repugnant to the Greeks, speaks face to face with Oedipus after the secret has come out, etc. It must be remembered that the play was almost certainly not meant to be produced. It abounds in rhetoric, dreary descriptions of necromancy and sacrifices, and is in every way inferior to the greatest of Greek dramas.

Officiis, de: Philosophical work by Cicero, dealing with Moral Duties. Book I is concerned with the *honestum* (virtue) with the four cardinal virtues of Plato described; Book II with the *utile* (expediency); and Book III with the conflict between *honestum* and *utile*.

Officiis Ministrorum, de: Work on the duties of ministers, by Ambrose (q.v.). The work is described by Rand as "a monument of Christian humanism."

Olbert, Abbot of Gembloux: b. ca. 980. Wrote a *Life of St. Veronus,* a hymn to the same, and other works.

Onulf of Blandigny: Wrote a *Life of the Abbot Poppo of Stablo,* ca. 1059. This is valuable not only for the individual but for the general cultural history. Its chief fault is an over-emphasis on miracles, legends, visions, etc. (Manitius)

Onulf of Speyer: Author (ca. 1050) of *Rhetorici Colores*.

Opalinski, Lukasz: 1612-1662. Polish poet. Wrote a *Defense of Poland* against the remarks of John Barclay.

Opicius, Johannes: fl. 1500. Panegyrist of Henry VII; he wrote many Latin poems celebrating the deeds of that monarch.

Opilius, Aurelius: See Aurelius.

Optatianus, Porfirius, P.: City Prefect under Constantine. His poetry is noted for its mannered artificiality. He wrote figure-poems, rhopalic verse, acrostics, palindromes, etc. (qq.v.). The fifteenth poem is the height of this sort of mannerism. The first four lines consist of words of two, three, four, and five syllables, respectively. The fifth line is rhopalic (q.v.) or cumulative, followed by a line which uses all the parts of speech, and concluding with a palindrome (q.v.). See Mannerisms, literary. (Curtius)

Optatus, St.: Bishop of Milan in the 4th century, contemporary of St. Augustine. Writer on religious subjects, e.g., the Donatist schism.

Optimo Genere Dicendi, de: See *Orator* (Cicero).

Optimo Genere Oratorum, de: Rhetorical work by Cicero: the picture of the perfect orator.

Opus Maius: See Bacon, Roger.

Opus Paschale: See Sedulius (1).

Opuscula Sacra: Theological treatises by Boethius (q.v.).

Ora Maritima: See Avienus.

Orator ad Brutum: Also called *De Optimo Genere Dicendi*. Perhaps the greatest of Cicero's rhetorical treatises. The work is largely autobiographical.

Oratore, de: Work on rhetoric by Cicero. An imaginary discussion on the requisites for orators and oratory.

Oratoribus, de Claris: See *Brutus* (2).

Oratoribus, Dialogus de: (Tacitus) See *Dialogus*.

Oratorum et Rhetorum Sententiae Divisiones Colores: The magnum opus of Seneca (1). The *Sententiae* are the main questions and the opinions of the speakers. The *Divisiones* map out the general lines of arguments; while the *Colores* are the "colors" or special arguments. The work is addressed to the author's sons, and consists of extracts from various speakers he has heard, interspersed with comments, digressions, etc. We possess five books of *Controversiae,* and one of *Suasoriae.*

Oratory: This art reached its height in the latter days of the Republic. The Empire, by its very nature, had a tendency to stifle the wellsprings of oratory, which was then replaced by declamations, rhetorical exercises, etc. Some of the great early orators are: Appius Claudius, Cato, Laelius, the Gracchi. Crassus and Antonius were probably the greatest of the pre-Ciceronian orators. Contemporary with Cicero himself (q.v.) was Hortensius whose skill as an orator was second only to Cicero's. Cicero's death might well be termed the death-knell of oratory. Pollio and Messalla bridge the gap between Republic and Empire. See Atticism, Asianism, rhetoric, Seneca (1), *Dialogus de Oratoribus,* epideictic oratory, Quintilian, etc.

Orbellis, Nicholas de: See Nicholas de Orbellis.

Orbilius Pupillus, L.: Grammarian and teacher of the first century B.C. Chiefly remembered as the severe teacher of Horace, who calls him "Plagosus," the Walloper.

Orderic: (Ordericus Vitalis) b. 1075. Wrote a *Historia Ecclesiastica* (History of the Church), beginning with Christ and the Disciples and ending with his own times. Of great historical value. (Manitius)

Ordo Nobilium Urbium: A work by Ausonius (q.v.) describing twenty famous cities.

Ordo Romanus: Any of several documents prescribing the ceremonies of the Roman Catholic Church (8th-15th centuries).

Ordo Vagorum: A mock order of the "Wandering Scholars" —the renegade monks, clerks and scholars—the "family of Golias." They wrote drinking songs, love-lyrics, invective and satire. More interested in the care of the body than that of the soul, they were a powerful force in the poetry of the 11th and

12th centuries. See Goliardic poets, Golias, Carmina Burana, Vagantenlieder, Hugh Primas of Orleans, Archpoet. (Waddell)

Organon: Collection of the works on logic by Aristotle. Includes the *Categories, Topics, Prior* and *Posterior Analytics*, and other works. Translated into Latin by Boethius (q.v.), it was of the utmost importance for the philosophy and Scholasticism of the Middle Ages. Cf. Bacon, *Novum Organon*.

Orientius: Christian-Latin poet of the early 5th century. Wrote *Commonitorium*, an exhortation, in elegiac distichs, to the Good (i.e., Christian) Life.

Origen: This Greek Father of the Church, also known for his excellent Latinity, has been preserved partly in Latin translations by Jerome and Rufinus (qq.v.).

Origines (1): Lost historical work by Cato (1), (q.v.).

Origines (2): Work by Isidore of Seville (q.v.).

Origo Gentis Romanae: Historical work falsely attributed to Aurelius Victor.

Ornithogonia: Work by Aemilius Macer: a didactic poem about birds. It has not survived.

Orosius, Paulus: Spanish author of the early 5th century, a friend of St. Augustine. Wrote a *History* in seven books to refute the charge that Christianity was the cause of wars. The work is not particularly noteworthy, except for its being the first Christian history, and for its use of now lost portions of Livy's epitomes and of Tacitus' *Histories*. It is similar in purpose to Augustine's *City of God*, though vastly inferior in merit.

Orpheus: Legendary Greek bard and singer. The story of his descent into the Underworld to bring back his wife, Eurydice, is well known. Ovid tells it in the *Metamorphoses*. Lucan wrote a (lost) work on Orpheus.

Orthographia, de: Work by Terentius Scaurus (q.v.). Two abridgements survive.

Orzechowski (Orichovius), Stanislaw: 1513-1566. Polish-Latin historian and polemist; wrote on celibacy, on the wars with the Turks, etc.

Osbern of Gloucester: 12th century English monk, wrote

Derivationes, a lexicon-cum-grammar, dealing with etymology, glosses, etc. Uses Isidore, Paulus, Macrobius and Priscian.

Osbert of Clare: Prior of Westminster in the 12th century who wrote hymns and other poetry.

Oscan: An Italic dialect of the P-Italic family (see Dialects, Italic). It had some influence on the development of the Latin language. Several of the early authors (e.g., Ennius, Pacuvius, and Lucilius) were Oscans. Ennius said that he had three souls: Oscan, Greek, and Roman. See *Tabula Bantina.*

Osorio, Jeronimo: 1506-1580. Portuguese historian; wrote the history of the reign of King Manuel, in Latin.

Ostentarium: See Tarquitius Priscus.

Ostroróg, Jan: 1436-1501. Polish-Latin political writer on matters such as universal military service, stronger royal power, various reforms, etc.

Otfrid of Weissenburg: 9th century author of a *Liber Evangeliorum.*

Othloh of St. Emmeram: 11th century monk, poet, and historian. Wrote hymns, *Life of Boniface,* etc.

Otho, Junius: See Junius Otho.

Otio, de: (Seneca 2) Partly mutilated work by the younger Seneca, defending the value of leisure.

Otto of Freising: b. ca. 1114. Wrote a *Gesta Friderici* (Deeds of Frederic Barbarossa) and a *Chronicle* of world history, which was sent to Frederic with a letter of dedication. The latter deals not only with historical subjects (using Augustine, Orosius, and later medieval sources), but also with philosophical, drawing on Plato, Aristotle, Boethius, and Cicero's *De Officiis.*

Otto Morena: b. ca. 1100. A judge in Lodi. Wrote *De Rebus Laudensibus,* which was finished and edited by his son Acerbus.

Ovid: (P. Ovidius Naso) 43 B.C.-A.D. 18. Greatest of the Augustan elegiac poets. Made elegy the meter of love, and gave it grace and dexterity. Also famous for his narrative skill. Knew Horace, Propertius, and other literary lights of the Augustan Age. He was exiled in A.D. 8 for a "carmen" (poem) and an "error." The former is probably the *Ars Amatoria;* the nature of the latter is unknown. He went to Tomis on the Black Sea, where he spent the last ten years of his life in misery. His works include the *Amores, Heroides, Ars Amatoria, Fasti, Metamorphoses, Tristia, Remedia Amoris, Medicamina Faciei Feminae, Epistula ex Ponto.* The love-poet par excellence, possessed of a grace and facility of expression that are at once his strength and his weakness. Ovid is capable of great beauty, and also of much shallowness. He was a great story-teller. His influence was felt almost immediately by such authors as Statius, Lucan, Martial, and Quintilian. In the Renaissance he was *the* Latin poet. He influenced art and music, Shakespeare (Pyramus and Thisbe, Venus and Adonis, Lucrece, etc.), Chaucer, Milton, Spenser, Tasso, Ariosto. Roman elegy, most short-lived of the poetic forms, may be said to have perished with Ovid. The story is told by Seneca that a friend asked for permission to destroy Ovid's three worst lines, and Ovid agreed on condition that he be allowed to exempt three lines from destruction. The three lines were the same in each case! One of the lines is: "Semibovemque virum, semivirumque bovem." (Duff, Golden Age)

"Ovidius": Author of a *De Mirabilibus Mundi,* a didactic poem in 126 leonine hexameters. The poem concerns strange beasts and men, and was probably written in the 12th century. (Manitius)

Owen, John: 16th century author of epigrams. In his most famous one, he compared his book to the world, and men to verses. In each case, he said, you could find a few good examples.

Oxyrhynchus Epitome: See Periochae, Livy.

Paccius: Tragedian of the Neronian Age. Author of *Alcithoë.*

Pacuvius, M.: 220-ca. 130 B.C. Nephew of the poet Ennius; one of the greatest of the Roman tragedians, and also a painter of renown. We have titles of 12 tragedies, including the *Armorum Iudicium* (the Ajax story), *Antiopa, Atalanta, Niptra, Hermione;* and one praetexta (*Paulus*). Much indebted to the Greeks, Pacuvius was known for his pompous style, his obscurities and embellishments. He was very popular. Cicero quotes a passage describing a storm. Varro speaks of his *ubertas* or richness.

Paetus Thrasea: A Stoic philosopher who modeled his life on that of Cato Uticensis. Tacitus tells the famous story of his suicide in 66 A.D. Wrote a panegyric on Cato (2).

Paganus Boletinus: Minor French poet of the early 12th century, school of Chartres.

Palaemon, Q. Remmius: fl. 48 A.D. Author of an *Ars* or handbook on grammar; perhaps the first systematic grammar. Teacher of Quintilian and Persius.

Palaeography: The study of documents on parchment, etc. (as distinguished from epigraphy, which deals with inscriptions on stone, metal, etc.) and the analysis of manuscripts in terms of date and place. Mabillon, a Benedictine monk of the 17th century and Montfaucon were two of the first scientific palaeographers.

Paleario, Aonio: 1503-1570. Italian humanist. Wrote a poem *De Immortalitate Animorum.*

Palimpsest: A manuscript that has been written over an older one. It is usually the latter that is of greater importance, and has been scraped away to make room for the later document. Important texts of Cicero, Plautus, the Bible, etc. have been recovered from palimpsests. See Mai, Cardinal.

Palindrome: A sentence that reads the same backwards and forwards. Eng. example: "Able was I ere I saw Elba." Latin example:
"Roma tibi subito motibus ibit amor" (Sidonius). See also Recurrent verse.

Palladius, Rutilius Taurus Aemilianus: 4th century author of an *opus agriculturae* in the manner of Columella and others. The last of the fourteen books is in elegiac verse.

Palliata: See *Fabula Palliata.*

Palmer, A.: British classical scholar, known for his work on Horace's *Satires,* Ovid, Plautus, and Propertius.

Pamphilus: 12th century comedy by an unknown author.

Pamphilus, Gliscerium et Birria: A comedy written about

1175 by an unknown clerk. Plot concerns efforts of Pamphilus and his servant Birria to find Gliscerium, Pamphilus' beloved.

Panaetius: 184-110 B.C. Stoic philosopher and teacher, whose work was used by Cicero in the latter's *De Officiis* (q.v.). Thus Panaetius influenced St. Augustine and the whole scholastic movement.

Pancratiastes: Lost comedy by Ennius. Enough fragments survive to show us that this poet's forte was not comedy. See Sedigitus.

Panegyric: A speech of eulogy, includes the *laudatio funebris* and the *gratiarum actio.* For examples, see Cicero, *Manilian Law,* Pliny's panegyric on Trajan, the *Panegyricus Messallae,* etc. Other examples are by Drepanius, Ausonius, Ennodius, Sidonius, Claudian, etc. The panegyric belongs to the genre of epideictic oratory. See also *Laus Pisonis.*

Panegyricus: 1. Claudian's panegyric on Stilicho.

2. Pliny's speech on Trajan, 100 A.D. Deals with Trajan's character, his public deeds—a fine, noble picture of the emperor, full of allusions to his wicked predecessor Domitian. On the whole, the speech is too long and over-fulsome.

Panegyricus Messallae: A verse panegyric in the *Corpus Tibullianum.* Almost certainly not by Tibullus.

Pange lingua gloriosi: A famous hymn. See Fortunatus.

Pangrammatic writing: An excessive alliteration. Cf. Ennius' line:

"O Tite, tute, Tati, tibi tanta, tyranne, tulisti." See also Hucbald's *Ecloga de Calvis.*

Pannonius: Hungarian author of the Renaissance (1434-1472). Wrote Martial-like epigrams.

Pantheon: A prose-verse composition by Godfrey of Viterbo. Deals with the Creation, soul, history, etc. A mixture of fable, allegory and fantasy.

Pantheon, Roman: The chief Olympian gods: Jupiter, Neptune, Pluto, Mars, Apollo, Bacchus, Mercury, Vulcan, Saturn, Juno, Minerva, Venus, Ceres, Diana, Proserpina (qq.v.). See also Mythology.

Pantomime: See Mime.

Papal Bull: The official documents of the popes. Cf. Encyclical.

Papias: A Lombard, middle of the 11th century, who wrote a lexicon (*Elementarium Doctrinae Rudimentum*) in roughly alphabetical order, comprising such varied fields as etymology, medicine, mythology, zoology, grammar, and Biblical commentary. (Manitius)

Papinian: Eminent jurist ca. 205. Executed by Caracalla in 212. His works include the *Responsa, Quaestiones, Definitiones.* Had a profound influence on later jurists.

Pappus: "Graybeard"—one of the stock characters of the Fabula Atellana (q.v.).

Papyrology: The study of papyrus documents, including legal and military works, scholastic documents, new parts of old authors, completely new works (e.g., the *Carmen de Bello Aegyptiaco*), texts already preserved, epitomes, etc. Although the field of Latin papyrology is not so fertile as the Greek, it nevertheless is responsible for the increasing of our store of knowledge in many areas.

Paracelsus: (i.e., Theophrastus Bombastus von Hohenheim) Renaissance author so called because he went "beyond Celsus" (q.v.). His work, in Schwyzerdeutsch, was translated into Latin. It is a strange combination of Neo-platonism, experimentalism, and superstition.

Paraclete: The hermitage founded by Abelard (q.v.).

Paraclitus: See Warnerius of Basel.

Paradoxa: Work by Cicero on the Stoic Paradoxes.

Parentalia: Work by Ausonius (q.v.).

Paris, Julius: See Julius Paris.

Paris, Matthew: Monk of St. Alban (d. 1257). Wrote (?) *Historia Major,* an account of the first eight Norman kings (1066-1259).

Parkhurst, John: 1512-1575. Bishop of Norwich; wrote Latin epigrams.

Parody: Following are examples of parody or pastiche: the tragic burlesque that is found in comedy, Petronius' description of the Sack of Troy; a satire of Catullus' poem to his

yacht in the *Appendix Virgiliana;* the *Antibucolica* of Numitorius; "Baldus"; the *Testamentum Porcelli;* the *Cena Cypriani,*
a bibical parody; the work of Surianus, etc.

Parthenius of Nicaea: Wrote elegiac poetry in the last
century of the Republic. Only a few fragments remain.

Partitiones Oratoriae: Rhetorical work by Cicero (q.v.).

Parvipontanus: See Adam of Petit-Pont.

Pasca, de: Poem on the Cross, ascribed to Victorinus (q.v.).

Passennus Paulus: Contemporary of Pliny (2), descendant
of Propertius. A minor poet who wrote elegies like Propertius
and odes like Horace.

Passieni: Two noted orators of the Augustan Age and after.
They were father and son.

Passienus, Crispus: Orator under Caligula and Claudius.
Suetonius wrote his biography.

Passion: Description of the suffering or martyrdom of Christ
or any other Christian martyrs. A common form of composition, from Prudentius to the great Passions of J. S. Bach.

Passion Plays: See Religious Drama.

Pastoral poetry: The important figures are (qq.v.) Virgil,
Calpurnius Siculus, Nemesianus, and the author of the *Einsiedeln Eclogues.* Christian eclogues were written by Endelechius, Theodulus, Dante, and others. See also Pollio, Valgius
Rufus, Bavius, Marsus, Baptista Mantuan, *Piscatory Eclogues,*
etc.

Patavinity: Pollio's imputation of foreignisms in the writing
of Livy. See Livy, Pollio, Morhof.

Pater Noster: The Lord's Prayer, so called from its first
two words in Latin.

Paterculus, Velleius: See Velleius Paterculus.

Patrick, St.: Bishop of the Irish in the 5th century. Converted the Irish to Christianity, and made Latin the language
of the Church in Ireland. Wrote a *Confessio* or autobiography,
and a *Letter to the Christians.*

Patristic: Pertaining to the writings of the Church Fathers
or Patres (e.g., Jerome, Gregory, Augustine, and Ambrose).

Patrizi, Francesco: 1413-92. Italian author of political treatises in Latin (*De Regno, De Institutione Reipublicae,* etc.).

Patrologia Latina: Huge corpus of patristic and theological writings of the Middle Ages, compiled by Migne (q.v.).

Patrology: A somewhat vague term, comprising the works of the Fathers of the Church (see Patristic), i.e., theological and ecclesiastical literature. No attempt is made to include all such literature in this dictionary, but only a representative selection.

Patronage, literary: An ordinary feature of Latin literature was the relationship between client and patron. The earliest writers had their patrons, e.g., Ennius, whose patron was one M. Fulvius Nobilior. The Scipionic Circle included Terence, Polybius, and others. Q. Lutatius Catulus also had a "circle." The Age of Augustus was the period when patronage was in its heyday, with the circles of Maecenas, Pollio, and Messalla fostering the works of Horace, Virgil, Propertius; and the emperor also known as a patron of literature. Nero, Titus, Domitian, and others were patrons of the arts. Vespasian was Quintilian's patron. Martial and Statius speak of their patrons. In the Middle Ages, writers would flock to courts, e.g., that of Charlemagne (see Carolingian Renaissance), who surrounded himself with many of the literary lights of his day; but the patronage of the Empire no longer existed. (Cf. Johnson's letter to the Earl of Chesterfield.)

Paul of Bernried: Wrote a biography of Gregory VII, in the early part of the 12th century.

Paula: Accompanied Jerome (q.v.) to Bethlehem, and with him, founded a school, one of the first co-educational schools we know of. Her letters are extant; they are full of charm and simplicity.

Paulinus of Aquilea: ca. 750-800. Poet and grammarian, contemporary of Charlemagne; author of poems on the *Passio*.

Paulinus of Nola: ca. 354-431. After an early career as a Roman Senator, Paulinus became a monk at the age of 40, "forsaking Apollo and the Muses for Christ and the angels." He was a student and friend of Ausonius, and corresponded with Jerome, who wrote him a famous letter on Education and

Sanctity. His letters are well known: Jerome compares him to
Cicero as an epistolary. He wrote verse in a variety of meters:
an *Epithalamium,* a paraphrase of the Gospel, etc., but his
poetry is not of the first rank. His preoccupation with things
spiritual led to his break with Ausonius, who was always more
interested in the secular world.

Paulinus of Pella: Grandson of Ausonius (q.v.). Poet,
author of *Eucharisticon* (q.v.).

Paulinus of Perigueux: Bishop in the 5th century. Wrote
a metrical paraphrase of Sulpicius Severus' *Life of St. Martin,*
which has the distinction of being called "the worst poetry
of the 5th century." (Raby)

Paulinus, C. Suetonius: A minor historian of the Neronian
period, who wrote on Mauretania, and was probably one of
the sources for Tacitus.

Paulinus and Polla: Comedy by Richard of Venosa (q.v.).

Paullus, L. Aemilius: Founded the first private library at
Rome in 167 B.C. with books from the collection of King
Perseus of Macedon.

Paulus: Title of a lost *praetexta,* or historical drama, by
Pacuvius (q.v.).

Paulus Albarus: fl. 850. Friend of Aldhelm and Theodulf
(qq.v.). Complained of rhyme in poetry. Wrote three poems
on the nightingale. Also a *Confessio,* and a *Life of Eulogius*
(q.v.).

Paulus Camaldulensis: 12th century monk and grammarian.
Wrote on prosody, quantity and accent, and other subjects.

Paulus Diaconus: (or Paul Warnefrid) 8th century author
(d. ca. 800) of the Carolingian Renaissance. Wrote a *History
of the Lombards,* and miscellaneous poetry, acrostics, etc.
Also epitomized Festus' abridgement of Verrius Flaccus
(qq.v.). (Manitius)

Paulus, Julius: fl. 200 A.D. One of the greatest of Roman
jurists, a pupil of Cervidius Scaevola. An extremely prolific
writer of monographs, commentaries, *Regulae, Institutiones,
Sententiae, Manualia.* He left over 300 volumes. Used by the

compilers of the *Digest*. Paulus was exiled by the emperor Elagabalus.

Pauly-Wissowa-Kroll: Editors of the great *Realencyclopädie der klassischen Altertumswissenschaft,* the most comprehensive encyclopedia on classical subjects, i.e., biography, history, antiquities, archaeology, mythology, etc.

Pax Romana: With the accession of Augustus and the beginning of the Principate, the Roman world saw peace for the first time in over a century. It was partly to commemorate the Pax Romana, or Pax Augusta, that Virgil was commissioned to write the *Aeneid*.

Pecham, John: Archbishop of Canterbury in the 13th century; wrote a Passion poem, the *Philomena*.

Pedianus, Q. Asconius: See Asconius.

Pedius, Sextus: Roman jurist, ca. 100. His treatise *De Stipulationibus* is quoted by Papinian and Ulpian.

Pedo, Albinovanus: See Albinovanus Pedo.

Pegasus: 1. Winged horse of mythology. 2. Jurist of the Proculian school, under Vespasian.

Pegavienses, Annales: By an unknown monk at the monastery of Pegau. Deals with the founding and history of the monastery, and general history besides.

Pelagius: fl. ca. 400. Author of the earliest surviving work from the British Isles: the *Expositions of 13 Epistles of St. Paul,* and the *Epistula ad Demetriadem*. His denial of original sin caused his excommunication and a long and bitter controversy.

Pelagius of Oviedo: See Sampirus of Astorga.

Pelagonius: 4th century author of a *Mulomedicina* or handbook of veterinary medicine.

Peleus and Thetis: Epyllion by Catullus. Shows much Alexandrine influence. See epyllion, Catullus, *Cantores Euphorionis*.

Penates: Roman household gods, brought anachronistically (?) by Aeneas to Italy.

Pentadius: African poet of the 3rd century; author of epigrams and epanaleptic verse (q.v.).

Pentheus: Lost play by Pacuvius.

Peregrinatio ad Loca Sancta: See *Itinerarium Aetheriae Abbatissae*. Description of a pilgrimage to the Holy Land by a 4th century abbess to her nuns.

Perfectione Monachorum, de: See Damiani, Peter.

Perilla: Poetess of the Augustan Age to whom Ovid wrote a letter. She has sometimes been identified as Ovid's daughter, but this is highly unlikely.

Perilla: See Ticidas.

Periochae: Summaries or epitomes, especially of Livy. Mentioned as early as Martial. The *Oxyrhynchus Epitome* is one source (for books 37-40 and 48-55).

Peripatetic: Aristotle's school of philosophy. Contrary to popular supposition, the name has nothing to do with "walking around," but derives from the "Peripatos" or colonnade, where Aristotle taught.

Peristephanon: Poems on the legends of the martyrs, in a wealth of meters, by Prudentius (q.v.).

Persa: (or, the Make-Believe Persian Girl) Comedy by Plautus.

Persius Flaccus, Aulus: 34-62 A.D. Roman satirist. Student of Remmius Palaemon. His lost works include a travel book and *praetexta*. His fame rests on a slim collection of 6 satires. Persius may be termed the first Stoic satirist. His style is extremely obscure, condensed, allusive; in fact, he is the most difficult of all Latin poets to read, but Persius wrote for the few, not for the many. His satires are really sermons, and are concerned with the right spirit in literature, right thinking and living according to the Stoic principles, the use of wealth, etc. The total extent of the 6 satires is 650 hexameters. (Duff)

Pervigilium Veneris: Poem in 93 trochaic lines, by an unknown author, and of unknown date. The tendency now is to place it rather late (perhaps as late as the 5th century). It is a romantic composition, full of the joy of spring and love. Raby calls it the "last flower of ancient verse and the first romantic poem of the new world." With its accentual, rather than quantitative verse, it is a fitting prologue to the Middle Ages. The haunting refrain is:

"Cras amet qui numquam amavit, quique amavit cras amet"
(Let the loveless love tomorrow; he who's loved shall love
again.) (Raby, OCD)

Petavius: French Jesuit; writer on chronology and theology.

Peter Aureoli: d. 1322. French Schoolman, philosopher
and theologian; lectured at Toulouse, Bologna, and Paris; archbishop of Aix. Called "Doctor Facundus" or Eloquent Doctor.

Peter of Blois: 1153-1204. Twelfth century scholar and
humanist; archdeacon of Bath. Wrote letters, sermons, *Libellus
de Arte Dictandi Rhetorici;* poetry, on the Struggle of the
Flesh and Spirit, and other works.

Peter Chrysologus: 5th century author of homilies and
commentaries on the Gospel.

Peter Comestor: 12th century author of an encyclopedia
of Biblical History.

Peter Damian: See Damiani.

Peter of Eboli: ca. 1160-ca. 1200. Twelfth-century poet,
author of the famous poem on the *Baths of Pozzuoli,* and the
Liber ad Honorem Augusti, to Henry VI.

Peter Lombard: Twelfth century Schoolman. Wrote commentaries on the Psalms, letters, and four books of *Sententiae,*
or opinions. The latter is a systematic exposition of Christian
doctrine in the manner of *Sic et Non* (q.v.), by assembling
statements, or sententiae, of the Church Fathers, e.g., Augustine.

Peter of Pisa: Grammarian in the second half of the 8th
century, brought by Charlemagne from Italy (See Carolingian
Renaissance). He wrote poetical letters.

Peter of Poitiers: d. ca. 1209. Author of *Aurora,* an allegorical Biblical poem, the *Floridus Aspectus, Vita Susannae,
Passions, Colores Verbarum et Sententiarum.* (Manitius)

Peter Riga: See *Aurora.*

Peter of Spain: 12th century scholar and logician; author
of *Summae Logicales.*

Peter the Venerable: ca. 1094-1155. Abbot of Cluny.
His letters are famous, especially the one to Heloise telling her
of the death of Abelard. He wrote the epitaph for Abelard.
His poem *Against Slanderers* is a defense of Peter of Poitiers.

Also wrote a *Rhythmus in Laude Creatoris,* poetry, sermons, and translated the Koran.

Petitionis Commentariolum: See *Commentariolum.*

Petrarch: (Francesco Petrarca) 1304-74. Great figure of the Italian Renaissance. One of the first and greatest of the Classical humanists.

Petronius Arbiter: Creator of the realistic novel (See *Satyricon*). Tacitus tells us of his death at Nero's invitation. Probably the "elegantiae arbiter" of Nero's court, until he lost the favor of the capricious emperor. His novel is a rollicking tale of adventure, with some elements of the Milesian Tales, interlarded with shrewd characterizations, epic burlesque, good humor, erotic stories, some penetrating literary criticism, hilarious satire of the nouveau-riche Trimalchio. It is most valuable for its preservation of *the sermo plebeius* (q.v.).

Petrus Alfunsi: A converted Spanish Jew, born ca. 1050. Wrote a *Disciplina Clericalis,* a *Dialogus.*

Petrus Cantor: 1125-97. Theological author of the 12th century; wrote *Verbum Abbreviatum, Summa de Sacramentis,* Biblical commentaries, sermons, *Quaestiones de Simonia.*

Petrus de Dacia: 1235-89. Swedish ecclesiastical writer (*Vita Christinae Stumbelensis*).

Petrus Helie: French grammarian, first half of the 12th century. Made an abridgement of Priscian (*Summa Prisciani*).

Petrus Pictor: 12th century monk, poet, and satirist; canon of St. Omer. Wrote works on simony, on the Eucharist, on Praise of Flanders, a Life of Pilate, miscellaneous poetry.

Peutinger, Konrad: 1465-1547. German humanist, historian, antiquarian, etc. (*Sermones de Germaniae Antiquitatibus*).

Phaedra: (Seneca 2) Play dealing with the love of the young Phaedra for her stepson Hippolytus, his spurning her, and her accusation of him to her husband Theseus. A distinctly inferior play to that of Euripides, on which it is based. For instance, Seneca has Phaedra personally accuse Hippolytus, instead of killing herself and writing a note. This play is the basis of Racine's *Phèdre,* but lacks the power and insight of the latter.

Phaedrus (1): Epicurean teacher who influenced Cicero in his youth.

Phaedrus (2): Author of "Aesopian" beast fables in iambic senarii. A native of Macedonia, he came to Italy and became a freedman of Augustus. His fables point out the foibles of society. Some of the best known ones deal with the Lamb and the Wolf, the Ape who was a Judge, the King of the Frogs, the Two Wallets, the Fox and the Grapes, the Lion's Share, etc. Martial is the only Roman who mentions him. His iambics are neat, if not inspired. See Fable, Avianus, etc.

Phaenomena: See Aratus.

Pharsalia: (*De Bello Civili*) Historical epic by Lucan (q.v.). Deals with the Civil War between Caesar and Pompey. It is difficult to tell who is the hero: Caesar, Pompey, or Cato. In parts the work is moving, eloquent and dramatic; at times it descends to the level of the grotesque. The poem was unfinished, and it would be interesting to know where Lucan meant it to end. Some have thought it was to end with the death of Cato in 46, some with the death of Caesar in 44, some with the battle of Actium. The historical value of the work is questionable. Because of the author's anti-Caesarian bias, he tends to whitewash Pompey. Much rhetorical influence (see Silver Latin), many nice lines, speeches, characterizations made this work popular in later times. Indeed, it is the best of the post-Virgilian epics. (Duff, Silver Age)

Philip de Grève: d. 1236/7. Author of many moral and satirical poems, including the *Bulla Fulminante*.

Philip the Chancellor: 1150/70-1236. Author of Latin hymns, *Summa de Bono*.

Philippics: Fourteen speeches by Cicero against Mark Antony. So called after the speeches by Demosthenes, the Greek orator. Full of bitter invective and vituperation (especially the Second Philippic), these speeches cost Cicero his life. Actually, they were not so much speeches as political pamphlets. Juvenal, in the Tenth Satire, refers to the Philippics, saying that if the hand which wrote them had confined itself to poetry (he then quotes a particularly unfortunate line of Cicero's poetry), it would not have been cut off.

Phillips: The nephew of Milton, he composed a travesty on Virgil.

Philoctetes: Title of a lost play by Accius, presumably based on the tragedy of the same name by Sophocles.

Philologus: See Ateius.

Philomela: See John of Hanville.

Philosopher, The: Medieval designation of Aristotle, showing his preeminence in the philosophy of the Middle Ages. (cf. Dante's "master of those who know.")

Philosophia, de: Lost work of Varro (q.v.).

Philosophiae Naturalis: See Newton.

Philosophy: See Lucretius, Cicero, Varro, Seneca (2), Boethius, Scholasticism, Realism, Nominalism, John of Salisbury, Aquinas, Abelard, Duns Scotus, Ockham, etc. Since the Romans were less philosophically-minded than the Greeks, they were usually obliged to furnish some sort of camouflage or sugar-coating for their works on philosophy, thus Varro used the form of the Menippean Satire, Lucretius the epic, Cicero the dialogue, Boethius a sort of Menippean Satire, and so forth.

Philosophy, Consolation of: See *Consolatio*, Boethius.

Phocas: 5th century grammarian; wrote a life of Virgil, in verse, and an *Ars de Nomine et Verbo.*

Phoenissae: Play by Seneca (2). Seems to be based partly on Sophocles' *Oedipus at Colonus,* partly on Aeschylus' *Seven Against Thebes.* Perhaps it really consists of fragments of two separate plays. The subject has puzzled scholars for a long time, and is by no means decided.

Phoenix: 1. Poem by Laevius in the shape of a wing (See Figure-Poems). 2. Allegorical poem, ascribed to Lactantius; the fable of the Phoenix symbolizes the Resurrection.

Phormio: Comedy by Terence about two cousins and the parasite who gets them out of their difficulty. The legal quibbling is in the best Gilbertian tradition.

Picaresque novel: See *Satyricon* of Petronius; *Metamorphoses* of Apuleius.

Piccolomini, Aeneas Sylvius: 1405-64. Italian humanist and Papal legate to Germany in the 15th century. Poetry: *Historia de Duobus Amantibus;* also wrote plays, historical and pedagogical works. Wrote a famous letter to a friend in which he expresses his fears for the future of the Latin-Christian world.

Pico, Giovanni: Count of Mirandola and Concordia. 1463-94 (Pico della Mirandola). Italian humanist (*Oratio de Hominis Dignitate; Apologia,* etc.)

Pierre de Bur: ca. 1427-1505. Neo-Latin poet (*Moralium Carminum libri IX*).

Pietas: Roman virtue of duty to the gods, one's country and family. More than the English derivative would imply. The outstanding quality of Aeneas, always attached by Virgil to the hero's name: *"pius Aeneas."*

Pirckheimer, Willibald: 1470-1540. German humanist, friend of Dürer. Wrote various works, including, perhaps, the satire *Eccius Dedolatus.*

Piscatory Eclogues: By Sannazaro (q.v.). Renaissance work, modelled on Virgil, but with Neapolitan fishermen substituted for the Virgilian shepherds.

Piso Frugi, Calpurnius: Consul of 133 B.C., who opposed T. Gracchus. Wrote a prose history, which is lost.

Pisonem, in: Speech by Cicero against his enemy Piso. The speech is full of invective and abuse.

Pitholaus, Voltacilius: See Voltacilius.

Pitra, J. B.: Benedictine who did much of editing for Migne (q.v.).

Pius, Cestius: See Cestius Pius.

Placidus (1): Grammarian of the 5th or 6th century. The glossary which bears his name is in reality two works. One of these is usually designated Pseudo-Placidus.

Placidus (2) Lactantius: 6th century grammarian, author of scholia on the *Thebais* of Statius. Not identical with Placidus (1).

Plagiarism: The Romans borrowed nearly all their literary forms, meters and mythology from the Greeks, and they were only too willing to acknowledge their debt. Besides, "plagiarism" was often regarded as a compliment. Horace warns Albinovanus Celsus against plagiarism; Terence rather curiously maintains that he did not borrow from Naevius and Plautus, but from Menander. Ennius takes lines from Naevius, Lucretius from Ennius, Horace from Lucilius, Virgil from Lucretius, Catullus, and others.

Plancio, pro: Speech by Cicero, 54 B.C. defending Plancius on a charge of electoral corruption.

Planctu Naturae, de: See Alan of Lille.

Planctus de Obitu Caroli: Lament on the death of Charlemagne by an unknown poet.

Platina, Il: (Bartolomeo Sacchi) 1421-81. Italian humanist (*Liber de Vita Christi ac Omnium Pontificum, De Optimo Cive, De Vera Nobilitate,* etc.).

Plato: Through Proclus, the neo-Platonists, and Pseudo-Dionysius, Plato had an extremely important influence on the philosophy and theology of the Middle Ages, beginning with Augustine and Boethius, and going on until the Twelfth Century Renaissance. The Realist school (q.v.) had important elements of Platonism and neo-Platonism.

Plautius: A jurist of the Vespasian period.

Plautus, T. Maccius: ca. 254-184 B.C. The most original genius of the Roman stage. His plays are vigorous, earthy, full of slapstick, mistaken identity, puns, etc. First and foremost a man of the theater like Shakespeare, Plautus has a comic force superior to that of Terence and Menander, though he lacks their polish. Among comic playwrights, Plautus ranks with Molière and Aristophanes. His humor is always robust. We have twenty plays and fragments of one more, which seem to tally with the 21 mentioned by Varro. They belong to the *fabula palliata,* and nearly all deal with romantic love. The stock figures are the youth, the parasite, the braggart soldier, etc. (see New Comedy). The dialogue is swift and snappy, the comic situations fresh and vigorous. Among the best plays are the *Aulularia, Amphitruo, Captivi, Mercator, Menaechmi, Mostellaria, Miles Gloriosus, Rudens.* Others include the *Trinummus, Pseudolus, Stichus, Asinaria, Bacchides, Casina, Cistellaria, Vidularia, Epidicus, Curculio, Persa, Poenulus, Truculentus.*

Plebeian Latin: See *sermo plebeius.*

Plemp, Cornelius Gijsbertsz: 1574-1638. Dutch poet and musician, and lawyer. Wrote poetry in Latin and Dutch.

Plinius Secundus, C. (Pliny the Elder) 23-79 A.D. Author of the gigantic *Natural History* (q.v.). Born at Comum. A cavalry officer and friend of Vespasian. Admiral of the Fleet in 79, the year of the great eruption of Vesuvius, in which he lost his life. The story of his scientific curiosity and death is admirably told by his nephew, the younger Pliny. A man of indefatigable energy and unquenchable thirst for knowledge, he had slaves read to him when he was dining, bathing, etc. No book, he said, is so bad as not to contain something of profit. His lost works include a manual of javelins, history, biography, and others; all of which, together with the *Natural History* were written in the time left over from his official duties. The History is full *of sententiae* and purple patches, but contain countless passages of interest and information. Pliny's love for nature, the earth, and for humanity, are unsurpassed. His philosophy is Stoic. (Duff, OCD)

Plinius Caelius Secundus, C.: (Pliny the Younger) 62-113?. Nephew of the Elder Pliny, adopted by him. Born at Comum. Studied under Quintilian; was an advocate under Nerva and Trajan. We probably know more about Pliny than about any other Roman, except for Cicero. He followed the regular civil career, surviving the dangerous era of Domitian. He was sent to Bithynia as the personal representative of Trajan. We have some of his official correspondence with the emperor. Wrote poetry, tragedy, epic, elegiac poetry, speeches, etc. His reputation as a man of literature, however, must rest on his letters (q.v.). They tell us a great deal about the Rome of his day, and about Pliny himself—genial, tolerant, kindly, a bit conceited—the perfect type of the Roman gentleman. (Duff, OCD)

Plinius Valerianus: See Medicina Plinii.

Plocium: (The Necklace) Comedy by Caecilius, based on one of the same name by Menander, but, as evidenced by a comparison of the fragments, quite inferior.

Plotius Gallus: A teacher of rhetoric in the second century B.C.

Plotius Tucca: See Tucca.

Pluto: God of the underworld in Roman mythology. Identified with the Greek Hades. Most familiar is his appearance in the myth of Proserpina.

Poenulus: "The Little Carthaginian." Minor comedy by Plautus.

Poeta Saxo: Anonymous epic poet of the 9th century, who wrote on the deeds of Charlemagne.

Poetae Latini Minores: See Anthologia Latina.

Poetis, de: Works with this title (On the Poets) were written by Suetonius, Varro, and Sedigitus (qq.v.).

Poetria: Title of a work on poetics by John of Garland (q.v.).

Poetria Nova: See Geoffrey of Vinsauf.

Poetry: See Epic, Lyric, Drama, Elegiac, Didactic, Pastoral, etc.

Poggio Bracciolini: 1380-1459. Great humanist and scholar of the Italian Renaissance, who discovered, among others, the MSS. of Quintilian, Silius Italicus, Vitruvius, Lucretius, Valerius Flaccus.

Polenton, Sicco: 1376-1447. Italian writer of literary history (*Scriptores Illustres*).

Policraticus: Work by John of Salisbury (q.v.).

Polignac, Melchior de, Cardinal: 1661-1742. Author of *Anti-Lucretius*, a famous diatribe against the *De Rerum Natura* of Lucretius.

Politian (Poliziano), Angelo: 1454-1494. Important figure of the Italian Renaissance; friend and adviser of Botticelli. Important for the history of Lucretian studies. Wrote creditable Latin verse: (*Sylvae*, etc.)

Pollio, C. Asinius: 76 B.C.-A.D. 5. Patron of an important literary circle in the Age of Augustus. Wrote history of the

Civil Wars; an orator of considerable ability, and no mean poet. His works are all lost. Pollio is said to have introduced public *recitationes* at Rome.

Polybius: Greek writer of Roman history, important as a source for other historians, e.g., Livy.

Polyhistor: See Solinus.

Pomerius, Henricus: 1382-1469. Dutch writer on theology and history.

Pompeius (1): Grammarian of the 5th century.

Pompeius (2) Lenaeus: Freedman of Pompey, who translated into Latin the work on poisons by Mithradates.

Pompeius (3) Saturninus: Contemporary of Pliny the Younger (100 A.D.). An orator, historian, and poet.

Pompeius (4), Sextus: Consul in 14 A.D. A friend of Valerius Maximus and a literary patron.

Pompilius (1): An early poet and writer of epigrams. Possibly he was a pupil of Pacuvius (q.v.).

Pompilius (2) Andronicus: An Ennian scholar of uncertain date; a Syrian.

Pomponazzi, Pietro: 1462-1525. Italian philosopher, wrote *De Immortalitate Animae, De Fato, De Causis,* etc.

Pomponius (1): A Jurist of the Age of Hadrian (mid-second century).

Pomponius (2): A Christian-Latin poet who wrote a cento "Tityrus"—a spiritual eclogue.

Pomponius (3), Bassulus: Wrote comedies and translations of Menander.

Pomponius (4), Bononiensis: Writer of literary Atellan farce. We have about 70 titles. His plays were very popular, even in imperial times.

Pomponius (5), Marcellus: A grammarian under Tiberius.

Pomponius (6), Mela: Author of an extant work on geography: the *Chorographia,* or *De Situ Orbis,* in which he follows the coastline of the Mediterranean, then deals with the interiors of the various countries, telling of legends, customs, in a manner recalling that of Herodotus. In spite of its many blunders, the work is readable and interesting.

Pomponius (7) Rufus: Author of anecdotes ("collecta"), used by Valerius Maximus (q.v.).

Pomponius (8) Secundus: Wrote tragedies and *praetextae* in the early empire (Julio-Claudian period). Quintilian had a high regard for his dramatic skill, as did Tacitus.

Ponce de Provence: fl. 1250. Author of an *Ars Dictaminis*, or letter-writer's manual.

Ponderibus et Mensuris, Carmen de: See Carmen de . . .

Pontano, Giovanni: 1426-1503. Italian humanist. Wrote idylls, elegies, dialogues, history, etc. One of the best poets of the Italian Renaissance.

Pontic Epistles: See *Epistulae ex Ponto* (Ovid).

Ponticus: An epic writer of the Age of Augustus; friend of the poet Propertius.

Pontius Glaucus: Title of a lost poetical work by Cicero, written in his youth.

Porcius Licinus: (Licinius ?) A minor poet, ca. 100 B.C., who wrote epigrams in imitation of the Greek. Aulus Gellius has preserved some small fragments.

Porphyrion, Pomponius: 3rd century scholar, author of a commentary on Horace which is still extant.

Porrée, Guibert de la: See Guibert de la Porrée.

Posidonius of Rhodes: Great Stoic philosopher and teacher, who influenced Cicero, Varro, and others.

Postgate, J. P.: English classical scholar. His edition of the *Corpus Poetaeum Latinorum* is an important landmark in classical scholarship.

Post Reditum: Two speeches made by Cicero, after his return from exile. The authenticity of the second has been doubted, but not recently.

Post-Renaissance Latin: Besides scholarly articles, books, dissertations; and papal communications, etc. consists largely either of erudite literary exercises or translations from the vernacular literatures *into* Latin; in either case, hardly belongs under the heading of Latin Literature. Jebb, Housman, Bury, etc. were excellent Latinists. See Neo-Latin.

Postumus Albinus: See Albinus.

Praeexercitamina: Title of Priscian's (q.v.) translation into Latin of the *Progymnasmata* of Hermogenes—a book of rhetorical exercises.

Praenestine Fibula: A brooch with a Latin inscription, dating from the 5th or 6th century B.C., consequently, the earliest extant piece of Latin. Of historical and linguistic, rather than literary interest. The inscription reads: Manios med fhefhaked Numasioi. ("Manius made me for Numerius")

Praeloquia: See Ratherius of Liége.

Praetexta: See *Fabula Praetexta.*

Praetextatus: See Vettius.

Pragmatica: Lost didactic work by Accius (q.v.), dealing with literature.

Praise of Folly: (*Moriae Encomium*). Erasmus' (q.v.) greatest work. Published in 1511, it is a gentle, humorous, but none the less thorough criticism of all of the follies of his age: ignorance, neglect, adherence to formalism, obedience to the letter rather than the spirit of Christianity, the evils of monasticism, etc. Folly, personified, speaks of her usefulness to mankind. The Latin title of the work is a play on the name of Sir Thomas More. This work, together with the author's *Colloquies,* had a great influence on the works of the literary giants of the Renaissance, e.g., Shakespeare, Rabelais, and Cervantes.

Pratum: Lost work by Suetonius; a miscellany of varia and curiosa; scientific and antiquarian lore, etc.

Praxidica: Title of a lost work on agriculture, by the tragedian Accius (q.v.). The title is identified with the name Persephone. (Duff)

Prayer: There were all sorts of formulae for Roman prayers. Some of our earliest remains of Latin consist of such formulae, as do the Tabulae Iguvinae for Umbrian. Generally they were very elaborately phrased. Appel's collection *De Romanorum Precationibus* is standard. For Christian prayer, see Mass, hymns, Missale, etc.

Precatio Omnium Herbarum: A short, post-Augustan prayer in iambic verse.

Precatio Terrae: A short iambic prayer to Mother Earth, of uncertain date.

Priam: King of Troy. Virgil (Aeneid, Book II) tells of his tragic death amid the ruins of his city. He is proverbial in classical literature for the individual who has known the greatest extremes of fortune (Juvenal, Aristotle, etc.).

Priapea: A collection of 85 poems, of which some are attributed to Tibullus, one to Ovid, probably all written in the Age of Augustus. As the name would imply (Priapus being the god of fertility), they are generally marked by their extreme obscenity, phallic motifs, etc. Some appear in the *Appendix Virgiliana.*

Priapus: Greek god of fertility, whose symbol was the phallus.

Priestly records: Important for the development of Latin prose. Include the *Libri Pontificum, Commentarii Pontificum, Fasti, Annales.*

Primas of Cologne: 13th century canon of Cologne, sometimes identified with the Archpoet, or with Hugh Primas of Orleans (qq.v.).

Primas, Hugh, of Orleans: See Hugh of Orleans.

Princeps: A rhetor of the first century.

Principate: This term is sometimes preferred to the term "Empire" for the first century or so of the "Empire." Augustus deliberately chose the title Princeps, rather than a less Republican or more autocratic-sounding name, to designate his position.

Prisca Virtus: The "old-fashioned" Roman virtue or virtues, of piety to the gods, family, and state; fortitude, *gravitas* or dignity, etc. Virtus means, literally, the quality of a *man.*

Priscian: Grammarian, ca. 500 A.D. Author of a comprehensive grammar in 18 books, which sums up all the grammatical learning of the previous centuries. The work is extremely rich in quotations; indeed this is one of the chief values of the *Institutiones Grammaticae,* which was widely used in the Middle Ages, until it was supplanted, in the 13th century, by works like those of Alexander of Villedieu and Eberhard of

Béthune (qq.v.). Priscian also wrote the following: *De Figuris Numerorum, de Metris Fabularum Terentii, Praeexercitamina Rhetorica,* works on pronouns and verbs, on the *Aeneid,* on accents, and miscellaneous poetry, including a panegyric on the emperor Anastasius.

Proba, Falconia: Poetess of the 4th century. Before her conversion to Christianity, she wrote an epic on the civil war between Constantius and Magnentius; after it, she produced a cento (q.v.) on Biblical subjects. Jerome was scathing in his denunciation of this and other such works; Isidore less so: he says that her ingenuity is to be praised, if not her conception. The work was fairly popular in the Middle Ages.

Probus, Valerius: Grammarian of the Neronian period and afterward. He is quoted frequently by later authors, e.g., Gellius, on points of grammar. He wrote on Terence, Lucretius, Virgil, Horace, Persius. The *Libri Iuris Notarum* attributed to him is not genuine. Various apocryphal works have come down under his name. In the Renaissance, a "younger Probus" was invented to explain these.

Procrustes: In mythology. He had two beds, which he would force passers-by to lie in, and either stretch them out to fit the longer one, or chop off feet (or heads?) to fit the shorter. He was killed by Theseus. The term "Bed of Procrustes" has passed into the language for an argument which will, willy-nilly, fit any circumstances.

Proculians: One of a pair of rival legal schools in the first century. See Sabinus, Labeo, Capito.

Proculus: Jurist of the early Empire. Leader of one of the two rival schools (see Proculians, etc.).

Prognostica: Work by Aratus, translated into Latin by Cicero.

Prologue: (Comedy) The prologue of Roman comedy was usually personal, like the parabasis of Greek comedy. The author would directly address his audience, speaking of the merits of his play. One is sometimes reminded, in this connection, of radio or television commercials.

Propemptikon: A sort of "bon voyage" poem. Horace wrote

one to Virgil, Cinna to Asinius Pollio. Other examples by Propertius, Tibullus, Ovid, Statius.

Propertius, Sextus: ca. 50-16 B.C. Augustan elegiac poet of love. Wrote four books of elegies. We know of his love for "Cynthia" (Hostia), who was probably as unworthy of his love as the notorious Lesbia was of Catullus'. He writes of his love, despair, joy at reconciliation; little vignettes of city life, etc. Martial says that Cynthia made Propertius a poet. Probably his best-remembered line is "Cynthia prima fuit, Cynthia finis erit." Propertius is a great poet of love, but he is also preoccupied with the idea of death. His elegiacs are smooth but not flawless. His erudition is almost Alexandrian; the metaphors are sometimes obscure. It has been thought that many lines are displaced or transposed, but the question is still a moot one. (Duff, Golden Age)

Prose, Latin: See under the various categories: Oratory, History, Grammarians, Learning, etc. The first writer of prose of whom we have any connected remains is Cato. His prose is crude and abrupt. That of Cicero is usually regarded as the high-water mark in the development of Latin prose. Later writers of artistic prose are Livy, Tacitus, Pliny (2).

Prose-rhythm: Latin authors (e.g., Cicero, Sallust, Caesar, Quintilian, etc.) gave much attention to the rhythm of their sentences, especially to the endings or *clausulae*. For instance, Cicero seems to have preferred sentences ending with "esse videatur" or words with the same or similar rhythm. Zielinski has made a study of prose-rhythm.

Proserpina: The Greek Persephone. Daughter of Ceres, abducted by Pluto, allowed to return to earth on a part-time basis. The whole is an etiological myth explaining the change of the seasons. Ovid and Claudian (qq.v.) tell her story. (Rose in OCD)

Prosimetron: A work composed in alternating prose and verse. See also Menippean Satire. Ancient examples: Petronius, *Satyricon*, Seneca (2), *Apocolocyntosis*. Late antiquity: Boethius, *Consolation of Philosophy*; Martianus Capella.

Medieval: the works of Alan of Lille, Bernard Silvestris, etc. See under these authors.

Prosper of Aquitaine: Early fifth century author. Versified some of the writings of Augustine of Hippo.

Protagoras: One of Plato's dialogues, translated by Cicero, probably in his youth.

Protesilaodamia: Title of a work (or part of a work?) by Laevius (q.v.). Possibly part of his *Erotopaegnia.*

Protrepticus: An exhortation to philosophy. The best-known one is that of Cicero, the *Protrepticus Hortensius,* the reading of which turned Augustine to the study of philosophy.

Proverbs: In late antiquity and in the Middle Ages there were many collections of proverbs (see *Disticha Catonis*). Other collections are the *Proverbia Heinrici,* the *Proverbia Rustici,* the *Salomonis Proverbia,* and many others.

Providentia, de: Dialogue by Seneca (2), addressed to his friend Lucilius. Replete with Stoic philosophy, the dialogue discusses the purposes of suffering, why misfortunes befall a good man, the nature of Providence, etc.

Provinces, Roman: Many Roman authors came from the provinces, especially the following: Spain (the Senecas, Lucan, Columella, Quintilian, Mela, Martial), Africa (Terence, Fronto, Apuleius), and Gaul (Nepos, Ausonius, etc.). Many of the Apologists (e.g., Tertullian, Lactantius, Minucius Felix) were African.

Provinciis Consularibus, de: Speech by Cicero, advocating that Caesar's Gallic command should be prolonged; a sharp volte-face from his earlier anti-Caesarian position.

Prudentius (1), Aurelius Clemens: 348-410? One of the best, and most prolific of the Christian-Latin poets. Born in Spain. Wrote many hymns; tales of the martyrs; poems on Church dogma (Rand calls him the "Christian Lucretius"); an epic, *Hexaemeron,* on Creation; the *Hamartigenia,* or Origin of sin; the *Psychomachia,* an allegorical epic; *Peristephanon, Cathemerinon,* etc. Prudentius reveals a great mastery of a wealth of meters, and a profound knowledge of the earlier Latin poets.

Prudentius (2) of Troyes: A bishop of the time of the Carolingian Revival. Wrote, or culled, a *Flores Psalmorum*.

Psalmodiae Bono, de: See Niceta.

Psalms: Many authors wrote commentaries on the Psalms, e.g., Cassiodorus, Jerome, and others.

Psalmus contra Partem Donati: Psalm against the Donatists, by Augustine, q.v.

Pseudepigraphic Literature: Works that have been proven not to be authentic: i.e., not to have been written by the person whose name is affixed to them. Of various types: deliberate forgeries; accidental copyings and juxtapositions; the tendency to ascribe unknown works to known authors of similar works; works of followers or members of a school ascribed to the master of the school; examples of each sort exist. Cf. the *Appendix Virgiliana,* the *Corpus Tibullianum,* the Sibylline books, the Clementine Recognitions, Pseudo-Dionysius, etc.

Pseudo-: Greek: "false." Prefixed to the names of supposed authors in the case of works of doubtful or spurious authenticity, e.g., Pseudo-Dionysius, Pseudo-Turpin.

Pseudo-Apuleius: Certain works attributed to Apuleius (q.v.): *Asclepius, Herbarius, De Remediis Salutaribus, Physiognomina.*

Pseudo-Asconius: 5th century author of a commentary on Cicero's Verrine orations, which has been incorporated with the works of Asconius (q.v.).

Pseudo-Dionysius: Unknown author of a work which attempts to reconcile Christian theology with Neo-platonic metaphysics. The work was probably written by a monk in the 5th century, and reflects the teachings of Proclus and the Neo-Platonists. It was translated by John Eriugena into Latin, and was of great importance for the development of scholastic thought in the Middle Ages.

Pseudo-Frontinus: The fourth book of Frontinus' Stratagems is clearly not by Frontinus, and the name of Pseudo-Frontinus has been given to its (unknown) author.

Pseudo-Ovidiana: See *Elegiae in Maecenatem.*

Pseudo-Placidus: See Placidus.

Pseudo-Plutarch: See Guarino.

Pseudo-Quintilian: See Quintilian, *Declamationes.*

Pseudo-Sallust: The *Invectiva in Ciceronem,* a piece of anti-Cicero vituperation, and Cicero's "answer," together with two anonymous suasoriae, *the Epistulae ad Caesarem senem de republica,* have all been transmitted to us along with the works of Sallust. Much doubt has been cast upon their authenticity, but the matter has by no means been decided.

Pseudo-Tibullus: See *Corpus Tibullianum.*

Pseudo-Turpin: Author of a history of Charlemagne (*Historia Karoli Magni*) which purports to be by Turpin, the legendary Archbishop of Reims. The work appears to be a deliberate forgery, written in the 12th century. Tells, among other things, the romantic story of Roland at Roncevalles. (Manitius)

Pseudo-Udalrich: Author of a letter, falsely ascribed to Bishop Udalrich of Augsburg, entitled *De Continentia Clericorum.* The letter is addressed to Pope Nicholas, but neither pope of that name was a contemporary of Udalrich. (Manitius)

Pseudo-Virgiliana: See *Appendix Virgiliana.*

Pseudolus: Play by Plautus, "the joy of his old age," as Cicero tells us. Pseudolus, the slave, outwits a rascally slave-dealer. It has elements of the Fescennine and of the Italian popular element.

Psychomachia: One of the earliest examples of Christian allegory, by Prudentius (q.v.). A series of epic combats between the vices and virtues personified (e.g., Pride vs. Humility, etc.).

Publilius "Syrus": Writer of mimes (q.v.) in the last century of the Republic. Small fragments are preserved, consisting mostly of maxims or *sententiae,* such as "avarus nisi cum moritur nil recte facit" (the only good miser is a dead one).

Pulcher: See Clodius. The cognomen has interesting modern parallels, cf. "Pretty-Boy Floyd."

Pullus, Robert: An early scholastic (d. 1150) who wrote on the doctrine of repentance.

Pumpkinification of Claudius: See *Apocolocyntosis*.

Punica: Epic on the Second Punic War by Silius Italicus. In 17 books. Some of the incidents are: the battle of Lake Trasimene; the affair of Regulus, the famous prisoner of war who kept his parole, though it meant his life; the great battle of Cannae; Hannibal and his elephants; the visit of Scipio to the Underworld (cf. the similar visit by Aeneas, depicted by Virgil); and the final Roman victory at Zama. Weaknesses are: a tendency to grotesque and monstrous incident, artificiality, woodenness of the characters. Some parts of it are rather good. One tends to have more sympathy with Hannibal than with Scipio, the hero. The *Punica* is the longest poem in the Latin language. (Duff, Silver Age)

Puns: The ancients were fond of plays on words. Plautus used them frequently. Cicero was given to making puns on the names of his friends (e.g., Rex, Brutus). Bede records the famous puns of Pope Gregory (angels-Angles). Christianity brought a new aspect into the field of puns: the reading of mystical significance into names by quasi-etymological explanations. Isidore does this (e.g., Paulus, the "minimus apostolorum"). Cf. also Erasmus' *Moriae Encomium* (Praise of folly), a pun on the name of Thomas More.

Pupius: A minor Augustan poet, lampooned by Horace.

Purchard: An 11th century monk of Reichenau, who wrote of the deeds of his abbot, in dialogue form.

Pyramus and Thisbe: This famous and tragic story is beautifully told by Ovid in the *Metamorphoses*. The young lovers, who have been forbidden to meet by their parents, assign a rendezvous. Thisbe arrives first, is frightened by a lion, and takes refuge in a cave, leaving her scarf, which the lion mangles. When Pyramus arrives, he sees the scarf, thinks Thisbe is dead, and kills himself. Thisbe, returning, does likewise. The story is burlesqued by Shakespeare. Matthew of Vendôme also dealt with it.

Pyrrhus, "Pyrrhic victory": Pyrrhus, king of Epirus, was the antagonist of Rome in the 3rd century B.C. He is said to have won a victory so costly that he said, "one more such victory, and I am ruined." Hence the term, Pyrrhic victory, is used for any victory so costly that it might as well be a defeat.

Quadratus: An apologist of the early second century. His work has not survived.

Quadrigarius, Claudius: See Claudius Quadrigarius.

Quadrivium: (or quadruvium) In medieval education, the mathematical "artes" or liberal arts. Consisted of arithmetic, geometry, music, and astronomy. Formulated by Boethius (q.v.). Together with the trivium (q.v.), the basis for all study and education in the Middle Ages. See Education, Artes.

Quaestiones: See Caecilius Africanus.

Quaestiones in decem libros Ethicorum Aristotelis: Work by Buridan, q.v.

Quaestiones in Vetus Testamentum: See Isidore of Seville.

Quaestiones Naturales (1): Work by Seneca (2). In seven books, it deals with matters of astronomy, meteorology, geography; i.e., with such phenomena as fire, air, thunder, lightning, rain, snow, the overflowing of the Nile, wind, earthquakes, comets, etc. His position is partly Stoic, partly eclectic. He often gives conflicting explanations. There are many unscientific but nonetheless interesting digressions.

Quaestiones Naturales (2): Work by Adelard of Bath (q.v.).

Quaestiones Plautinae: Lost work of Plautine scholarship by Varro (q.v.).

Qualitate Vitae, de: Poem by Florus (q.v.).

Quaternuli: Work by David of Dinant (q.v.) in which he sums up his doctrine of materialistic pantheism.

Quedlinburgenses, Annales: A big historical work written at the convent of Quedlinburg under Adelheid. Mostly in praise of the ruling house of Saxony, the deeds of Otto, etc., the work is indebted to the Annals of Einhard, and has frequent quotations from Virgil and other authors. Valuable as source material, but written with no real historical understanding. Style is affected and clumsy. (Manitius)

Querolus: A late adaptation of Plautus' *Aulularia* (q.v.) used by Vitalis of Blois for his *Aulularia* (qq.v.).

Quindecim Gaudia: "Fifteen Joys of the Virgin Mary." See John of Hoveden.

Quintilian: (M. Fabius Quintilianus)—ca. 35-ca. 100 A.D. Rhetor and teacher, born in Spain, brought to Rome by the emperor Galba. Held a chair of rhetoric, which brought him fame and fortune. Elevated to the consulate, he was appointed tutor to the grand-nephews of Domitian. His one extant work is the great *Institutio Oratoria* (q.v.), which depicts the complete education of a Roman citizen, not only in rhetoric, but in all the liberal arts. Quintilian ranks as one of the world's great teachers, along with Socrates. The work is full of common sense, humanity, and all-pervading sanity. Many of his gems of literary criticism have become proverbial. He helped to establish the canon of great authors. The two Declamations which appear under his name are almost certainly spurious. His other work, the *De Causis Corruptae Eloquentiae*, is lost. Quintilian's influence on literature has been great. Tacitus owes much to him, as do Juvenal and Suetonius. In later times, Jerome and Lactantius, Cassiodorus and Isidore, all are indebted to Quintilian. The manuscript of Q.'s work was discovered by Poggio at St. Gall in 1416. (Duff, Silver Age)

Quintuplex Psalter: See Lefèvre d'Étaples.

Quirinus: An Italian deity, who regularly forms a third, with Jupiter and Mars, in prayers, formulae, rituals, etc.

Quispiam ad Quandam Virginem: See Gilbert.

Quodlibeta: See Godfrey of Fontaines.

Quotations: Following is a partial, but representative list of famous Latin quotations, which have become part of the heritage of western civilization. It will be noted that Horace, Juvenal, and Virgil predominate. Horace: *carpe diem* (snatch the day), *nil admirari* (nothing is to be admired, i.e., set no store by external goods); *auream mediocritatem* (the Golden Mean); *odi profanum vulgus* (I hate the common throng); *dulce et decorum est pro patria mori* (it is sweet and fitting to die for one's fatherland); *purpureus pannus* (the purple patch); *non omnis moriar* (I shall not altogether perish); *ars est celare artem* (art consists in concealing art); *in medias res* (plunging into the middle of the story); *laudator temporis acti* (one who praises bygone days); *parturiunt montes, nascetur ridiculus mus* (the mountain labors and gives birth to a ridiculous mouse); *Eheu fugaces, Postume, Postume, labuntur anni* (Alas, Postumus, the years are fleeting). Virgil: *timeo Danaos, et dona ferentes* (I fear the Greeks, even when they bear gifts); *dux femina facti* (a woman was leader of the deed, or, "cherchez la femme"); *hoc opus, hic labor est* ("there's the rub!"); *facilis descensus Averni* (the road to Hell is easy); *forsan et haec olim meminisse iuvabit* (some day, perhaps, it will be pleasing to remember these things too); *sunt lacrimae rerum* (lit. there are tears for things). Juvenal: *panem et circenses* (bread and circuses); *nemo repente fuit turpissimus* (nobody gets wicked overnight); *mens sana in corpore sano* (a sound mind in a sound body); *quis custodiet ipsos custodes?* (who will watch the watchmen?). Catullus: *odi et amo* (I love and hate); *Vivamus, mea Lesbia, atque amemus* (let us live and love, my Lesbia). Martial: *Non amo te, Sabidi* ("I do not like thee, Dr. Fell"); *Sera nimis vita est crastina: vive hodie* (Tomorrow's too late to live: live today!). Tacitus: *ubi solitudinem faciunt, pacem appellant* (they make a wilderness and call it peace). Seneca: *peccavimus omnes* (we have all sinned); Accius: *oderint, dum metuant* (let them hate me, so long as they fear me). Ennius: *amicus certus in re incerta cernitur* ("a friend in need is a friend indeed"). Cicero: *O tempora, O mores* (Shame on the times and customs!). Terence: *homo sum, humani nil a me alienum puto* (I am a man; nothing human is alien to me). Cato: *rem tene, verba sequentur* (know your facts and the words will come); *vir bonus dicendi peritus* (a good man who is skilled at speaking—Cato's definition of an orator). Ambrose: *Nolo episcopari* (I don't want to be a bishop—cf. "I do not choose to run"). Anselm and/or Augustine: *credo ut intellegam* (I believe that I may understand). Tertullian: *credo quia absurdum est* (I believe because it is absurd). Descartes: *cogito, ergo sum* (I think, therefore I exist).

The above, it must be emphasized, is not intended to be a complete list of such quotations; there are hundreds more; it is merely an indication of the more frequent ones, and the most oft-quoted authors.

Raban Maur: See Hrabanus Maurus.

Rabienus: See Labienus.

Rabirio, pro; Rabirio Postumo, pro: Speeches by Cicero.

Rabirius (1): Wrote an epic on Antony's defeat, possibly identical with the *Carmen de Bello Aegyptiaco* (q.v.).

Rabirius (2): Epicurean teacher who influenced Lucretius.

Radbertus, Paschasius: 9th century theologian; wrote *De Corpore et Sanguine Domini* (on the body and the blood of Christ).

Radbod, bishop of Utrecht: German poet (d. 917). Wrote a famous poem on the swallow.

Radewijns, Florens: 1350-1400. Dutch writer of devotional works. See *Devotio Moderna*.

Radolf of Liége: Teacher and mathematician of the early 11th century. See Ragimbold of Cologne.

Radulf of Caen: b. ca. 1080. Wrote a *Gesta Tancredi*, partly in prose and partly in hexameters. His style is lively, and shows the influence of Virgil and Horace.

Radulf of La Tourte: Wrote, ca. 1100, a versified edition of the work of Valerius Maximus (q.v.), and other poetry.

Radulfus de Diceto: Wrote *Abbreviationes Chronicorum*, a huge compilation of miscellaneous pieces from ancient and medieval sources; and *Ymagines Historiarum*, a continuation of the *Abbreviationes*.

Radulfus Glaber: 11th century author of a lively history. He was driven out of one monastery after another, and must have been an extremely unpleasant individual. (Waddell)

Ragimbold of Cologne: Early 11th century teacher and mathematician, wrote a series of letters to Radolf of Liége (q.v.).

Rahewin of Freising: Continued the *Gesta Friderici* of Otto of Freising (q.v.). Other works: *Versus de Vita Theophili* in 651 rhymed hexameters; a poem *De Deo et Angelis.*

Rainaldus: 11th century scholar; pupil of Fulbert, teacher of Baudry (qq.v.).

Ramus, Petrus: 1515-72. French humanist and philosopher. Wrote numerous philosophical works on Aristotle.

Ramusio, Girolamo: 1450-1486. Italian poet, friend of Pico della Mirandola. Wrote Latin lyrics.

Rand, Edward K.: (1871-1945) Late Professor of Latin at Harvard University. Author of *Founders of the Middle Ages,* and co-editor of the Loeb Boethius.

Rangerius: Bishop of Lucca 1097-1112. Wrote poetry, notably one poem on the *Ring and the Staff.*

Rape of the Sabines: One of the most familiar legends in Roman literature and history. The Romans, after inviting the neighboring Sabines to a festival and games, made off with their women. The story is treated in Livy. Ennius (q.v.) wrote a *praetexta* on the subject. At the time of writing (fall, 1954), a motion picture is being shown ("Seven Brides for Seven Brothers") which is, in effect, a modernized version of the same story.

Rapin, René: 17th century Jesuit and humanist. Wrote a *Hortorum Libri iv,* and works against the Jansenists.

Raptu Proserpinae, De: Mythological epic by Claudian (q.v.).

Ratherius of Liége: b. ca. 887, came to Italy in 926, appointed bishop of Verona in 931. Imprisoned for his support of Arnold of Bavaria. Wrote his most famous work, *Praeloquia,* in prison. A call to all men of whatever rank, occupation, sex and age, to fight against evil and sin, the work is one of the most subjective of all medieval documents. Ratherius shows much acquaintance with classical authors and the Fathers. He writes with much self-revelation and criticism. Manitius calls the work a "Weltspiegel" (Mirror of the world). Other works by Ratherius: *De Contemptu Canonum, De Otioso Sermone, De Nuptu Illicito,* and many others. (Manitius)

Ratpert: Scholar and historian of St. Gall in the 9th century (d. 890). Wrote elegiac poetry with leonine rhyme.

Ratramnus: fl. 850. Friend of Gottschalk. Rejected Radbertus' (q.v.) explanation of the Eucharist.

Raymond of Agiles: Chaplain of Count Raymond of Toulouse, whom he accompanied on the First Crusade. He wrote a history of this Crusade.

Raymond of Sabunde: d. 1436. Wrote prose sermons. Condemned by the Council of Trent.

Re Coquinaria, de: See Apicius.

Re Rustica, de (1): Cato's treatise on agriculture. See Cato (1).

Re Rustica, de (2): Treatise by Varro (q.v., 1) on agriculture. Although the prose style is not very artistic, the treatise is not without its charm. Varro writes on crops, cattle, game, fish, etc. with a real feeling for the land and for nature. More literary and learned than the treatise by Cato, as one would expect.

Re Rustica, de (3): Treatise on agriculture in prose (except for book X, which is in verse), by Columella, written in the Neronian period. He deals with the following subjects: choosing the land; water supply; ploughing and fertilizing; vines and vineyards; trees, livestock; cheese-making; poultry, fish, and bee-keeping; pickling, preserving, etc. The prefaces, and book X, on gardens, are especially good. (Duff, Silver Age)

Realism: A medieval school of philosophy: the doctrine that universal concepts have objective existence; in opposition to the *Nominalist* school, which maintained that only individuals exist. Plato was the first to set forth the doctrine of Realism, in his Theory of Ideas, which was modified by Aristotle. The Platonic version was current in the Middle Ages, until Aquinas (q.v.) adopted Aristotle's version. See Nominalism, Universals, and for full discussion, see Runes, Dictionary of Philosophy.

Recension: See Textual Criticism.

Recitationes: Public readings by authors of their works. Common in the Empire. Pliny frequently mentions them. The practice appears to have been introduced by Asinius Pollio (q.v.).

Recurrent Verse: There are two types of recurrent verse, which means verse that reads backwards or forwards. The first is the palindrome (q.v.), in which the *letters* are read backwards; in the second, the *words* are read from end to beginning, with no alteration of meter or sense:

> "Praecipiti modo quod decurrit tramite flumen
> Tempore consumptum, iam cito deficiet."

and

> "Deficiet cito iam consumptum tempore flumen
> Tramite decurrit quod modo praecipiti."

This example is by Sidonius Apollinaris, who was also fond of the palindrome.

Reditu Suo, de: See Rutilius Namatianus.

Rege Deiotaro, pro: Speech by Cicero in 45 B.C. to disprove the alleged attempt by Deiotarus, the tetrarch of Galatia, on Caesar's life.

Reginald of Canterbury: 1040?-1109? 11th century poet, author of a Sapphic ode; of a metrical *Life of St. Malchus*; and other miscellaneous poetry.

Reginald von Dassel: Chancellor of Frederic Barbarossa. Mentioned by the Archpoet (q.v.) for his unreasonable demand of an epic on Barbarossa's Italian campaign, to be finished in one week.

Registrum Multorum Auctorum: Catalogue of 80 curriculum authors by Hugh of Trimberg (q.v.).

Regius of Prüm: Author of *De Armonica Institutione; Chronica; De Synodalibus Causis et Disciplinis Ecclesiasticis.*

Regula Pastoralis: See Gregory I.

Regulus (1), M. Atilius: Semi-legendary figure of the Punic War. Sent to Rome to negotiate an exchange of prisoners, he voluntarily returned to Carthage, where he is said to have been tortured and killed. Mentioned as a national hero, and exponent of the *prisca virtus* (q.v.) by Cicero, Horace, and others.

Regulus (2), M. Aquilius: An unscrupulous informer or *delator* in the Neronian period and afterward. Known as "vir malus dicendi imperitus" (the exact opposite of Cato's famous dictum), and hated by Pliny (2) as the biggest rascal on two feet. Wrote a lament on his dead son.

Reichenau: A famous German monastery.

Reinald von Dassel: See Reginald von Dassel (the more usual form of the name).

Reiner of Liége: 12th century writer of biography, history, hagiography, etc. An extremely prolific author, if not an original or significant one. Was fond of making poetical paraphrases of the works of others. (Manitius)

Relatio de Legatione Constantinopolitana: See Liutprand of Cremona.

Religion, Roman: Originally quite different from the Greek anthropomorphic religion. The Roman gods were personifications of the powers of Nature, as Jupiter, the sky, Dianus (Janus) the sun, Diana, the moon, etc. They were worshipped for practical purposes, hence the importance of the Lares (ancestral spirits of the home) and the Penates (keepers of the storehouse). Other important deities were Tellus (Earth), Saturnus (seed), as well as evil divinities that had to be propitiated: Robiga (blight), and Febris (malaria). Religion was a family, rather than a state function in the earliest times. The formulae, prayers, and rituals were very explicitly laid down. The tendency to deify abstractions, like Virtus, Fides, Honor, etc. is a particularly Roman one. The identification with Greek deities and the taking over of the whole body of Greek mythology with the Roman names of the gods, was a relatively late phenomenon, and resulted in a fusion of Greek and Roman, as well as Etruscan, features. (OCD)

Religious Drama: (Medieval) The first Passion, or Chancel, plays were very primitive. In the 9th and 10th centuries, the Saints' Plays were performed, consisting of dramatizations from the lives of the various saints. The Mystery Plays came later (not from *mystery*, but from *mestier*, or trade, as they were performed by the guilds). Each guild would enact the portion of the Old or New Testament most intimately connected with its own trade or function. The term *Miracle Plays* is sometimes used for these. Eventually they were performed on rolling platforms (*Pageants*). Gradually these dramas became more secular until, with the Reformation, they disappeared. However, the Morality Plays (e.g., *Everyman*) persisted in allegorical form.

Remacle d'Ardenne: 1482-1524. French Neo-Latin poet. Wrote epigrams, *Amores,* and a comedy, *Palamedes.*

Remedia Amoris: Work by Ovid on the ways of stifling love and obtaining relief from passion. On the whole, a rather inferior work.

Remigius of Auxerre: A theologian and philosopher of the 9th century. He was a Christian Platonist, a realist, following Eriugena.

Remiremont, Love Council of: See under Council.

Remus: See Romulus.

Renaissance: (Fr. "rebirth"). In addition to the commonly-known Renaissance which began in Italy and gradually spread to France, England, Germany and the Lowlands, there should be noted two other periods of revival and "rebirth." First, the flowering of culture and letters ca. 800 (See Carolingian Renaissance), and second, the period of humanism and enlightenment in the 12th century that centered in the great cathedral schools such as Chartres.

Renatus, P. Vegetius: See Vegetius.

Reposianus: Third century author of an artificial work: *De Concubitu Martis et Veneris.*

Republica, de: A work by Cicero, on political science and the happy life; broadly modeled on Plato's *Republic,* but not very much like that masterpiece. The work except for the famous *Somnium Scipionis* (Dream of Scipio) was lost until 1822, when portions of it were discovered. In addition to Plato, Cicero draws from Aristotle and from Roman history.

Requiem Mass: The Catholic Mass for the dead. Incorporating the famous sequence *Dies Irae* (q.v.), the Requiem has inspired some of the world's greatest religious music (e.g., Mozart, Verdi, Fauré, but not Brahms).

Rerum Natura, de: (see also Lucretius) One of the greatest works in the Latin language. Lucretius' magnificent didactic epic on the atomic theory, and the universe. Based on the works of Epicurus, the poem's chief purpose is to free mankind from the ignorance and fear brought about by superstition and religion. After a beautiful invocation to Venus the life-giver, L. says that the terrors of the mind must be banished by an understanding of the laws of Nature, just as childish fears of the dark disappear with the rays of the sun. He complains of the difficulty of expressing these matters in the inadequate Latin language, and the necessity of inventing new terms to describe the atoms. He then discusses the nature of matter and space, developing the doctrine of "Nothing from nothing," or the Law of Conservation of Matter. He describes the atoms, their movement in the void, their swerve, their combinations; the senses, the soul, the folly of fearing death, the sources of the various natural phenomena; the history of the human race, and the incursions of religion. "Eat, drink, and be merry, for tomorrow we die!" is *not* the motto of Lucretius and the Epicureans; we shall not be hungry and thirsty when we are dead. Concerning the gods, Lucretius is not an out-and-out atheist; the gods exist, but they are powerless to help or harm men. His explanations are always rational and natural, if sometimes improbable. One of the best portions is that dealing with human evolution from the primitive state. The (probably unfinished) work ends with a description of the Plague of Athens, taken bodily out of Thucydides. (Duff, Golden Age)

Res Gestae Divi Augusti: See *Index Rerum Gestarum.*

Res Urbanae: Lost historical work by Varro (1).

Restoration: See Textual Criticism.

Reticus: Bishop of Autun in the early 4th century. Wrote a (lost) commentary on the *Song of Songs.*

Retractations: Late work of St. Augustine (q.v.). Gives a complete chronological catalogue of all his works, correcting the errors in them.

Rettenbacher, Simon: 1634-1706. Austrian-Latin dramatist, professor at Salzburg. Wrote 20 Latin plays.

Reuchlin, J.: 1455-1522. Great humanist and scholar of the

Renaissance. Particularly noteworthy for his work in Hebrew.

Reynardus Vulpes: 13th century version of the beast-epic of Reynard the Fox. Cf. *Ysengrimus.*

Rhadamanthus: Mythological son of Zeus and Europa; judge of the dead in the underworld. Appears as such in Plato, Virgil, etc.

Rhapsodomancy: See *Sortes Virgilianae.*

Rhetor: Teacher of rhetoric, or the equivalent of a college professor. He taught oratory, political science, law, debating. See Education, declamationes, Seneca (1), suasoria, etc.

Rhetoribus, de: Work by Suetonius on professors of rhetoric. Incomplete list of famous teachers.

Rhetoric: Of tremendous importance for the study of Roman education and literature during the Empire. Equivalent of a university education plus law school. The students were given exercises such as *suasoriae, controversiae, declamationes,* etc. (qq.v.). The influence of rhetorical training is most strongly felt in the literature of the Silver Age, when poetry became more prosaic, and prose more poetic. The five parts of rhetoric are: *inventio* (subject-matter), *dispositio* (arrangement), *elocutio* (speaking), *memoria* (learning the speech by memory), and *actio* (delivery). See also Cicero, Quintilian, Oratory, Seneca (1). Cf. Cato's famous definition of the orator as "a good man skilled at speaking."

Rhetorica: (Cicero) See *Inventione, de.*

Rhetorica ad Herennium: A manual on oratory in four books. Previously ascribed to Cicero, and often printed with his works, it is now believed to have been written by Cornificius, a contemporary of Sulla. The work generally follows the Greek models, except that there is much native material introduced, e.g., quotations from Ennius, Plautus, and Pacuvius. Quintilian's quotations from the *Rhetorica* of Cornificius corresponds to our text. The style is not particularly excellent, but the work is important for our knowledge of the history and practice of oratory.

Rhodian: A style of Roman oratory midway between the

florid Asian and the bald, restrained Attic. Cicero's style was
said to be Rhodian (he studied at Rhodes).

Rhopalic verse: A form of affectation in which the first
word of a line of verse has one syllable, the second two, and
so on. The following examples are from Ausonius (q.v.):

"Spes deus aeternae stationis conciliator."

"Lux verbo inductas peccantibus auxiliatrix."

Rhyme in Latin Poetry: In prose, the device of using words
with similar endings (i.e., *homoeoteleuton*) is a favorite with
Cicero. Classical poetry has no rhyme, except accidentally. In
late antiquity, with the change to accentual rather than quantitative verse, rhyme begins to be seen, especially in the hymns
of Ambrose, Prudentius, etc. In the later Middle Ages it
became more frequent, not only in the hymns and sequences,
where leonine rhyme often appears, but in secular poetry as
well. The standard form of goliardic verse is a rhymed
quatrain.

Rhythmical Verse: In late antiquity, the change from a
quantitative verse-form was gradually replaced by one in
which the ictus coincided with the accent of the word, as,
indeed, is the case in modern poetry. The transition can be
seen in such works as the *Pervigilium Veneris*.

Ribbeck, Otto: German classical scholar, known for his
work on Virgil and Juvenal.

Richard of St. Victor: 12th century Scottish scholar, pupil
of Hugh of St. Victor (q.v.). Wrote works on theology, commentaries on the Psalms and Song of Songs, etc.

Richard of Venosa: Early 13th century. Wrote a comedy
De Paulino et Polla.

Richer of Metz: Wrote a poem in praise of his city (*In
Laude Urbis Metensis*) and a *Life of St. Martin*.

Richer of St. Remi: Pupil of Gerbert (q.v.). Author of
Historiae dealing with Karl the Simple and Ludwig IV.
Written in a brisk, interesting style, the work is chiefly interesting for its great emphasis on medical lore, descriptions of ill-
nesses and cures, etc. Richer has a good historical perspective
and a good sense of cause and effect. (Manitius)

Riddles: Never as popular in Latin literature as they were with the more speculative and fun-loving Greeks. Isolated examples appear, e.g., in Petronius, in Varro (quoted by Gellius), etc. In the Middle Ages, however, riddles became more popular. Aldhelm (q.v.) made a collection of 101 riddles in hexameters, based on the collection of the African Symphosius (q.v.). See also *Versus Cuiusdam Scoti,* Tatwine, Eusebius (2), Notker Balbulus.

Ripoll, MS. of: A collection of medieval love-poems.

Ritschl, F.: Great German classical scholar, most famous for his work on Plautus.

Robert II, King of France: 970-1031. A poet and hymnodist of considerable repute.

Robert of Cricklade: Twelfth century author of *Defloratio,* nine books excerpted from Pliny's *Natural History.*

Robert of Melun: d. 1167. Writer of *Sententiae* of the school of St. Victor. Wrote a *Summa Sententiarum* and *Quaestiones de Epistolis Pauli.*

Robert of St. Remi: (or, Robert of Reims) Late 12th century. Wrote a *Historia Hierosolymitana* (q.v.) in prose and perhaps one in verse. The whole question, however, of the identity of the author, as well as whether he wrote either or both of these works, is still moot. (Manitius)

Robert de Sorbon: Great preacher and theologian (1201-1274), founder of the college which bears his name. Author of many sermons. Grammar and dialectic, while they have their uses, he said, should be subordinated to the study of theology.

Roger of Caen: 11th century monk who wrote a long poem *De Contemptu Mundi.*

Roger of Hoveden: Late 12th century author of a *Chronicle* which contains much important material on the Crusades, etc.

Roger of Wendover: d. 1236. English monk. Wrote a Chronicle from the Creation to the year 1235.

Romance: See Novel, Milesian Tales, Petronius, Apuleius.

Romanticism: Romantic influence can most clearly be seen in the Alexandrine school and the Milesian tales (qq.v.).

Petronius, for example, has much of a romantic nature. So have Catullus and even Virgil. The Dido episode of the Aeneid (Book IV) is romantic in concept and execution. Ovid might also be termed a romantic. Many of the comedies of the Middle Ages, as well as those of Plautus and Terence, deal with romantic themes. The *Metamorphoses* of Apuleius is full of romance. See also *Ruodlieb, Waltharius*.

Romanus: See Vergilius, Voconius.

Romanus, C. Julius: Third century grammarian.

Rome: The Third Satire of Juvenal. A bitter and realistic picture of life in a crowded, slum-ridden metropolis. The author describes the current xenophobia (i.e., his own), the all-powerful influence of money, the crowds, the fires, the filth, the danger of robbers, accidents, the noise, etc. etc. He ends with the ironic observation that there is a shortage of iron for agricultural implements, because it is all being used for fetters in the prisons. With a few small changes, the satire could refer to modern London, New York, Shanghai, etc. Cf. Johnson's *London*.

Romoald of Salerno: Wrote *Annales* (middle of the 12th century), beginning with the Creation of the world, drawing on all the usual sources: Bede, Jerome, Einhard, etc. The part dealing with the 11th century is particularly useful, for it uses (lost) Italian sources.

Romulea: The non-sacred verses of Dracontius, including epithalamia, works on Hylas, Orestes, Medea, and others.

Romulus: Legendary founder of Rome, with his brother Remus. Cast out by Amulius, the twins were reared by a she-wolf and found by the shepherd Faustulus. When they came to manhood, they killed Amulius, and made Numitor king. Then they founded their own city, and according to one version of the story, Romulus killed his brother for leaping over the wall.

"Romulus": Author of a collection of fables; a prose paraphrase of the iambics of Phaedrus. See *Fable*.

Roncevaux: (or Roncevalles): Scene of the *Chanson de Roland,* i.e., the disastrous defeat of Roland by the Saracens.

Written in Latin by an unknown poet of the 12th century. See Pseudo-Turpin.

Roscelin: Theologian and philosopher, d. 1120. An early nominalist, perhaps founder of the nominalist school (q.v.).

Roscio Amerino, pro: One of Cicero's earliest speeches.

Roscio Comoedo, pro: Speech by Cicero in defense of the actor Roscius.

Roscius, S.: One of the greatest of comic actors, he kept alive the *togatae* of Atta (q.v.). Defended on a charge of damages by Cicero.

Rubicon: Famous river that flows into the Adriatic; the boundary between Italy proper and Cisalpine Gaul. Caesar's crossing this river in 49 B.C. with his army was the first step in the civil war. Hence the expression, "crossing the Rubicon," i.e., taking an irrevocable step.

Rubrenus Lappa: See Lappa.

Rudbeckius, Johannes: 1581-1646. Swedish scholar; wrote *Logica, Controversiae Logicae.*

Rudens: One of the most romantic comedies of Plautus. The scene is a wild seacoast. The villain Labrax is trying to recover the two girls who have escaped from the wrecked ship. The play has the classic elements of the long-lost daughter, the *gnorismata* or tokens, the recognition scene, the lovers happily united at the end.

Rudolf of St. Trond: b. ca. 1070. Wrote a history of his monastery (*Gesta Abbatum Trudonensium*), and some poetry.

Rue, Dom Charles de la: 1684-1739. French Neo-Latin poet. Author of two tragedies (*Cyrus, Lysimachus*), after Corneille and Seneca.

Rufinus (1): A minister of the emperor Theodosius. A hateful monster, he was killed by a mob at Byzantium. Claudian makes allegorical use of him in the poem *In Rufinum;* as does Alan of Lille in his *Antirufinus,* which depicts the ideal man.

Rufinus (2): A fifth century grammarian. Wrote about the meters of Terence and the orators.

Rufinus (3): Translated Eusebius and Origen into Latin.

Rufius Festus: Author of an abridged history (*Breviarum*), ca. 400.

Rufus, Cluvius: See Cluvius Rufus.

Rufus, Curtius: (or Sulpicius, Rutilius, etc.) See Curtius Rufus, Sulpicius Rufus, Rutilius Rufus, etc.

Rufus, Varius: See Varius Rufus.

Rule of Benedict: See Benedict, St.

Rules: Several works of this name were written, dealing with the Rules for the conduct of monks. Besides the famous Rules of Benedict, Caesarius and Columban have left sets of Rules.

Rullum, in: Speeches by Cicero. The first was delivered to the Senate, the second and third, to the people. The fourth is lost.

Ruodlieb: A romance in Latin verse, written ca. 1050, by an unknown monk of Tegernsee; previously ascribed to Froumond (q.v.).

Ruopert: Late 10th century. Wrote a *Life of St. Adalbert*, full of miracles, legends, etc.

Ruotger: A cleric of Cologne, wrote the *Life of Bruno* (brother of Otto the Great), an encomium in praise of Bruno and the whole royal house. Influenced principally by Sallust, Ruotger quotes from such classical authors as Virgil, Terence, Persius, Juvenal, and from later authors like Prudentius. (Manitius)

Rupert of Deutz: Early 12th century author of historical, exegetical, biographical, theological and philosophical works: Chronicles, commentary on the *Song of Songs*, works on the minor prophets, etc.

Rupert of Liége: Author of an allegorical poem, or series of poems, in which (going back to Horace or even Alcaeus) he pictures the Church as a ship riding the stormy seas. He complains of the unworthiness of the monks, priests, etc.

Rusticitas Latina: The rustic quality, or provincialism, in Latin. Partly the result of Italic dialects (i.e., Oscan and Umbrian) on Latin, partly of the speech of the provinces. Especially marked in the Vulgar Latin of the Empire. The basis of the modern Romance languages.

Rusticius Helpidius: 6th (?) century poet; author of *Carmen de Christi Jesu Beneficiis.*

Rusticus: See Fabius, Arulenus, etc.

Rutilius (1) Lupus: See Lupus.

Rutilius (2) Namatianus: Possibly the last of the pagan poets (5th century). Prays that the Dea Roma will be rejuvenated. Wrote *Itinerarium, De Reditu Suo,* etc.

Rutilius (3) Rufus: Consul 105 B.C. Wrote memoirs, which have not survived.

Sabellico, Marcantonio: 1436-1506. Italian humanist and historian (*Historiae Rerum Venetarum*). Also wrote a universal history in 92 books.

Sabine Women: See Rape of Sabines.

Sabinians: Members of one of the two rival schools of jurisprudence (See Jurisprudence, Sabinus, Proculians). Included Cassius, Gaius, Javolenus, and many others.

Sabinus (1): A minor Augustan poet. He wrote a work modeled on Ovid's *Fasti,* and answers to the *Heroides.*

Sabinus (2) Angelus: 15th century poet who also wrote answers to Ovid's *Heroides* (e.g., Ulysses to Penelope, Paris to Oenone, etc.). These were included in old editions of the *Heroides.*

Sabinus (3), Georg: 1508-1560. German Neo-Latin poet. Wrote elegies, poemata, etc. His Latinity is good.

Sabinus (4) Masurius: A jurist in the Claudian period. His most famous work consisted of three books on the *ius civile.* The Sabinian school took its name from him.

Sacerdos: Third century grammarian, author of our oldest extant Latin grammar.

Sacra Historia: See *Euhemerus.*

Sadoleto, Jacopo, Cardinal: 1477-1547. Italian humanist. Wrote a Ciceronian Latin.

Saevius (or Sevius) Nicanor: Early Roman grammarian, ca. 100 B.C. A famous teacher, he wrote commentaries and a satura.

St. Albans: Famous English monastery. Matthew Paris,

Alexander Neckham, and many others received their training there.

St. Gall: Great German monastery, founded by Irish monks in the 7th century. One of the most important centers of learning, poetry, and music during the early Middle Ages.

St. Victor: Abbey at Marseilles, founded by Cassian. Important for the development of the Sequence (q.v.). Many poets, scholars, etc. are associated with St. Victor, e.g., Adam, Hugh, Andrew, et al.

Sainte-Beuve, C. A.: A great French literary critic.

Sainte-Marthe, Scévole de: 1536-1623. French-Latin poet; author of a didactic poem on the care and feeding of infants (*De Puerorum Educatione*).

Saintsbury, G.: Great British scholar and critic. His *History of Literary Criticism* is a classic.

Saleius Bassus: Wrote epic poetry based on mythology, in the Flavian period.

Salian Hymns: See *Carmina Saliara*.

Salimbene: 1221-ca. 1287. Thirteenth century author of *Chronicles,* cited by Curtius as example of "numerical composition." He writes of ten "infortunia" which befell Frederic II, and adds two more to bring the number up to 12. (Curtius)

Sallust: (C. Sallustius Crispus) 86-35 B.C. Roman historian who was the first Roman completely to abandon the annalistic method and raise the level of history to a literary form. He had a good grasp of causes and party politics, and a philosophical concept of history akin to that of Thucydides, who was his model. He made use of documentary sources, and reveals a sound insight into human psychology, although he is generally considered inferior to Thucydides in profundity. Sallust was popular in the Middle Ages. Works: *Bellum Catilinae,* a terse account of the conspiracy of Catiline, told, however, with a pro-Caesarian bias; *Bellum Jugurthinum,* which, except for chronological difficulties, ranks as a masterpiece of vivid description and character study; *Historiae,* only fragments of which have been preserved. See Pseudo-Sallust for disputed works. Sallust was the inventor of the historical monograph, and was highly praised by Quintilian, Tacitus, and Martial. (OCD)

Salmon, Jean: 1490-1557. French Neo-Latin poet, called the "French Horace."

Salomon: ca. 860-920. Bishop of Constance, Abbot of St. Gall; author and poet.

Salus: Roman goddess, personification of Health, identified with the Greek Hygeia.

Salutati, Coluccio: 1331-1406. Italian humanist; wrote Latin verse, political and philosophical works.

Salvianus (Salvian): ca. 400-470. Presbyter of Marseilles, author of *De Gubernatione Dei,* contrasting the government of God with the corruption of man. Salvian also wrote letters, nine of which are preserved.

Salvius Julianus: Great jurist of the time of Hadrian. Wrote many important works on jurisprudence, including a *Digesta, Responsa, De Ambiguitatibus,* and others. Noted for his clarity of style and precision of exposition.

Sammonicus, Serenus: Author, in Caracalla's time, of *De Medicina Praecepta,* based on Pliny's *Natural History.*

Sampirus of Astorga: Middle of the 11th century. Wrote a chronicle of the Kings of Spain. This was continued by Pelagius of Oviedo in the 12th century.

Samson: 9th century author of an *Apologeticum.*

Sandys, J. E.: Noted British scholar and critic. His *History of Classical Scholarship* is still regarded as definitive. He divided classical scholarship into four main periods: Italian, French, English and Dutch, and German. (See Scholarship)

Sannazaro, Jacopo: Italian humanist and author of the *Piscatory Eclogues,* as well as *De Partu Virginis,* a story of the Incarnation of Christ, which mentions the Fourth, or Messianic Eclogue of Virgil.

Santeul, Jean-Baptiste de: 1630-1697. French-Latin poet; author of hymns. Translated Corneille into Latin. The unofficial poet laureate of Louis XIV.

Santra (1): A Roman writer of tragedies. Little more than his name has survived.

Santra (2): Grammarian, author of a (lost) work *De Antiquitate Verborum.*

Sappho: Perhaps the greatest of the Greek lyric poets. Her works were imitated by Horace and Catullus. The latter, in his poem "ille mi par esse deo videtur," literally translated one of Sappho's odes, using the same meter.

Sarbiewski, Maciej Kazimierz: 1595-1640. Polish-Latin poet, called "Horatius Christianus" because of his imitation of Horace.

Sardus: Minor prose author, ca. 100 A.D., whose works delighted the younger Pliny.

Sasernae: A father and son, both writers on agriculture, whose works were used by Columella (q.v.).

Satira in Mettensis: A satire by an unknown clergyman, written in 1097, against the inhabitants of Metz. In rhymed (sometimes leonine) hexameters. (Manitius)

Satire: The one form of literature that was truly a Roman invention. A highly individualized form, it was never quite the same with any two authors. The name is most plausibly explained as meaning a mixture or hodgepodge (satura), unless it derives from Etruscan *satir* (speech); and it seems to contain elements of the Old Comedy, the Menippean type of satire (q.v.), and the diatribe. The first examples to be noted are in the fragments of Ennius (e.g., the debate between Life and Death, the fable of the Lark, etc.) and of Lucilius, the real inventor of satire, of whom Horace said, "He rubbed the city smartly down with salt." Highet's definition of the Satire is: "a piece of verse, or prose mingled with verse, intended to improve society by mocking its anomalies, and marked by spontaneity, topicality, ironic wit, indecent humor, colloquial language, frequent use of dialogue, constant intrusions of the author's personality, and incessant variety of tone and style." (Highet, OCD). Varro's Menippean satires were without a sting (Lucilius has been compared to the wasp, Varro to the bee, and Horace to the dragon-fly), and were in the nature of a sugar-coating for his philosophy, as Cicero used the

dialogue and Lucretius the epic. Horace's satires are genial
commentaries on types (the "Bore"), human ambition, city
and country life, etc. Seneca's *Apocolocyntosis* differs from
the foregoing in its great bitterness against Claudius. The
satires of Persius are crabbed, obscure, and full of Stoic
philosophy. The *Satyricon* of Petronius is directed mainly
against the pretensions of the nouveaux-riches. Perhaps the
greatest master of satire is Juvenal, who felt that he was
impelled to use this form ("difficile est saturam non scribere,"
i.e., the difficulty is *not* to write satire), and whose satires are
marked by the same kind of gloomy bitterness that characterize the works of Swift. (See Satires, Juvenal.) Claudian's
"satires" are not really satires, any more than are Cicero's
Philippics. In addition to works of soi-disant satire, other
authors, e.g., Lucretius, often made use of satirical material.

In the Middle Ages, mention should be made of Matthew
de Vendôme, Bernard de Morlaix, Nigel Wireker's *Mirror of
Fools,* John of Hanville and especially, the poems of the
Goliardic poets, Hugh Primas, the Archpoet, *Carmina Burana,*
Apocalypse of Golias, etc., which are frequently full of satire
and invective. In the Renaissance, Erasmus' *Praise of Folly,*
and the *Epistulae Obscurorum Virorum* are further examples.
See under individual works and authors herein mentioned.
See also, *Ysengrimus,* Amarcius, Arnulf (3), *Satira in Metten-
sis.* (Duff, Golden and Silver Ages, OCD)

Satire, Menippean: See Menippean Satire.

Satires: (Horace) Horace's satires are marked by a cheer-
ful, tolerant urbanity, and are completely without the political
invective of Lucilius on the one hand, and the vitriol of
Juvenal on the other. Some subjects are: the Bore; a Journey
to Brundisium; the Praise of Country Life, containing the fable
of the Town and Country Mouse, the former an Epicurean
type, the latter a Stoic; the Folly of Ambition, etc. There is
little or no personal invective here, but rather, commentaries
on universal types and foibles, and above all, revelation of
Horace himself. The hexameters are smooth.

Satires: (Juvenal) On the whole, they are marked by bitterness, irony, and gloom. Unlike those of Horace, Juvenal's satires tell us little of himself. Among topics he treats are: philosophical hypocrisy, patronage, women, genealogies, corruption, the over-emphasis on money, and many others. The best are III (*Rome*, q.v.), VI, on Women, and X (*The Vanity of Human Wishes*, q.v.).

Satisfacio: An elegiac poem written by Dracontius (q.v.) in prison, asking forgiveness of God and king.

Satrius Rufus: A rhetor of the first century, mentioned by Pliny the Younger.

Satura: (See Satire) A medley or hodgepodge; the satire. Another explanation for the origin is the Etruscan "satir" or speech.

Saturio: A lost play of Plautus.

Saturn: One of the oldest of Roman deities. The father of Jupiter, identified with the Greek Kronos. The festival of the Saturnalia was in his honor.

Saturnalia: 1. See Macrobius.

2. See Lucan.

Saturnian verse: The native Italian meter, used in the older poets' works, but replaced by the hexameter (Ennius). Example:

Dabúnt malúm Metélli// Naévió poétae

cf. "The quéen was ín the párlor,// eáting bréad and hóney." (Macauley's famous example.) Actually, we do not know how this verse was scanned.

Satyricon: The great picaresque novel of Petronius. In form a Menippean Satire (q.v.), it tells of the adventures of Encolpius and his friends, and is full of stories, episodes, Milesian tales, literary criticism, social satire, and interspersed with poetic fragments. There is much indecency and coarseness. The *Satyricon* might be called the spiritual ancestor of Rabelais and Fielding. Especially interesting is the use of the *sermo plebeius* (q.v.). The Banquet of Trimalchio is the central portion, telling of the sumptuous dinner of the nouveau-riche, the outlandish dishes, the abysmal ignorance, the complete emphasis on money. There are large lacunae in the work.

Saxo Grammaticus: A Dane, b. ca. 1150. Wrote a history

of the Danes (*Historia Danorum*) in 16 books. It smacks of
the rhetorical style of a Valerius Maximus. (Manitius)

Scaeva Memor: A tragedian in the reign of Domitian. We
have titles of some of his works (e.g., *Hercules, Hecuba*).

Scaevola, C. Mucius: Legendary hero of Roman antiquity.
Rather than betray military secrets to the Etruscan Porsenna,
he held his right hand in the fire until it was burned off, hence,
by popular etymology, the name Scaevola, or "Lefty."

Scaevola, Q. Mucius: Great jurist and orator, ca. 100 B.C.
Murdered by Marius. He wrote the first systematic treatment
of civil law, wills, damages, court procedures, inheritance, etc.
and is thus the founder of a long tradition in civil law. See
Jurisprudence.

Scaliger: Father (Julius) and son (Joseph). Both great
French classical scholars.

Scauro, pro: Speech of Cicero, 57 B.C.

Scaurus (1), Aemilius: Wrote memoirs, second century
B.C.

Scaurus (2), Mamercus: Orator during the reign of
Tiberius, criticized by Seneca (1) for his laziness. Wrote a
tragedy, *Atreus*, which, together with his friendship for the
ill-fated Sejanus, led to his downfall.

Scaurus (3), Terentius: Grammarian of the second century. His *Ars Grammatica* is now lost, but the *Liber de
Orthographia* attributed to him may well be genuine. He also
wrote a commentary on Horace.

Scazons: "Limping iambics," introduced by Matius, used
by Catullus ("Misér Catúlle, désinás inéptíre") and other
poets. The first five feet are iambics, the sixth is a trochee.

Schanz-Hosius-Krüger: The most comprehensive history of
Roman Literature to the time of Justinian. See *Handbuch der
klassischen Altertumswissenschaft.*

Scholarship, in antiquity: See Grammar, Learned and technical prose, Isagogic works. Early scholars were Stilo, Varro
(1), Cicero, Valerius Cato, and Nigidius Figulus. In the
Augustan Age: Hyginus, Fenestella, Verrius Flaccus. The first
systematic grammar was by Palaemon. See also Quintilian,

Probus, Suetonius, Gellius, Festus, Solinus, Nonius, Donatus, Jerome, Macrobius, Boethius, Martianus Capella.

Scholarship, Classical, in Modern Times: Sandys' division into the four periods (Italian, French, English-Dutch, and German) still may serve as a rough outline. Little more can be done here than a mere mention of some of the outstanding names of modern classical scholarship. The Italian period begins with the Renaissance and includes Petrarch, Valla, Politian, Ficino, etc. The earliest printed editions of classical texts belong to this period. The French period begins in the 16th century with such names as Budé, Scaliger, Casaubon, Lipsius, Salmasius, Heinsius. The English group consists of Porson, Bentley, Holland, Dryden. The German school, in the 19th century, includes Lachmann, Ribbeck, Reuchlin, Müller, and such gigantic works as Pauly-Wissowa, Müllers *Handbuch,* Bursians *Jahresbericht,* Mommsen and Wilamowitz, Boeckh and Jacobs; and in the 20th century, Christ, Schmid, Stahlin, Buecheler, Diels, Meyer, Leo, and others. Modern British scholars include Housman, Conington, Munro, Palmer, Postgate, Bury, Sandys, Jebb, Leaf, etc. American scholarship has contributed such names as Gildersleeve, Rand, Pease, Goodwin, Gulick, Shorey, Tenney Frank, Shipley, etc. (OCD, Sandys)

Scholarship, Medieval: See Scholasticism, Boethius, Isidore, Cassiodorus, Martianus Capella, Aldhelm, Bede, Alcuin, the Carolingian Renaissance, Anselm, John Eriugena, John of Salisbury.

Scholastica Historia: Encyclopedia of Biblical history by Peter Comestor (q.v.).

Scholastics or Schoolmen: Generally speaking, a group who applied the logic of Aristotle and the sophists to Christian theology. Denotes a narrow, rather than a humanistic study of the Classics. Albertus Magnus and Aquinas in the 13th century represent the full flowering of scholasticism, to which should be added such names as John Eriugena, Anselm, Abelard, Hugh of St. Victor, etc. Boethius has often been called the first of the Schoolmen.

Scholia: Notes preserved in the margins of texts. Include the *lemma* (a word or phrase from some author with the interpretation), *gloss* or separate word, and *commentary*, a continuous passage of explanation or exegesis. The scholia go back to the third century.

Schools: See Education.

Schoon of Gouda: 16th century author of six "Terentian" plays on Biblical subjects (cf. Hroswitha). The plays, a strange mixture of sacred and profane, are on the following subjects: *Naaman, Tobaeus, Nehemias, Saulus, Josephus,* and *Juditha.*

Schwarzerd: (Schwarzert) See Melanchthon.

Scipio the Younger: See Literary circles, patronage.

Scipio Nasica: An early Roman jurist.

Scipio: Title of a work, perhaps a *satura,* by Ennius.

Scipionic Circle: Included all the greatest minds of the mid-second century B.C., for instance, Laelius, Terence, Lucilius, etc.

Scotist, Scotism: Follower of, or teachings of Duns Scotus (q.v.).

Scotus: Medieval agnomen signifying Irish or Scottish. See Duns Scotus (a Scot), John Scotus Eriugena (Irish), Sedulius of Liége, Josephus Scottus, etc.

Scribonius Largus: Court physician to the emperor Claudius. Author of *Compositiones* or prescriptions.

Scripturarum Claves: See Ebarcius of St. Amand.

Scriverius, Petrus: 1576-1660. Dutch scholar and Latin poet. Wrote *Saturnalia* (A Latin eulogy on tobacco). Friend of Heinsius (q.v.).

Scrofa, Cn. Tremellus: Early writer on agriculture, used by Varro, Pliny, and Columella.

Scylla: In mythology, 1. A monster in the Odyssey.

2. Daughter of Nisus, who steals his lock of hair. See *Ciris.*

Secundus: See Pliny (1) and (2), Julius Secundus, Pomponius.

Secundus, Janus: 1511-1536. Neo-Latin poet. Wrote *Basia, Elegies, Odes, Epistolae, Funera, Itineraria,* etc.

Sedigitus, Volcatius: Quoted by Gellius as listing the ten best Roman authors of comedy, as follows: Caecilius Statius,

Plautus, Naevius, Licinius, Atilius, Terence, Turpilius, Trabea, Luscius Lanuvinus, and Ennius, admitted only because he is so old! The modern "Ten-Best" craze is thus not without classical precedents.

Sedulius (1): Mid 5th-century author of *Carmen Paschale*, on the life of Christ, and a prose version of the same work, *Opus Paschale*. Sedulius was one of the first authors to use rhyme consciously.

Sedulius (2) of Liége: Also known as Sedulius Scotus. Ninth-century Irish scholar, poet, and philosopher, author of commentaries on the Psalms, lyric and satirical poetry, and a poetical debate or *Streitgedicht* between the Lily and the Rose.

Sejanus: A powerful personage who was executed by Tiberius for treason. Used by Juvenal as proverbial for "the mighty fallen." See "Vanity of Human Wishes."

Sellyng, William: d. 1494. Early English humanist. Famous for his Latin orations.

Seneca, L. Annaeus (1) ("The Elder"): Born in Corduba, Spain in 55 B.C. Lived nearly a century. Composed the *Suasoriae* and *Controversiae* in his old age, relying on a prodigious memory. An old-fashioned Roman of the type of Cato, he deplored the new-fangled education and moral decadence of his day. His works are chiefly interesting for their significance in the history of education, and for the many anecdotes with which they are interlarded, and they are the *locus classicus* for the Roman educational system. Seneca is the link between the Golden and Silver Ages, bridging the century between Cicero and Claudius.

Seneca, L. Annaeus (2) ("The Younger"): Second son of Seneca (1). One of the most versatile of Latin authors, he was a philosopher, poet, dramatist, essayist, natural scientist and satirist. He came to Rome as a child, and quickly was won over to Stoic philosophy, which remained his first love. Exiled to Corsica by Claudius for immorality, he was recalled and made tutor to the young Nero. During the five years of his influence, Nero's reign was milder than at any other time. Even so, there were murders, which Seneca had to justify or condone. He was forced to commit suicide in 65 as a result of the Pisonian conspiracy. Tacitus tells beautifully the story of his death. He left a huge fortune at his death, and there is something rather paradoxical about this wealthy Stoic, who could not or would not practice what he preached.

Accused by his detractors (e.g. Rose) of being a moral coward, he is hardly deserving of their scorn and loathing. The extenuating circumstances of the times must be considered, as well as Seneca's own, highly neurotic personality. He was aware of his own shortcomings. (cf. his phrase "peccavimus omnes")

Works: Philosophical: Dialogues *De Providentia, De Constantia Sapientiae, De Ira, De Vita Beata, De Otio, De Tranquillitate Animi, De Brevitate Vitae,* and the *Consolations* to Marcia, Helvia, and Polybius; *De Clementia, De Beneficiis,* and 124 *Epistulae Morales.* Scientific: Seven books of *Quaestiones Naturales.* Satirical: *Apocolocyntosis Divi Claudii* (q.v.). Plays: *Hercules Furens, Hercules Oetaeus, Troades, Phoenissae, Medea, Phaedra, Oedipus, Thyestes,* and *Agamemnon.* Lost or fragmentary works on geography, astronomy, fish, superstitions, customs of the Egyptians, speeches, letters, etc.

His prose style is clear but not ornate. His writing is full of blemishes, which Quintilian says are his greatest charm. Seneca created the philosophical essay, and ranks with Montaigne and Bacon. His influence was great and varied, upon such figures as Juvenal and Tacitus, Tertullian and Lactantius, Jerome, and others. His plays are full of rhetoric and frigid mythology, and were obviously never intended for performance. They are mostly indebted to Euripides, but fall far short of the works of the Greek dramatist. Even so, they contain some rather fine passages, speeches, and are good in their psychological insight. The *Troades* is perhaps the best. The philosophy of the Stoics, modified by Roman common sense, is found in most of his works, and had a profound influence on early Christianity. His poetry, in the *Anthologia Latina,* consists mostly of elegiac pieces, not bad, but not spectacular.

Above all, he is known for his proverbs or *sententiae*. His language is partly literary, partly plebeian. In the field of drama, Seneca forms a bridge between Greek and modern drama, and is necessary for an understanding of Corneille, Racine, and Shakespeare. (Duff, Silver Age, OCD)

Seneca (3) "Grandio": A rhetor, mentioned by Seneca (1).

Senectute, de: Dialogue by Cicero on old age. One of his most charming works.

Sententiae: Little proverbs or maxims, tersely expressed. Horace was a master of the form, and was highly prized for his *sententiae* in the Middle Ages, as was Ovid. Seneca is also known for his *sententiae*. See also the *Disticha Catonis*.

Sententiae: Theological work by Isidore of Seville (q.v.). See also Peter Lombard.

Septimius, L.: Translated the "Trojan Diary" of Dictys Cretensis into Latin.

Septimius, P.: Author of a lost treatise on architecture, used by Vitruvius.

Septimius Serenus: A minor poet of the age of Hadrian, one of the "neoterici" (q.v.).

Sepúlveda, Juan Ginés de: 1490?-1573. Spanish humanist and historian. Attacked Erasmus and Las Casas. His Latinity was excellent.

Sequence (Sequentia): A musical term, referring to the music of the prolonged final "a" of the Alleluia, and the text adapted to this melody. Its invention is ascribed to Notker Balbulus, who is supposed to have developed the text to facilitate the memorization of the long series of notes. For important sequences see *Dies Irae, Stabat Mater*.

Serenus, Annaeus: Pupil of the younger Seneca (2), and recipient or addressee of some of the latter's philosophical essays (*De Constantia Sapientiae, de Otio, de Tranquillitate Animi*).

Sergius: Author of *Explanationes in Donatum* (4th century). Often confused with Servius.

Serius Augurinus: See Augurinus.

Serlo of Bayeux: 12th century author and satirist. Wrote in leonine hexameters on the Council of Clermont.

Serlo of Fontain: Wrote various grammatical works: *De Differentiis Verborum: De Dictionibus Disyllabis,* etc. Also a didactic epic, *De Dictionibus Aequivocis.*

Serlo of Wilton: English scholar of the mid-12th century. One of the "Wandering Scholars." A great teacher and logician. Became a monk in the Cistercian monastery at L'Aumone in 1171. (Waddell)

Sermo cotidianus: The everyday speech of the educated Roman. Cicero's letters are a good example.

Sermo plebeius: The speech of the common people. Found in such authors as Petronius. Certain differences of vocabulary, e.g., "caballus" for "equus," foreshadow the development of the Romance Languages.

Sermo rusticus: The everyday language of the farmers. Like the *sermo plebeius,* but not of the city.

Sermones: See *Satires* and *Epistles,* Horace.

Serranus: Minor epic poet of the Neronian Age.

Servasius, Sulpicius Lupercus: 4th century poet. We have a Sapphic ode *De Venustate* and an elegiac poem *De Cupiditate* of his.

Servatus Lupus: Abbot of Ferrières, d. 862. A humanist who made a great collection of manuscripts of classical texts.

Servetus, Michael: Sixteenth century heretic and anti-Trinitarian. Wrote *De Trinitatis Erroribus* and *Christianismi Restitutio.* He was burned at the stake in Geneva in 1553.

Servilius Nonianus: Minor historian under the emperor Claudius. Wrote of recent and contemporary history.

Servius: ca. 400 A.D. One of the greatest of ancient grammarians and commentators. He had a wide knowledge of history and literature. In addition to various works on meters, etc., his chief work is the great commentary on Virgil, which relies partly on the earlier commentary of Donatus.

Servius Clodius: See Clodius.

Sestio, pro: Speech by Cicero, in defense of Sestius, who was charged with *vis* (public violence).

Setina: Title of a play by Titinius.

Severus (1), Cassius: An outspoken orator of the Augustan Age. His books were burned and he was exiled. This shows the stifling effect of the Empire on oratory, which soon degenerated to the point of rhetorical exercises.

Severus (2), Cornelius: Augustan poet who wrote an epic on the *Bellum Siculum.*

Severus (3), Septimius: Grandfather of the emperor. A famous rhetor.

Severus (4), Sulpicius: ca. 360-410. Author of a Life of St. Martin, which was later versified by Paulinus of Périgueux, and still later by Fortunatus (qq.v.).

Seville, Isidore of: See Isidore.

Sextii: Father and son were both philosophers and teachers.

Sextus: Author of a collection of *sententiae* or "gnomes," translated into Latin by Rufinus, who called the work *Anulus.*

Shepreve, John: 1509-1542. Oxford scholar and Latin poet of great renown.

Ship of State: A favorite allegorical subject or cliché. Horace wrote an ode in imitation of one by the Greek poet Alcaeus on this topic. See also Rupert of Liége and cf. Whitman's "O Captain, my Captain."

Shorthand: Cicero's freedman Tiro invented a system of shorthand or tachygraphy (*Notae Tironianae*).

Sibyl: Latin name for a prophetess. The Cumaean Sibyl appears in Virgil (*Aeneid* and *Eclogues,* IV). The Messianic interpretation of the latter gives the Sibyl a place in Christian literature and art, so that she appears in the famous sequence *Dies Irae,* as prophesying the Last Judgment, as well as in Michelangelo's Sistine Chapel.

Sibylline Books: Ancient books of prophecies, inscribed on palm leaves. Many forgeries were circulated. The official collection was burned in time of Stilicho.

Sic et Non: ("Yes and No") See Abelard.

Siculus, Calpurnius: See Calpurnius Siculus.

Siculus Flaccus: 2nd century writer on gromatics, or surveying.

Sidonius Apollinaris: Fifth century author of nine books of letters modeled on those of Pliny; traditional panegyrics; and poems. The latter reveal all sorts of mannered artificiality, much mythological allusion. As a poet, Sidonius was mediocre. As an indication of the literature of the fifth century, he is important.

Sigebert (1) of Gembloux: One of the more important authors of the 11th-12th centuries. Chiefly active in the fields of biography and history. Wrote biography of Dietrich, bishop of Metz, Wicbert, and a *De Viris Illustribus.* Also a *Chronicle* beginning with the year 381, and hagiographic writings.

Sigebert (2) of Liége: 1030-1112. 11th century lyric poet.

Sigehard: Middle of the 10th century. Wrote a life of Maximinus, or rather, an appendix to the life by Lupus of Ferrières (q.v.) of that saint, telling of the miracles he worked after his death. Written in a lively, graphic style. Later translated into elegiac verse-form as rubrics for a series of paintings (11th century).

Siger of Brabant: 13th century philosopher and Averroist (q.v.).

Silius Italicus, Ti. Catius: 25/6-101. An informer under Nero; proconsul of Asia. Loved Virgil so much that he made religious pilgrimages to that poet's tomb in Naples. A true Stoic, Silius starved himself to death because he had an incurable disease. Silius is the author of the *Punica,* an epic in 17 books on the Second Punic War, which has the distinction of being the longest poem in the Latin language. Pliny the Younger says of Silius that he wrote "maiore cura quam ingenio" (with more pains than genius); and he is, in fact, a diligent but uninspired writer. His chief literary models were Virgil and Lucan, but he is sadly inferior even to the latter of these. See *Punica.* (Duff, Silver Age)

Silius Proculus: Minor poet, contemporary of Pliny the Younger.

Silo, Gavius: Spanish rhetor mentioned by the elder Seneca.

Silus, Albucius: See Albucius.

Silvae: Collection of miscellaneous verses by Statius (q.v.).

Some deal with: sleep, the birthday of the dead Lucan, a complaint to Domitian, a parrot. Some of the poetry is nice, most of it is rather artificial. Duff calls them "hothouse blooms." Silvae, or Sylvae, remained until the Renaissance a term for miscellaneous verses. (Duff, OCD)

Silvanus: Italian god of the forest or any uncultivated land. Actually Silvanus is an epithet, rather than a name. He was identified with Pan and the Greek satyrs.

Silver Age: Followed the Golden Age of literature. The usual limits are from the reign of Tiberius to that of Hadrian (A.D. 14-138), although the latter limit is sometimes stretched. For characteristics, see Silver Latinity. In general, the philosophy was stoic, the oratory consisted of literary exercises, rather than speeches, which were much too dangerous, unless they were epideictic or show-pieces. Provincial influences became more marked, especially Spain, Gaul and Africa. The Silver Age ends in increasing sterility, conscious archaisms, and the "elocutio novella" (q.v.). Poetry becomes either very long (Silius) or very short (Martial): there is more of a tendency to extremes. However, silver has a glow of its own, even if it does not shine so brightly as gold. (Duff)

Silver Latinity: The best authors of the Silver Age are Tacitus and Petronius, Juvenal, Pliny (2) and Martial. Silver Latinity is characterized by: great range in quality and subject matter; increasing influence of rhetoric and declamation, resulting in more poetic prose, and more prosaic poetry; a good deal of artificiality, allusiveness, circumlocution and frigid mythology; a tendency toward the grotesque; changes both in syntax and vocabulary; a propensity to extremes (very long works, like the *Punica* and the *Natural History* on one hand, very short ones like Martial's epigrams, on the other); and much miscellaneous learning (Celsus, Mela, Columella, Suetonius, Frontinus, etc.).

Silvestris, Bernard: See Bernard Silvestris.

Simony: See Guido of Arezzo, Humbert, Bruno, et al. for works dealing with this practice, which may be defined as the purchase or sale of ecclesiastical preferment.

Simon Aurea Capra: (or Chèvre d'Or) 12th century author of an abbreviated *Aeneid,* and a Latin *Iliad.*

Simulans: A play by Afranius (q.v.), in 57 B.C. A performance of this play caused a political demonstration during which Clodius (q.v.) was driven from the theater.

Sinnius Capito: See Capito.

Siro: An Epicurean philosopher; teacher of Virgil.

Sisebut: King of the Visigoths 612-620. Wrote poetry on the eclipses of the sun and the moon; letters; biography.

Sisenna (1), L. Cornelius: 119-67 B.C. A historian of the Sullan era. Also translated Milesian tales into Latin.

Sisenna (2): A Plautine commentator.

Sisyphus: Title of an Atellan farce (q.v.). Presumably a parody or satire on the well-known mythological figure who is shown in Tartarus pushing a giant stone uphill, which, when it reaches the top, rolls downhill again.

Situ Orbis, de: See Pomponius Mela.

Situ Urbium Italiarum, de: See Hyginus (1).

Smaragdus of St. Mihiel: Ninth century author of a didactic poem on grammar.

Smyrna: See *Zmyrna,* Cinna.

Sobrietate, de: Didactic poem by Milo of St. Amand (q.v.).

Solimarius: Epic on the Crusades by an unknown author; a versification of the Historia Hierosolymitana by Robert of Reims (or Robert of St. Remi). Written in the latter part of the 12th century.

Solinus, C. Julius: Third century epitomizer. Wrote a *Collectanea Rerum Memorabilium,* or geographical description of the world. It is all taken from Pliny and Mela. Solinus was the first to call the Mediterranean Sea by that name.

Somnium Scipionis: "The Dream of Scipio"—Part of Cicero's philosophical work *De Republica*—an imitation of Plato's *Vision of Er.* The only part, in fact, of the *Republica* that was known until Cardinal Mai's discovery of the famous palimpsest in 1822.

Sorbon, Robert de: See Robert de Sorbon.

Sortes Virgilianae: (or Biblicae, etc.) The medieval use of Virgil (or the Bible) as a magical source of prophecy. A person would consult these books at random for prophetic advice. This practice is called bibliomancy or rhapsodomancy.

Sosii: Well-known Roman booksellers, mentioned by Horace.

Sota: Title of a lost work by Ennius.

Spain: Birthplace of many Roman authors; e.g., the Senecas, Lucan, Pomponius Mela, Quintilian, Columella, Martial, Prudentius, Orosius, Isidore, etc.

Spartianus, Aelius: See Aelius Spartianus.

Spectacula: See *Liber Spectaculorum.*

Spectaculis, de: Book by Tertullian, modeled on Suetonius.

Speculum: (Lat. "mirror"). A favorite metaphorical title in the Middle Ages (cf. *Speculum Stultorum, Speculum Regum,* etc.).

Speculum Naturale, Historiale, Doctrinale: See Vincent of Beauvais.

Speculum Regum: See Godfrey of Viterbo.

Speculum Stultorum: See Nigel Wireker.

Spelman, Sir Henry: 1564-1641. English historian and lawyer; wrote on church history and jurisprudence.

Spinoza, Benedict: 1632-1677. This great philosopher wrote chiefly in Latin (*Ethica, Tractatus, De Intellectus Emendatione,* etc.).

Spiritalis Historiae Gestis, de: See Avitus.

Spiritu Sancto, de: See Ambrose.

Spurinna, Vestricius: A lyric poet of the Vespasian period.

Stabat Mater: One of the most beautiful of the medieval Sequences, it grew out of the Franciscan veneration of Mary. It has been attributed to everyone from Gregory the Great to Bernard of Clairvaux. Perhaps the most plausible attribution is to Jacopone da Todi. The Stabat Mater has inspired some of the most beautiful of church music (e.g., by Palestrina, Pergolesi, Haydn, and Rossini).

Staberius Eros: Famous teacher of Brutus and Cassius.

Stabili, Francesco: 1269-1327. Italian poet. Wrote (in Latin) on astrology.

Stadiasmus Maris Magni: A fourth-century account of the Mediterranean, its coasts, harbors, peoples, distances, etc.

Starowolski, Szymon: d. 1656. Polish-Latin writer; wrote polemics against the detractors of Poland, and a survey of Polish literature.

Statius (1) P. Papinius: ca. 45-96. Silver Age author of epic and occasional poetry. Works (qq.v.): *Thebaid, Achilleid, Silvae.* Lost works include an *Agave* and an epic on the German campaigns of Domitian. Statius was a man of considerable learning and great appreciation of beauty. He was not above flattery of the emperor Domitian. His non-mentioning of Martial and the latter's reciprocation argue a mutual dislike. Statius' verses are smooth and polished, and full of Virgilian echoes. He was popular in the Middle Ages, and Dante places him in Purgatory with Lucan and Horace, and regards him as a Christian. He was also very popular with Chaucer. (Duff, Silver Age)

Statius (2) Ursulus: Gallic rhetor, mentioned by Jerome, and confused with Statius (1), who is therefore sometimes called Sursulus (cf. Agellius for A. Gellius, etc.).

Statius (3), Caecilius: See Caecilius Statius.

Stella, Arruntius: Poet, contemporary of Statius. He wrote passionate love-poetry to one Violentilla, which seems to have been successful, for she later became his wife. He was a patron of both Martial and Statius.

Stemmatics: See Textual Criticism.

Stephan of Rouen: Monk of the monastery of Bec. Wrote an elegiac poem on the death of the King's son-in-law; an historical epic (*Draco Normannicus*) about the Normans on French soil—of historical importance; and other miscellaneous poetry.

Stephanus: (Father and son, Robert and Henri Estienne). Sixteenth century French scholars. Authors of the *Thesaurus Linguae Latinae* (Robert), the *Thesaurus Graecae Linguae* (Henri), and of many editions of classical texts.

Stephen: Italian poet, ca. 700. Wrote a rhythmical poem, containing reminiscences of the *Aeneid.*

Stephen of Tournai: Abbot of St. Genevieve in 1176; bishop of Tournai 1192-1203. Wrote poetry and letters, in which he complained of the sad state of learning in Paris.

Stertinius: Augustan philosopher who is said to have written 220 books on Stoic philosophy.

Stichus: A comedy by Plautus. Two "grass widows" are awaiting the return of their husbands. The parasite Gelasimus, is a familiar type.

Stilicho: Gothic general eulogized by Claudian (q.v.).

Stilo, Aelius: See Aelius Stilo.

Stoicism: A school of philosophy advocating self-sufficiency, fortitude, and philosophic indifference. Founded by Zeno of Citium, taught by Posidonius and Panaetius, it had an important and enduring effect on Roman literature. Cicero's works are deeply influenced, as are those of Virgil, Seneca, Lucan, and many others. There is a good deal of Stoicism in the works of the early Christian writers. The emperor Marcus Aurelius was a Stoic philosopher, and wrote, in Greek, a book of *Meditations.*

Strabo, C. Julius Caesar: Tragic poet and orator, d. 87 B.C. None of his works has survived.

Strabo, Walafrid: See Walafrid Strabo.

Stratagems: (*Stratagematon Libri iii*) Book by Frontinus, illustrating various principles of warfare, tactics, strategy, by examples from Greek and Roman history. The work is, on the whole, quite readable. It is roughly arranged according to strategy before, during, and after the battle. The authenticity of the fourth book, with examples of justice, discipline, restraint, etc., has been challenged (see Pseudo-Frontinus).

Streitgedicht: A poetical debate. These were extremely common in the 12th-13th centuries, and, indeed, even in late antiquity. See Vespa (Cook and Baker), *Conflictus Veris et Hiemis,* Sedulius Scottus, etc. Other topics for these debates are: *Wine and Water; Wine and Beer; Summer and Winter;*

Ganymede and Helen; Acis and Polyphemus; Body and Soul; Justice and Mercy; Man and Death; Jew and Christian; Fortune and Philosophy; Flora and Phyllis; the King of France and the King of England; the *Poor Scholar and the Rich Man;* and many others. (Manitius)

Stress-accent: See accent.

Stromateus: See Caesellius Vindex.

Studiosi iii Libri: ("the Student") Lost work by the elder Pliny, on the education of an orator. Quintilian said that it contained much wisdom, but also much superstition.

Suarez, Francisco: 1548-1617. Spanish Jesuit, founder of a school which bears his name. His chief work: *Disputationes Metaphysicae.*

Suasoria: A rhetorical exercise, see Seneca (1) or deliberation. Usually taken from history or mythology, e.g., Agamemnon debates whether he should sacrifice Iphigenia; Alexander debates whether he shall cross the ocean; etc.

"Subtle Doctor": See Duns Scotus.

Sueius: A writer of idyllic poetry. Possibly (Ribbeck) the same as Seius, a friend of Cicero and Varro.

Suetonius Tranquillus, C.: ca. 69-140. Roman biographer of the Caesars (See Lives of the Caesars). Lost works by Suetonius include: Games and Spectacles, the Roman Year, on Proper Names, on Cicero's Republic, On Abusive Terms, on Blemishes, on Manners and Customs, on Eminent Courtesans, etc. Suetonius' influence on later biographers was tremendous. 700 years later, Einhard used him as a model for his Life of Charlemagne. The style of S. is chatty, informal, and pleasant. Also surviving is the section *De Grammaticis et Rhetoribus* from his work *De Viris Illustribus.*

Suffenus: See Alfenus Varus.

Suger: ca. 1081-1151. French clergyman and historian. Wrote panegyrics, and architectural descriptions.

Sulla, L. Cornelius: 138-78 B.C. Aside from his military and civil exploits, the dictator wrote verses, and memoirs, or

Commentarii Rerum Suarum, in 23 books, which were completed on his death by his freedman Epicadus.

Sulla, pro: Speech by Cicero.

Sulpicia (1): Poetess, niece of Messalla. Author of six elegies in the *Corpus Tibullianum.*

Sulpicia (2): Poetess who wrote erotic verses in the Flavian period.

Sulpiciae Fabella: A satire of uncertain date, ascribed to Sulpicia (2).

Sulpicius (1) Apollinaris: Second century author, teacher of Aulus Gellius. Wrote verse summaries of the *Aeneid,* and the metrical summaries, or "arguments" for the plays of Terence.

Sulpicius (2) Blitho: See Blitho.

Sulpicius (3) Camerinus, Q.: A minor epic poet of the Augustan Age.

Sulpicius (4) Galba: Noted orator of the mid-second century B.C.

Sulpicius (5), Servius: Augustan poet, author of love-lyrics. The son (or grandson?) of Sulpicius (6).

Sulpicius (6) Rufus, Servius: Most illustrious authority on jurisprudence of the Ciceronian Age; a friend of Cicero, and author of a famous letter to the orator (Fam, 4.5), a consolation on the death of Tullia, his daughter.

Sulpicius (7) Severus: See Severus.

Summa: An exposition, or comprehensive treatment of a subject. Cf. *Summa Theologica* (Aquinas).

Summa Aurea: See William of Auxerre.

Summa contra Gentiles: See Thomas Aquinas.

Summa Sacramentorum: Work attributed to Hugh of St. Victor (q.v.).

Summa Theologica: See Thomas Aquinas.

Summa Universae Theologicae: See Alexander of Hales.

"Summum Bonum": The highest good; a subject of much philosophical speculation, cf. Cicero, *De Finibus.*

Sunesen, Anders: 1167-1228. Chiefly remembered for his poem on Creation, the *Hexaemeron* (cf. Prudentius).

Supplementum: See May, Thomas.

Sura, Licinius: See Licinius Sura.

Surianus: The "Archbishop" of the Wandering Scholars (q.v.), author of a remarkable document, parodying Eberhard II of Salzburg. (Waddell)

Suso, Henry: ca. 1295-1366. A German mystic, author of an autobiography and a Book of Heavenly Wisdom.

Sussaneau, Hubert: b. 1512. French Neo-Latin poet. Wrote on the siege of Peronne; epigrams; grammatical and critical works.

Swedenborg, Emanuel: 1688-1772. Swedish scientist, philosopher, and mystic. Wrote many important works: *Opera Philosophica et Mineralia, Arcana Coelestia, Vera Christiana Religio, Doctrina Vitae pro Nova Hierosolyma,* etc.

Sylvester II, Pope: See Gerbert.

Symmachus, Q. Aurelius: Roman aristocrat and orator of the late 4th century. Successfully opposed by Ambrose in the Affair of the Altar of Victory (q.v.). Following in Pliny's footsteps, he wrote literary epistles, nine books of private, and one of official correspondence. One of the leading opponents of Christianity.

Symphosius: Author of the African Anthology. Collected 100 versified riddles, the basis for the later collection of Aldhelm. See *Riddles.*

Synodicus: Poem by Warnerius of Basel (q.v.).

Syntagma Tragoediae Latinae: See Delrio.

Syrus, Publilius: See Publilius Syrus.

Szymonowicz, Szymon: 1558-1629. Polish-Latin poet. Wrote plays in imitation of Euripides, and miscellaneous poetry.

Tabernaria: See *Fabula Tabernaria.*

Tabula Bantina: A set of municipal regulations; our chief source for the Oscan (q.v.) language.

Tabulae Iguvinae: Bronze tablets containing formulae for priestly ritual in the Umbrian language. Of great linguistic importance for the study of P-Italic.

Tachygraphy: See Shorthand.

Tacitus, P. Cornelius: ca. 55-117. The life of the greatest of Roman historians is almost a complete mystery to us. His very dates are a matter of conjecture. He studied rhetoric in his youth with Julius Secundus, and may have been a pupil of Quintilian himself. His *Dialogus de Oratoribus* (q.v.) reveals his early interest in oratory. The *Agricola,* an idealized portrait or "profile" of his illustrious father-in-law, and the *Germania,* monograph about the people of Germany, their customs, warfare, economy, etc.—these are also early works. He wrote the *Histories* (Domitian to Nerva), and followed this work with his greatest, the *Annals* (q.v.). His style is a masterpiece of compression and brachyloquy. Difficult though it is, it offers rewards because of the author's penetrating insight into human psychology and historical causes, which make him and Sallust the only Roman historians to approach Thucydides in scope and depth. (Duff, Silver Age)

Taio: Bishop of Saragossa in the 7th century. Wrote epigrams in hexameters, and *Sententiae,* a theological treatise.

Tanusius Geminus: A historian mentioned by Suetonius and Seneca.

Tarentilla: ("The Girl from Tarentum") Comedy by Naevius, of which one considerable fragment survives.

Tarpeian Rock: Famous cliff in Rome from which traitors and murderers were thrown.

Tarquitius Priscus: Roman source for Etruscan lore. Mentioned by Pliny and Macrobius. He wrote a work called *Ostentarium,* a translation of an Etruscan work on divination.

Tatwine of Canterbury: Monk from Mercia; became Archbishop of Canterbury in 731. Wrote on grammar, and made a collection of riddles. (Manitius)

Te Deum Laudamus: Great Christian hymn. See Niceta.

Tebaldeo, Antonio: 1463-1537. Italian poet much admired for his Latin epigrams, pastoral eclogues, etc.

Technical prose: To be distinguished from learned prose (i.e., grammar, history). Deals with such subjects as Agriculture (Cato, Varro, Columella, etc.); Architecture (Vitruvius); Medicine (Celsus, Pliny the Elder); Military Science (Frontinus, Vegetius); Gromatics (Hyginus 3, Siculus Flaccus, etc.). Of a more vocational nature than "learned prose," these works tell "how to do" something. See the subjects and authors herein mentioned, and also Isagogic Literature.

Technopaegnion: Verses by Ausonius (q.v.) ending in monosyllables, and other mannered artificiality. A triumph of triviality.

Tegernsee: Famous monastery in Bavaria.

Telamo: A tragedy by Ennius. A famous fragment from this play says that the gods do not care what happens to men; if they did, the good would fare well, the bad ill; but this is not the case.

Telesio, Antonio: 1482-1534. Italian humanist; writer of Latin lyrics, a play (*Imber Aureus*), treatises, speeches, etc.

Telesio, B.: Renaissance scholar and scientific empiricist. Wrote *De Natura Rerum juxta Propria Principia.*

Telestich: A kind of acrostic in which the last letters of the lines, read from top to bottom (sometimes from bottom to top) spell a word or words, frequently the author and title of the work.

Tellus: Roman goddess of the earth.

Temporibus Meis, de: Lost work by Cicero.

Terence: (P. Terentius Afer—195?-159 B.C.) Roman comic playwright of the second century B.C. Born in Carthage, he was brought to Rome as a slave, manumitted, and soon became a member of the famed Scipionic Circle (q.v.). His first play, the *Andria,* was written in 166. He departed for Greece in 160/59. His six plays were written in those six years. The time and manner of his death remains a mystery. Some have said he was lost at sea, some that he died broken-hearted, etc. (A modern parallel is the disappearance of Ambrose Bierce). Works: *Andria, Adelphoe, Hecyra, Hautontimoroumenos, Eunuchus, Phormio.* Terence achieved a much higher degree of polish than had Plautus, but he lacked the "vis comica" (comic force or élan) of the latter. Caesar called Terence "dimidiate Menander" (Menander halved). His characters are the stock figures of New Comedy, the love-lorn youth, the courtesan with a heart-of-gold, the kidnapped maiden, the parasite, etc., and the plots deal with intrigue, romance, and love. Terence seems to have captured better than any other ancient playwright (with the possible exception of Menander, about whose fragmentary works no true estimate can be formed) Meredith's "Spirit of Comedy"; he is the spiritual ancestor of Molière. His plays are comedies of manners. The prologues tell us a lot about Terence, his rivalries, the charges of "contaminatio" or spoiling the Greek originals. Above all, he is famous for the humanity of his plays and characters. (Beare, The Roman Stage, Duff, OCD)

"Terentianus Christianus": Another name for Schoon or Schonaeus (q.v.).

Terentianus Maurus: Third century grammarian, author of a verse treatise of nearly 3000 lines on the letters, syllables and meters of Horace.

Terentianus Scaurus: Grammarian of Hadrian's time. Wrote commentaries on Plautus, Virgil, and Horace, as well as a *Liber de Orthographia* which is extant. His *Ars Grammatica* is lost.

Tereus: Lost play by the Neronian tragedian Faustus. Also, there are recorded plays of this title by Livius and Accius.

Terminism: Another name for the school of Nominalism (q.v.).

Tertullian: (Q. Septimius Florens Tertullianus, 165-220) African ecclesiastical writer and apologist. Wrote in Greek and Latin, but only the latter works have survived. Tertullian may be said to have created the language of ecclesiastical Latin. Dogmatic in faith, earnest in moral tone, rhetorical in style, he has left us a number of works, the most important of which is the *Apologeticum,* refuting the usual charges made against Christianity. The *Ad Nationes, De Testimonio Animae, De Baptismo, Adversus Judaeos, De Spectaculis, De Cultu Feminarum, De Poenitentia, De Pallio, De Corona,* these are other well-known works. Tertullian is the first writer on the Trinity, and is important as the creator of Christian-Latin terminology.

His tone is often rather satirical, and he is one of the most difficult Latin prose authors to read. (OCD)

Testamentum Porcelli: A satirical work by an unknown author of the third or fourth century, the will of a pig about to be killed. Jerome mentions it as popular with schoolboys.

Testicularia: Title of a lost play by Naevius.

Textual Criticism: The study dealing with the settlement and restoration of classical texts, by comparing manuscripts consists of the following: *Recension,* or restoration of a text, so far as possible, to the form intended by the author. 1st step: *Collation* of MSS. 2nd, *Stemma* showing relation of MSS. 3rd, Arrival at "transmitted text" (i.e. oldest, least interpolated, and freest from copyist errors). 4th, *Restoration* of corrupt or missing portions. The study demands a rather specialized knowledge, as the textual critic must not only be completely familiar with the vocabulary, syntax, etc. of the language, and the variants of monastic hands, but also, well-versed in the style of the particular author in question. The errors in transmission are often valuable in determining interrelationship or independence of MSS. and a missing *archetype* must often be found or conjectured. Important figures in recent textual criticism are: Bentley, Porson, Lachmann, Hermann, Housman, and Wilamowitz-Moellendorff.

Thangmar of Hildesheim: Head of school at Hildesheim (Saxony), wrote biography of Bishop Bernward, ca. 1015, and a *Translatio St. Epiphanii.* In both style and content, his work is a valuable addition to the biography of the period. (Manitius)

Theater, Roman: The first theaters were temporary wooden structures with no seats. Mummius, in 145 B.C. built the first wooden theater with tiers, and Pompey the first stone one in 55 B.C. The stage (*pulpitum*) was elevated, and was long and narrow. The background or *scaena* represented two houses with an alley (*angiportus*) between them. The dress was roughly modeled on the Greek, with stylized colors representing various characters. The production was in the hands of the *dominus gregis* (producer), and actors were usually of low social status. The performance was continuous without intermission, and the audiences were frequently noisy and ill-behaved. In the Empire, the emphasis was more on the spectacular and grotesque than on dramatic representations.

Thebae: Play by the Neronian tragedian Faustus (q.v.).

Thebaid: (or Thebais) Epic by Statius on the Theban Cycle. The story, which is quite diffuse and lacking in unity, deals with the blinding of Oedipus; the quarrel of his sons; the Lemnian women's murder of their husbands; the Antigone story; the Seven Against Thebes; etc. It is a mélange of the plots of several Greek dramas. The mythology is frigid, but individual passages are often vivid and striking. The work was a great favorite in the Middle Ages (see Statius).

Thegan: Author of a biography of Louis the Pious.

Theobald: Author of a work entitled *De Naturis Animalium.* Written in the 11th century, the work consists of twelve poems, each dealing with one animal.

Theoderich of Fleury: b. ca. 950. Wrote a *Life of Pope Martin I,* a book on the laws and customs of the monastery of Fleury, and many biographies, passions, commentaries, hymns, etc. (Manitius)

Theoderich of St. Trond: Wrote lives of various saints, versified parts of Solinus' *Collectanea* (q.v.), and wrote a rather fine poem on the death of a little dog, full of classical allusions (Virgil-Culex, etc.).

Theodofrid: 7th century Gallic monk, probable author of two alphabetical poems (q.v.) one on the Six Ages of the World; the other on Asia and the World.

Theodore of Tarsus: Archbishop of Canterbury in the 7th century, leader of the Cathedral school there.

Theodoreans: One of the two schools of oratory that flourished in the early empire, named after Theodorus (q.v.).

Theodorich of Chartres: 12th century scholar, wrote on Creation, on Cicero's *De Inventione*; and other works dealing with grammar, rhetoric, dialectic, and astronomy.

Theodorus of Gadara: Famous rhetor; teacher of the emperor Tiberius. Leader of the school of rhetoric which bears his name.

Theodosiani Libri XVI: Decrees of various emperors pertaining to education, gathered in the Theodosian Code. Contains much important information about Roman education.

Theodulf: d. 821. The poet-laureate of the Carolingian Renaissance. A Visigoth, he became bishop of Orléans. Among other works, he is famous for his panegyric on Charlemagne, his hymn *Gloria, Laus* (Glory, praise, and honor), and his poem on the contents of his library.

Theodulus: Author of an *Eclogue* consisting of a debate between Christianity and Paganism. It has been suggested (see Raby) that Theodulus is none other than Gottschalk of Fulda, whose name is the literal translation of Theodulus (i.e., "servant of God"). (Raby, Manitius)

Theologica Germanica: A 14th century work by an anonymous clergyman. It abounds in mysticism. Placed on the *Index* (q.v.) in 1621.

Theological Treatises: Works by Boethius (q.v.) on the Trinity, on the Catholic Faith, and on various heresies. Although their authenticity has been challenged, they are now generally accepted as genuine.

Theriaca: Didactic poem about serpents, by Aemilius Macer.

Thesaurus Linguae Latinae: Thesaurus of the Latin language, produced in the middle of the 16th century by the elder Stephanus (Robert Estienne).

Theseis: Lost epic by Albinovanus Pedo (q.v.).

Thierry of Chartres: 12th century humanist of the school of Chartres; brother of the celebrated Bernard of Chartres. Thierry lectured on Aristotle, and wrote a *Heptateuchon,* or handbook of the seven liberal arts.

Thietmar: 11th century bishop, author of a *Saxon Chronicle.*

Thierry Ruinart: Associate of Mabillon (q.v.) in editing *Acta Sanctorum ordinis Benedicti.*

Thiofrid of Echternach: b. 1030-40. One of the early Schoolmen. Wrote *Flores Epitaphii Sanctorum,* a *Vita Liutwini,* and some poetry, sermons, etc. (Manitius)

Thomas Aquinas, St.: 1224-1274. Dominican friar whose great work was the welding of Aristotelian philosophy and Christian theology into one harmonious whole. His *Summa*

Theologica is his greatest work, and mention should also be made of his commentary on the *Sententiae* of Peter Lombard, his *Summa contra Gentiles,* and *Questiones Disputatae.* To Aquinas, Aristotle is *the* philosopher. Thomas dealt with the problem of universals, of substance and accident, of Nature and the existence of God, which he proved in five ways. He is generally regarded as the greatest of the Scholastics (q.v.), along with his teacher, Albertus Magnus. Aristotle's ethics, teleology, and metaphysics, as well as his logic, all find their way into the system of Aquinas. (Ferm, Encycl. of Relig.)

Thomas a Becket: Archbishop of Canterbury in the 12th century. Under his leadership, Canterbury became one of the great centers of learning, rivalling even that of Chartres. He wrote a well-known hymn on the Seven Joys of Mary, as well as letters, and a satire against the practice of simony (q.v.).

Thomas of Cantimpré: Dominican friar in the first half of the 13th century, author of an encyclopedia *De Naturis Rerum.*

Thomas of Celano: Probable author of the great hymn *Dies Irae* (q.v.).

Thomas a Kempis: Author (or editor?) of the Imitation of Christ (q.v.).

Thomism: The philosophy of Aquinas and his followers (who were called Thomists). A merging of Christianity and Aristotelianism.

Thule: (Ultima Thule) In antiquity and the Middle Ages, the most distant conceivable part of the world. An early voyager, Pytheas, decribes it as being six days North of Britain. It has variously been identified with one of the Shetlands, Norway, or, most probably, Iceland.

Thyestes: In Greek mythology, the brother of Atreus, who served to him a meal consisting of his (i.e., Thyestes') own children, as an act of vengeance. A favorite subject for Roman tragedies. The following authors wrote plays on the subject: Ennius, Varius Rufus, Curiatus Maternus, and Seneca (2). Only the latter's play has survived.

Tiberianus: 4th century poet, chiefly famous for his poem

Amnis ibat, a lovely description of a river. It was conjectured (by Baehrens) that Tiberianus was also the author of the *Pervigilium Veneris.*

Tiberius: This emperor was a skilled orator, though overfond of cryptic utterances. He wrote love stories and poetry, including a lament on the death of L. Caesar.

Tibullus, Albius: 48?-19 B.C. Elegiac poet of the Augustan Age, belonging to the literary circle of Messalla. His elegies are addressed to two mistresses, Delia (Book I), and Nemesis (Book II). The former is unfaithful, the latter is greedy as well. Book III is probably not by Tibullus (see Corpus Tibullianum and Pseudo-Tibullus). T. is characterized by smoothness of line, simplicity and clarity, and by great depth of feeling, passion, love, joy, despair. He longs for the idyllic life of the country, as did Horace. His popularity has been virtually unchallenged from his day to ours.

Tibur (Tivoli): Location of Horace's famous Sabine Farm. Catullus, Augustus, and Hadrian also had villas there.

Ticidas: One of the Cantores Euphorionis or "neoterici." Wrote love-poetry to one Perilla.

Timaeus: Dialogue of Plato dealing with cosmology. The only one of Plato's works that was really known during the Middle Ages, it had considerable influence on medieval philosophy.

Timone Comite, Carmen de: See Minor Carolingian Poetry.

Tiro: Cicero's loyal and capable freedman. Edited his letters and speeches, wrote a biography of the orator, and also a treatise on the Latin language. Tiro is perhaps best known for the system of shorthand he devised (see shorthand, *Notae Tironianae*).

Tiro Prosper: See Prosper of Aquitaine.

Titianus (1): 2nd century grammarian and epistolographer, who wrote "Ciceronian" letters.

Titianus (2): Son of Titianus (1), a writer of prose fables.

Titinius (1): The first writer of *fabulae togatae* (q.v.). We have fifteen titles and a few fragments. He was favorably compared with Terence.

Titinius (2) Capito: Historian, ca. 100 A.D., who wrote *Exitus Inlustrium Virorum* (the Deaths of Famous Men).

Titius (1): Contemporary of Cicero. Wrote speeches and plays.

Titius (2): Augustan poet; author of tragedies and "Pindaric odes."

Titius (3) Probus: An epitomizer.

Titus: This emperor wrote a poem on a comet. It has not survived.

Tityrus: A Virgilian cento (q.v.) by Pomponius in the 4th century.

Tmesis: The separation of parts of a word (usually prefix and root) by another word or words. The classical example is Ennius' "cere comminuit brum." English example (humorous): "Such influences are rep, I might say, rehensible." (W. Kelly)

Tobit (Tobias): A long elegiac poem by Matthew of Vendôme (q.v.).

Togata: See *Fabula togata.*

Trabea, Q.: Early writer of palliatae; a contemporary of Plautus.

Tractatus de Amore: Treatise on love by Andreas Capellanus (q.v.).

Tragedy, Roman: Never as popular or as inspired as the Greek tragedy, Roman tragedy came to an early bloom in the Republic, and then slowly died away. Early authors of tragedy are Livius, Ennius, and Naevius, all of whom wrote plays based on Greek originals or on Greek mythology. Only scanty fragments remain. Accius (q.v.) was the greatest of the tragedians; and Pacuvius also enjoyed a good reputation. In the Ciceronian period, the decline began. We have titles of a few plays after this, e.g., the Thyestes of Varius Rufus and that of Maternus; the Medea of Ovid, etc. The only Roman tragedies that have been preserved are those of Seneca (q.v.). See also Praetexta; *Octavia,* pantomime.

Tragedies (Seneca): We have nine plays by Seneca: the

Hercules Furens, Hercules Oetaeus, Agamemnon, Thyestes, Oedipus, Medea, Phaedra, Troades, and *Phoenissae.* Intended for recitation rather than performance, they are at best, frigid imitations of the Greek masterpieces that inspired them. Individual parts, speeches, characters stand out now and then, well-expressed *sententiae,* shrewd pieces of characterization, etc.

Tranquillitate Animi, de: Philosophical essay by Seneca (2) on the subject of Peace of Mind. It contains a good deal of practical wisdom, and Stoic philosophy, modified by Roman common sense. The mind, Seneca says, should find its pleasures in itself. He speaks of the worthlessness of the artificial life and the vanity of human wishes.

Transalpine humanism: Differed from the humanism of the Italian Renaissance, in that the transalpine humanists (e.g., Reuchlin, Agricola, Erasmus) were often religious teachers and even ascetics.

Translations: For most classical authors, the Loeb Classical Library, which combines a scholarly edition of the text, incorporating the latest results of textual criticism, with a readable translation, will be found useful.

Traube: Collected and edited the poetry of the Carolingian Age.

Trebatius Testa, C.: Jurist of the Augustan Age; a friend of Cicero and Horace. Wrote *De Religionibus* and *De Iure Civili.* Teacher of Labeo (q.v.).

Trebellius Pollio: One of the authors of the *Historia Augusta.*

Tribonian: (Trebonianus) Friend and collaborator of the emperor Justinian in the composition and editing of the great codes of law (i.e., the Digest, Institutes and Novella).

Tribus Puellis, de: Late 12th century "comedy" by an unknown French author.

Trimalchio: Prototype of the vulgar, ostentatious, self-made nouveau-riche in Petronius' *Satyricon.* He wears outlandish clothes, deliberately comes late to his own banquet, makes tasteless and ill-bred comments, pretends to culture, etc.

Trinitate, de: Works of this title were written by Boethius, Hilary of Poitiers, and Novitian (qq.v.).

Trinummus: A comedy by Plautus. The characterizations are rather fine. The loyalty of old Callicles in caring for the son, daughter, and treasure of his friend Charmides is the chief topic of the play. The slave Stasimus is also a faithful and sympathetic character.

Tripertita: See Aelius Paetus.

Tristia: (Ovid) Collection of elegiac letters written by the poet from his place of exile on the Black Sea. The *Tristia* are of biographical interest, but too tinged with self-pity to have much literary worth. See also *Epistulae ex Ponto*.

Trithemius, John: 1462-1516. Renaissance humanist and historian.

Trivium: The three basic subjects of the medieval curriculum: grammar, rhetoric, and dialectic. Together with the *quadruvium* (q.v.) this made up the "Liberal Arts." See Education, Martianus Capella, Liberal Arts.

Troades (Seneca): Combines the *Trojan Women* and the *Hecuba* of Euripides, but without either the pathos or the social consciousness of the Greek playwright. Nevertheless it has some fine scenes, and is perhaps Seneca's best play.

Trochaic tetrameter: (Catalectic) A brisk marching meter, used in the comedies of Plautus and Terence, as well as in various other works, such as the *Pervigilium Veneris* ("crás amét qui númquam amávit, quíque amávit crás amét.") and the Bible version of Hilary of Poitiers. English example: "In the spring a young man's fancy Lightly turns to thoughts of love."

Trogus, Pompeius: Augustan scholar. Wrote a comprehensive history of the world (*Historiae Philippicae*) in 44 books. The narrative was rather elaborate, full of moralizing speeches; it was abridged by Justinus in the Antonine Age.

Troiae Halosis: (Sack of Troy) A poem from the *Satyricon* of Petronius; perhaps a parody of Seneca.

Troica: Nero's epic on the sack of Troy, verses from which he is said to have chanted during the Fire of Rome.

Trollus: See Albert of Stade.

Trope: A text used with musical accompaniment as either an introduction or addition to the Catholic liturgy.

Truculentus: Minor comedy of Plautus, which, Cicero tells us, was a great joy to the author in his old age.

Tubero, Aelius, L.: Historian, ca. 60 B.C. His son, Q. Aelius Tubero, was also an historian and jurist, and one of Livy's sources.

Tucca, Plotius: A member of the Maecenas circle. After Virgil's death, he helped to edit the *Aeneid.*

Tuditanus, C. Sempronius: Consul 129 B.C. Wrote a history of Rome, and a treatise on the functions of Roman magistrates. It has not survived.

Tullio, pro: Early speech by Cicero. It survives, but in a mutilated condition.

Tully: The name by which Cicero was known in England. Comes from Tullius, the *nomen gentilicium,* or family name, of the orator.

Turnus (1): A poet and satirist of the Flavian period.

Turnus (2): The enemy and chief antagonist of Aeneas (q.v.), by whom he is finally defeated (*Aeneid* XII).

Turpilius, S.: d. 103 B.C. Writer of palliatae. We have fragments of two plays: *Leucadia,* a burlesque of the Sappho story, and *Epicleros* (the Heiress).

Turpin: See Pseudo-Turpin.

Turpio, L. Ambivius: See Ambivius.

Turranius (1) Gracilis: Date unknown. Used by the elder Pliny as an authority on Spain.

Turranius (2): Tragic playwright of the Augustan Age.

Turrinus, Clodius: Two rhetors of this name are mentioned by Seneca (1). They were father and son.

Tusculanae Disputationes: Philosophical work of Cicero (q.v.). On happiness and the *vita beata.* Written in the last year of Cicero's life.

Tusculum: Fashionable resort, 15 miles southeast of Rome. Cato was born there, and Cicero, Lucullus, and Maecenas had villas there.

Tuscus, Clodius: Writer on astronomy, used by Ovid (*Fasti*).

Tuticanus: Friend of Ovid; minor Augustan poet who wrote of Homeric themes (e.g., the Nausicaa story from the *Odyssey*).

Tutilo (or Tuotilo): Monk of St. Gall, friend of Notker Balbulus (q.v.); composer of tropes.

Tutulius: Grammarian and rhetor of the first century. Mentioned by Martial and Quintilian.

Twelfth Century Renaissance: Great period of humanism, when the Cathedral Schools (e.g., Chartres) became the chief centers of culture and learning. Abelard, Bernard Sylvestris, John of Salisbury are figures associated with this period.

Twelve Tables: Early collection of Roman law, dating from the 5th century B.C. The original tables were destroyed when Rome was sacked by the Gauls. Our fragments represent a later, modified version. The tables dealt with lawsuits, court procedure, property damage, etc. They were memorized by every schoolboy and were called the "fons omnis publici privatique iuris." In fact, the Twelve Tables are the beginnings of the development of Roman law.

Ulgerius of Angers: Clergyman and teacher, first half of the 12th century. Wrote poetry, epigrams, etc. He was a pupil and friend of Marbod (q.v.).

Ulpian: One of the greatest of Roman jurists. A pupil of Papinian (q.v.), he was a voluminous writer, producing ca. 280 books. Much of his work is included in the *Digest* of Justinian. Ulpian was murdered by the Praetorian Guards in 228.

Ultima Thule: See Thule.

Umbrian: One of the important languages of the P-Italic branch. See Italic dialects, Iguvinian Tables.

Unam Sanctam: A bull issued by Pope Boniface VIII in 1302, against Philip the Fair. A classical defense of the rights of the Church.

Uncials: Large, or majuscule letters used in manuscripts.

Universals: The dispute over universals goes back to Plato and Aristotle, with Aristotle's rejection of Plato's Theory of Ideas. During the Middle Ages, the argument between the Realists and the Nominalists was over the question of universals, that is, the objective existence of universals or abstractions, with the Realists claiming (as had Plato) that universals do exist, and the Nominalists taking the opposite viewpoint. See William of Champeaux, Abelard, Nominalism, Realism, Ockham. (Runes, Dict. of Phil.)

Universities: Many of the great European universities of today were founded in the Middle Ages (e.g., Paris, Bologna, Oxford, etc.).

Universo, de: Encyclopedic treatise by Hrabanus Maurus, based on the work of Isidore of Seville (qq.v.).

Urbanus: Grammarian and Virgilian scholar, ca. 100 A.D., quoted by Servius.

Urbe Condita, ab: Livy's great history of Rome from its origins to his own day. It came out in installments. We have only books 1-10, 21-45, and summaries or *periochae* of the rest. Enough of the work has survived (approximately one quarter) to give us a good idea of the whole. It is a wonderful picture of the Roman character and the "grandeur that was Rome." Livy is an artist rather than an historian. He deals lovingly with the old-time glories of his city, the *prisca virtus* (q.v.) that made the men of olden times the great heroes of legend. He writes with a "lactea ubertas" (milky richness), according to Quintilian. We are indebted to him for such episodes as the story of Romulus and Remus, Horatius at the Bridge, Cincinnatus, the Punic Wars and Hannibal, the sack of Rome by the Gauls. Livy is more akin to Herodotus than to Thucydides. That is to say, he is more interested in telling a noble story than in inquiring into historical truth, cause and effect, etc. Livy influenced all subsequent writers of history: Valerius Maximus, Florus, Plutarch, Dio Cassius, Lucan, Silius, etc. From the time of Priscian in the 6th century until John of

Salisbury in the 12th, we lose sight of Livy entirely. He was accused by Pollio of "Patavinity" (q.v.). The summaries (*periochae*) were already in vogue by Martial's time, as we learn from one of that poet's epigrams. (Duff, Golden Age)

Urseius Ferox: Jurist of the period of Vespasian.

Ursinus, Kaspar Velius: 1493-1539. Silesian humanist and historian. Wrote *De Bello Pannonico Libri X.*

Utopia: Literally, "nowhere" (cf. Butler's *Erewhon*). A work of social criticism by Thomas More. The complete title is "De optimo rei publicae statu deque nova insula Utopia." It was published in Latin in 1516 under the supervision of Erasmus.

Vacca: A sixth century grammarian, author of *a Life of Lucan.* Vacca seems to have known the lost works (see Lucan).

Vagantenstrophe: Goliardic verse (q.v.).

Vagantes: The "wandering scholars" of the 12th-13th centuries. Some were renegade monks and clerks, some genuine scholars and teachers. They wrote a body of miscellaneous verse, some tender, some satiric and scurrilous. See Goliards, Goliardic verse, Carmina Burana, etc. Their poetry was the last flowering of the Latin language. (Waddell)

Vagellius: Poet of the Neronian age; friend of Seneca (2).

Valerand de la Varenne: fl. ca. 1500. Neo-Latin epic poet. Wrote on the life of Joan of Arc (*De Gestis Joanne Virginis*).

Valeriano, Pierio: 1477-1551. Italian humanist and poet. Wrote love-poetry and scholarly works, in Latin.

Valerius (1): Author of palliatae (q.v.). Ribbeck identified him with a Valerius (2) Aedituus who wrote erotic epigrams.

Valerius (2) Aedituus: Writer of erotic epigrams in the Greek style, ca. 100 B.C.

Valerius (3) Antias: See Antias.

Valerius (4) Cato, P.: One of the *neoterici* or Cantores Euphorionis (q.v.). The *Lydia* and the *Dirae* of the Appendix

Virgiliana have been attributed to him, but on very questionable grounds.

Valerius (5) Flaccus: Epic poet of the Flavian period. Author of the *Argonautica* (q.v.), which is somewhat indebted to the epic of Apollonius Rhodes. The poem is incomplete; parts of it are very fine, parts seem over-rhetorical, and have the usual faults as well as the virtues of Silver Latinity.

Valerius (6) Licinianus: A fellow-townsman of Martial, from Bilbilis in Spain. A rhetor, exiled by Domitian, but under Nerva, he became a professor of rhetoric in Sicily.

Valerius (7) Maximus: Author of *Facta et Dicta Memorabilia*. Nothing is known of his life. He probably lived during the age of Tiberius. His work is a huge collection of stories and anecdotes to be used by speakers. The stories are loosely arranged according to subject-matter. He draws on Cicero, Livy, Sallust, etc. In spite of the artificiality and bombast of the work, it was popular in antiquity, and more so in the Middle Ages. Its popularity is shown by the fact that two epitomes were made of it, one by Julius Paris, the second by Nepotianus.

Valerius (8) Soranus: A didactic poet, linguistic and antiquarian scholar of the early first century B.C.

Valgius Rufus: Member of the literary circle of Maecenas. Wrote epigrams, also works on grammar and herbs.

Valla, Lorenzo: Important figure of the Italian Renaissance. His *Annotationes* on the Vulgate are significant.

Vallius Syriacus: Rhetor, pupil of the great Theodorus (q.v.). Mentioned by the elder Seneca.

Vanity of Human Wishes: Samuel Johnson's title for the great Tenth Satire of Juvenal. The theme is: the malignant gods overthrow people by granting their requests. What do people pray for? Wealth? Political power, Eloquence? Military glory? Long life? Beauty? Each of these has ruined those who were unfortunate enough to possess it. (Sejanus, Cicero, Demosthenes, Hannibal, Alexander, etc. are briefly and brilliantly dealt with, to prove these points.) At the end, he asks: is there nothing that man may safely wish for? and the answer: "mens sana in corpore sano" (a sound mind in a sound body).

Vargunteius, Q.: Grammarian of the second century B.C. who lectured on Ennius and edited his works.

Varius Rufus, L.: ca. 74-14 B.C. The dean of Augustan poets. He wrote an epic on Caesar's death (*De Morte Caesaris*); a panegyric on Augustus; a tragedy (*Thyestes*). He was a friend of Horace and Virgil, and, after the latter's death, helped to edit the *Aeneid* (See also Tucca).

Varro (1), M. Terentius: 116-27 B.C. In his long life, which nearly spans the last century of the Republic, Varro left virtually no subject of human learning untouched. He was a man of encyclopedic learning and indefatigable energy. Augustus said that Varro's reading was so wide, that it was a wonder that he ever wrote anything; and his writings so numerous that no one could ever read them through. Varro wrote 490 volumes, as follows: Menippean Satires, tragedies, miscellaneous poetry; *Annals, Res Urbanae, De Gente Populi Romani,* and other historical and antiquarian works; *Disciplinae* (nine books, embracing the *trivium* and *quadruvium* qq.v., plus medicine and architecture); miscellaneous letters, speeches; works of Plautine scholarship; works on law, philosophy, geography, linguistics, agriculture, poetry, rhetoric, grammar, astronomy, etc. All that have survived are the *De Lingua Latina* and part of the *Rerum Rusticarum libri iii* (de re rustica, q.v.). The former is chiefly valuable for the many quotations Varro has preserved from the older poets; the latter has some charm, although it is rather pedantic. Varro was not a profound thinker, but he tried to keep abreast of all the learning of his times and record it for posterity. His prose is rather bald. (Duff)

Varro (2), P. Terentius, "Atacinus": b. 82 B.C. Wrote elegies, a geographical poem (*Chorographia*), a translation of the *Argonauts* of Apollonius of Rhodes, an historical epic, the *Bellum Sequanicum,* and some satire. Only very meager fragments remain.

Vatican collection: A group of Latin lyrics, goliardic poetry, satire, etc. from the 12th-13th centuries.

Vatinium, in: A speech by Cicero, full of invective against Vatinius. Two years later (54) Cicero defended Vatinius.

Vatronius: A writer of palliatae. Nothing is known of him except his name.

Vegetius, Renatus Flavius: Military writer of the 4th century (ca. 380). Besides his *Epitoma Rei Militaris,* he wrote on diseases of cattle and mules.

Vegio, Maffeo: 1407-1458. Italian humanist; author of an educational treatise *De Educatione Liberorum.* Also wrote a thirteenth book for the *Aeneid.*

Veiento, Fabricius: Wrote satirical books or *Codicilli* against the senators and priests. He was banished by Nero and his books were burned.

Velius Longus: Second century grammarian and Virgilian scholar. Also wrote on Ennius, Lucilius and Accius. His *De Orthographia* is the only extant work.

Velleius Paterculus, C.: ca. 19 B.C.-post A.D. 31. Historian during Tiberius' reign. Had an honorable military career as prefect and legatus in Pannonia and Germany. His history is a compendious affair in two books. Most of the first is lost. The second covers the period from 146 B.C. to A.D. 30, with great brevity until we come to Caesar. His sources: Cato, Hortensius, Nepos, Trogus, and Sallust. The work is full of rhetorical flourishes and apostrophes, such as his diatribe against Mark Antony for the murder of Cicero. He is fond of epigrammatic utterances, balanced antitheses, etc. but seems to have little real understanding of history. His method is chiefly biographical, and his prejudices are always evident, e.g., his adulation of the emperor Tiberius whom, as Duff says, "he praises not wisely but too well." The faults of Silver Latinity are already evident in Velleius (rhetoric, purple patches, sententiousness, etc.). He is a writer of little profundity or discrimination, but he is quite readable, on the whole. The digressions are particularly interesting. His rosy-colored picture of Tiberius makes an interesting contrast and antidote to the gloomy depiction of Tacitus. (Duff, Silver Age)

Vellius, C.: Early Roman exponent of the Epicurean philosophy.

Venantius Fortunatus: See Fortunatus.

"Venerable": A medieval title of respect, usually given to an abbot or clergyman (e.g., the Venerable Bede, Peter the Venerable, etc.).

Veni, Creator Spiritus: Famous hymn ascribed, without much foundation, to Hrabanus Maurus, but certainly a product of the Carolingian Renaissance.

Vennonius: Early Roman historian, mentioned by Cicero.

Venus: Mythology—the goddess of love and beauty, identified with the Greek Aphrodite. Mother of Cupid. She occupies a special place in Roman mythology and legend, since she is the mother of Aeneas, the legendary founder of the Roman people. It is to her, the goddess of nature and fertility, that Lucretius addresses his epic on the Nature of Things.

Venustate, de: See Servasius.

Verborum Significatu, de: The huge lexicon of Verrius Flaccus (q.v.), which survives only in the abridgment of Festus (2nd century), and in the later abridgment by Paulus Diaconus in the Carolingian period.

Verecundus: Bishop of Junca, wrote poems on the Resurrection and the Last Judgment, and prose works of commentary, allegory, and exegesis.

Vergil: See Virgil.

Vergiliomastix: "Scourge of Virgil." A name given to critics of Virgil.

Vergilius Romanus: A writer of comedies in the style of Menander, and the old satyric comedy. Mentioned by the younger Pliny.

Verginius Flavus: See Flavus.

Verginius Rufus: Minor Flavian poet; author of erotic verse.

Verres: Governor of Sicily, noted for his rapacity, corruption, double-dealing, and total disregard of the rights of citizens. He was successfully prosecuted by Cicero in 70 B.C.

Verrine Orations: Cicero's speeches against Verres. Only the first was delivered, as Verres then fled. Cicero's victory over his rival, the more experienced Hortensius, made his name in politics. The speeches contain some of Cicero's best oratory. His swift, graphic narratives are especially fine.

Verrius Flaccus: Freedman in the Augustan Age, tutor to the Imperial children, who wrote the first alphabetical lexicon of the Latin language (*De Verborum Significatu,* q.v.). His other works include a *De Orthographia,* a *De Obscuris Catonis, Libri Rerum Memoria Dignarum,* and *Fasti.* These are all lost.

Versus Cuiusdam Scoti de Alphabeto: Riddles on the letters of the alphabet by an unknown Irish monk of the 7th (?) century.

Versus de Verona: A 9th century poem in which the (unknown) author is naively amused that the Pagans were able to build such beautiful structures.

Versus Eporedienses: A long love-poem, probably dating from the latter part of the 11th century, by an Italian clergyman.

Versus Fescennini: A type of rustic banter, in which may be found the most primitive ancestor of the Roman comedy. Originating in some sort of harvest celebration, the verses were noted for their license and ribaldry; probably a form of sympathetic magic. They were used at marriages and festive occasions, written in meter, and the name probably derives from the Etruscan town of Fescennium or Fescennia. It is interesting to note that Claudian, one of the last of the pagan Roman poets, also wrote Fescennine verses.

Verus, Cloatius: An Augustan scholar who wrote a book on Latin's debt to Greek (*Libri Verborum a Graecis Tractorum*).

Vespa: Third century poet, author of the *Contest between Cook and Baker,* a poetical debate or *Streitgedicht.* The work is a masterpiece of affectation and triviality.

Vespasian: 9-79. Like most of the emperors, Vespasian tried his hand at letters. He was an orator of no mean ability, and wrote memoirs.

Vesta: Roman goddess of the hearth, to whose worship the Vestal Virgins (q.v.) were consecrated. Identified with the Greek Hestia.

Vestal Virgins: First four, then six maidens, dedicated to the worship of Vesta, whose task it was to guard the sacred fire of that goddess. They were buried alive for unchastity, and beaten for allowing the fire to go out. They served for 30 years, after which they were allowed to, but seldom did, marry. They were preceded by lictors in the streets, and had reserved seats at games and festivals. If a condemned criminal met them, on his way to the place of execution, he was immediately set free.

Vesuvius: Famous volcano near Naples. Its eruption in 79 buried Pompeii, Herculaneum, and Stabiae, and killed the elder Pliny, as is described in two famous letters (6.16,20) by his nephew.

Vettius Agorius Praetextatus: 4th century opponent of Christianity. Translated Aristotle's *Categories* and wrote a long iambic epitaph.

Vettius Valens: A second century writer on astrology.

Vetus, L. Antistius: A minor Neronian historian.

Vibius Crispus: An informer (*delator*) with a very pleasant style of oratory.

Vibius Maximus: Author of a (lost) *Universal History* much admired by Statius.

Vico, Giambattista: 1668-1744. Italian philosopher, historian, poet, etc. Wrote *De Antiquissima Italorum Sapientia, De Nostri Temporis Studiorum Ratione*, etc.

Victor, Aurelius: See Aurelius Victor.

Victor of Tonnenna: Chronicler and historian of the 6th (?) century.

Victor (Vita?): 5th century African bishop; author of a history of the African persecution of Christians under Gaiseric.

Victorinus, Marius: 4th century grammarian and neo-Platonist. Most of his translations from Plato and Aristotle are lost. His *Ars Grammatica* was popular in the Middle Ages. (See Aphthonius)

Victorinus, Maximus: Grammarian of unknown date; author of various works on metrics and prosody.

Victorius Marcellus: Orator to whom Quintilian (q.v.) dedicated his *Institutio.*

Vida, Marco Girolamo: 1485-1566. Italian humanist, poet. Wrote an epic (*Christiados*), an *Ars Poetica,* and treatises on chess and silkworms.

Vidularia: Play by Plautus (q.v.) surviving only in fragments.

Vigiliis, de: See Niceta.

Villedieu, Alexander of: See Alexander of Villedieu.

Vincent of Beauvais: d. 1264. Author of a voluminous encyclopedia: *Speculum Naturale, Historiale, Doctrinale,* dealing with nature, history, and theology.

Vincent of Lerins: 5th century clergyman (d. ca. 440), author of *Commonitorium,* a discussion of Christian faith and tests of orthodox belief.

Vincent, St., Poem to: A poem of 14 strophes, written around the middle of the 11th century at St. Bertin. The poem displays great metrical ingenuity, and is in a variety of lyrical meters. (Manitius)

Violentilla: See Stella, Arruntius.

Vipstanus Messalla: Orator and historian of the first century. A friend of Tacitus, and one of the interlocutors in the latter's *Dialogus de Oratoribus* (q.v.).

Vir Bonus: A minor poem of the *Appendix Virgiliana.* Not even Augustan, it probably dates from the fourth century.

Virgil: (P. Vergilius Maro, 70-19 B.C.) Life. Born in Mantua, educated in Cremona and Milan. At Rome he studied rhetoric and philosophy. He became a member of the circle of Maecenas, and was friendly with Horace. His first published work was the *Eclogues,* which took him three years to write. He worked for seven years on the four books of the *Georgics* (an average of about a line a day), and devoted the last 11 years of his life to the composition of his magnum opus, the *Aeneid* (q.v.). He died in Brundisium, and was buried in Naples (see Epitaphs), requesting that the unfinished *Aeneid* be destroyed. Augustus overruled this request, however, and caused the manuscript to be edited by Varius and Tucca. His works (see under the separate titles) are indebted to Theocritus, Hesiod, and Homer, respectively, but Virgil was no slavish imitator. He molded the Latin hexameter into an instrument of lofty, poetical expression never again equalled, and his position in Latin poetry is comparable to that of Cicero in prose: he is *the* Latin poet, bar none. He is the poet of Rome, who most keenly realized the imperial importance of that city, and expressed it in never-to-be-forgotten language. Augustus realized this, which is why the emperor was so interested in the *Aeneid.* Virgil's popularity has remained unchallenged from his own day to the present. He was widely read and studied in the Middle Ages, and the number of commentaries and centos attests to this. All subsequent epic poets more or less imitated him (Lucan, Statius, Valerius Flaccus, Silius Italicus, etc.). He was held in the Middle Ages to have foretold the coming of Christ (Eclogue IV), and Dante's use of Virgil as his guide is a glowing testimony to the poet's position in medieval times; a position accorded to him for his tenderness, his humanity, his religious feeling, and his command of the Latin language. Tennyson sums it up with the words:

"Wielder of the stateliest measure ever moulded by the lips of man." (Duff, Golden Age, OCD)

Virgilio, Giovanni del: See Giovanni del Virgilio.

Virgilius Maro of Toulouse: A grammarian of the 7th century (fl. ca. 630).

Virginitate, de: See Aldhelm.

Viris Illustribus, de: The title of a number of series of biographies of famous men. See Nepos, Isidore of Seville, Suetonius, Jerome, Sigebert (1).

Virtus: Literally, the quality of a *man.* A cardinal Roman virtue and essential quality of a Roman. Together with *pietas* (q.v.) this represented the character of Aeneas, and replaced the Greek quality of *kalokagthia* (beauty and goodness).

Vita: "Life" or biography. Used by Suetonius, Jerome, etc., and especially in the Middle Ages, for Lives of Saints.

Vita Beata, de: Seneca's dialogue on the Happy Life: what qualities make for it (sound mind, courage, peace of mind, virtue), and how to attain this life. Addressed to his brother Novatus.

Vita Caesarum, de: See Lives of the Caesars (Suetonius).

Vita Columbani: Biography of the great Irish monk Columban, by Jonas, a monk of Bobbio in the 7th century.

Vita Heinrici IV: Written shortly after the emperor's death in 1106 by an unknown monk. In spite of the good style, the work is full of errors and omissions. (Manitius)

Vita Karoli: See Einhard.

Vita Merlini: Biography of Merlin, by Geoffrey of Monmouth (q.v.).

Vita Populi Romani: Lost treatise by Varro (q.v. 1) on the evolution of the Roman people. Interesting, in that Varro has the philosophical concept of the organic growth of the nation.

Vitae Sanctorum: Lives of the Saints. See Jerome, Jacopo da Voragine, etc.

Vitalis of Blois: 12th century author of comedies. See *Geta* (Amphitryo), *Aulularia*.

Vitiis Corporalibus, de: Lost work by Suetonius, on physical blemishes.

Vitruvius Pollio: Military officer and architect in the Age of Augustus. Author of *De Architectura* in ten books. The work deals with types of architecture, location, materials, temples, water-supply, pavements, private dwellings, etc. Drawing mostly from his own experience, Vitruvius has created a work that, although it is highly technical, is not unattractive. The garrulous prefaces and philosophical reflections are noteworthy. The work is of great value to anyone interested in re-creating the physical aspects of the Augustan Age.

Vittorino da Feltre: 1378-1446. Great teacher and humanist of the Italian Renaissance, who combined love of the classics with Christian learning.

Vives, Juan Luis: 1492-1540. Spanish humanist and philosopher. Works: *De Anima et Vita,* Commentary on the *City of God,* Latin *Dialogues, Defensio Fidei Christianae,* etc. All his works are in Latin.

Voconius Romanus: Orator, contemporary of Pliny the Younger, who said that his letters sounded as if the Muses were speaking Latin.

Volcacius: A rhetor from Pergamum. He was exiled for poisoning, and opened a school in Marseilles.

Volcatius Sedigitus: See Sedigitus.

Voltacilius Pitholaus, L.: The first freedman to write works of history, he had a school of rhetoric in 81 B.C. He was Pompey's teacher, as well as his biographer.

Volumnius, P.: Philosopher and friend of Brutus. Wrote about the latter's last battle, prodigies, etc.

Voragine, Jacopo da: See Jacopo.

Voss, G. J.: 1577-1649. Author of a *De Historicis Latinis*. He definitely established Caesar's authorship of the *De Bello Civili*.

Votienus Montanus: An orator mentioned by Seneca (1). Convicted of treason, he died in exile. Because of his love of repetition, he was called "the Ovid of speakers." (Cf. Ovid's famous line: "Semibovemque virum, semivirumque bovem"—a man, half-ox; an ox half-man)

Vulcacius Gallicanus: One of the six authors of the *Historia Augusta* (q.v.).

Vulcan: (Volcanus) Roman god of the forge, volcanoes, etc. Identified with the Greek Hephaistos.

Vulgar Latin: The common, every-day Latin spoken in the Empire. Of great importance for the student of the Romance languages.

Vulgari Eloquentia, de: Treatise by Dante on the theory of language. It is interesting that this work, demanding a common Italian language, was written in Latin.

Vulgate: The official Latin version of the Bible used by the Roman Catholic Church. Made by Jerome (q.v.), who revised the Latin translation, by comparisons with the Hebrew and Greek. It was officially adopted by the Council of Trent in 1546.

Vulteius Remensis: d. 1542. French Neo-Latin poet. Wrote epigrams, *Xenia*, etc.

Waddell, Helen: Author of *The Wandering Scholars,* a delightful book, which recaptures the spirit of the Goliards or Vagantes, as well as being a good résumé of learning and literature in the Middle Ages. A scholarly and readable work.

Waifarius of Salerno: See Guaiferius.

Walafrid Strabo: Author of *Glossa Ordinaria,* an abridgement of the patristic commentaries; *De Cultura Hortorum* (or *Hortulus*) on gardens. An erudite imitator of Virgil in the Carolingian Renaissance.

Walo of St. Arnulf: Late 11th century. Wrote letters to Pope Gregory VII, wishing him good fortune, reproaching the Archbishop for his wicked ways, etc. A very lively and spirited letter-writer.

Walter of Châtillon: 12th century author of an epic on Alexander (*Alexandreis*), based largely on Curtius Rufus (q.v.); a lament on the death of Thomas a Becket; goliardic lyrics (perhaps he is the author of the *Apocalypse of Golias*); *Tractatus Contra Judaeos; Georgics,* and other miscellaneous poetry. (Manitius)

Walter of Compiègne: Monk of Tours, 12th century. Wrote *Otia de Machomete,* a poem on the life of Mohammed.

Walter of Mortagne: Theologian of the school of Chartres, who opposed both William of Champeaux and Abelard on the question of Universals (qq.v.).

Walter of St. Victor: A polemicist of the 12th century, who condemned all natural knowledge, speculation, etc.

Walter of Speyer: fl. 982. German scholar and author of *Scholasticus,* and of a prose and a verse *Vita* of St. Christopher.

Waltharius: A lively epic poem by Ekkehard I of St. Gall. Written as a schoolboy's exercise, it tells of the adventures of Waltharius (Walther) and his lady-love, their escape from the Huns, etc.

Wandalbert of Prüm: 9th century monk; wrote poetry on the Mass, on martyrs, on divisions of time, etc.

Wandering Scholars: See Vagantes, Goliards, Goliardic verse, *Ordo Vagorum, Carmina Burana,* etc.

Warnefrid, Paul: See Paulus Diaconus.

Warnerius of Basel: Middle of the 11th century. Author of *Paraclitus,* a didactic poem on theology, and *Synodicus,* an imitation of the *Eclogue* of Theodulus.

Wedding of Philology and Mercury: One of the most important textbooks of the Middle Ages. See Martianus Capella.

Weigel, V.: German mystic of the 16th century; author of *Dialogus De Christianismo.*

Whitby, unknown monk of: Author of a biography of Gregory the Great.

Wibald of Corvey: 12th century statesman and orator (d. 1158). In his letters he bemoans the lost art of oratory, for which there was no use in the monasteries.

Wibert: Wrote, in the middle of the 11th century, the life of Pope Leo IX. Of good Latinity, the work has the usual amount of emphasis on miracles, visions, etc.

Wichram of St. Gall: 9th century. Wrote a work on Christian chronology, which shows its indebtedness to Bede (q.v.).

Wido: (or **Guy,** or **Guido**) Bishop of Amiens, d. 1076. Author of an historical epic on the Battle of Hastings (*De Hastingae Proelio*).

Wido of Ferrara: Wrote of the struggle between Henry IV and Hildebrand (Gregory VII), taking the part of the King and endeavoring to prove that Clement (Wibert) is the rightful Pope. His style is lively and has reminiscences of Sallust. (Manitius)

Wido of Ivrea: Author of hymns and idylls. 11th century.

Widow of Ephesus: A lively example of the Milesian Tale in the *Satyricon* of Petronius (q.v.).

Widukind: Monk of Corvey; author of *Res Gestae Saxonicae,* a history of the Saxons.

Wilfrid: ca. 634-705. Bishop of York, important influence at the Synod of Whitby.

William of Apulia: Author of an epic poem in five books on the deeds of the famous prince Robert Guiscard. Poem was written ca. 1110, and is one of the best pieces of historical poetry of its period. (Manitius)

William of Auvergne: d. 1243. Augustinian scholar and theologian of the 13th century. Wrote on the independence of religious certainty.

William of Auxerre: 13th century scholastic (d. ca. 1231). Influenced by the Peripatetic school. Wrote a *Summa Aurea.*

William of Blois: Author of a "comoedia," *Alda.*

William le Breton: Author of a life in verse of Philip Augustus (13th cent.).

William of Champeaux: d. 1120. Philosopher and theologian. Taught at the Cathedral School of Paris; Bishop of Chalons-sur-Marne. A realist, one of the early scholastics, he had a famous controversy with Abelard (q.v.) on the question of universals (q.v.).

William of Conches: 12th century grammarian, philosopher, astronomer, etc. of the school of Chartres. Wrote *De Philosophia Mundi*; a commentary on the Timaeus; *Dragmaticon Philosophiae;* a commentary on Boethius; a *Moralium Dogma Philosophorum,* etc. (Manitius)

William of Hirsau: 11th century. Wrote on astronomy, music, the customs of his monastery, etc.

William of Jumièges: Second half of the 11th century. Wrote *Gesta Normannorum Ducum,* a history of the Norman kings from the establishment of Christianity. A work of considerable historical value. (Manitius)

William of Malmesbury: 1080-1142. Learned monk and historian of the 12th century. Works: *De Gestis Regum Anglorum* (449-1126), *Historiae Novellae, De Rebus Gestis Pontificum Anglorum,* and other historical writings.

William de la Mare: An Oxford Franciscan of the 13th century, opponent of Thomas Aquinas. Wrote a *Correctorium Fratris Thomas.*

William of Newborough: 12th century English monk, author of a *Historia Rerum Anglicarum* from the Norman Conquest to 1197.

William of Ockham: See Ockham, William of.

William of Poitiers: Wrote *Gesta Willelmi Conquestoris*— the history of William the Conqueror. Compares the struggle between William and Harald with those between Aeneas and Turnus, and Achilles and Hector. (Manitius)

William of St. Amour: d. 1273. French theologian, author of *De Periculis Novissimorum Temporum.*

William of St. Thierry: 12th century monk, friend and disciple of Bernard of Clairvaux; consequently, an opponent of Abelard. Wrote *Disputatio adversus Abaelardum,* and *Libri ii de Natura Corporis et Animae* (on the nature of the body and soul).

William of Tyre: b. 1130. Born in Syria, but of Western parentage. Wrote (a) *Historia de Gestis Orientalium Principum.* (b) *Historia Rerum in Partibus Transmarinis Gestarum.* The latter is one of our best authorities for the Crusades.

Willibald: Author of a Life of St. Boniface.

Williram of Ebersberg: Monk at Fulda, middle of the 11th century. Wrote a Latin versification and a German paraphrase of the *Song of Songs,* as well as other poetry. (Manitius)

Wimpfeling, Jakob: 1450-1528. German humanist and Neo-Latin author. Wrote a Terentian comedy (*Stylpho*), a *History of Germany,* poems, theological works, etc.

Wine and Water, debate of: One of the innumerable medieval debates; see *Streitgedicht.*

Winrich: Teacher in the cathedral school of Trèves in the 11th century, who was demoted to the kitchen, whereupon he wrote a poem of complaint, chiefly interesting for the catalogue of authors it contains. (Waddell)

Wipo of Burgundy: Wrote the Easter Sequence *Victimae Paschali,* around which miracle and morality plays grew. Also wrote *Gesta Chuonradi* (biography of the emperor Conrad III), and verses on the emperor's death; *Tetralogus;* collections of *Proverbia,* and other miscellaneous prose and poetry.

Wireker, Nigel: See Nigel Wireker.

Wit, Roman: Wit was more akin to the Roman spirit than humor. Even the older Romans had a nice sense of wit. Cicero tells a story about the pointed wit of Cato. Cicero himself was extremely witty. Plautus has more wit than Terence. In the Empire, Seneca, Petronius, Martial, and even Juvenal are noted for their witty sallies. Horace is less witty than humorous. In the Middle Ages, wit is not the rule, especially in the theological writings, until one comes to the satirical works of the Goliardic poets.

Witelo: 13th century philosopher and physicist. Studied refraction (cf. Grosseteste).

Wolfhere of Hildesheim: Wrote, in the first half of the 11th century, a Life of Godehard (Bishop of Hildesheim), whose long preface is a masterpiece of bombast, prolix, long-winded, and full of difficult explanations. (Manitius)

Wulstan of Winchester: Second half of the 10th century. Wrote lives of Ethelwold and St. Swithin.

Wyclif, John: 1324-84. His early works, before the great Bible-translation, were written in Latin.

Xenia: Poems by Martial (q.v.) written to accompany presents or party-favors.

Xenophobia: Fear and hatred of foreigners. In his Third Satire, Juvenal discussed the prevalence of this (cf. "Graeculus esuriens"—the "hungry Greekling").

Ximenes: Spanish cardinal in the 16th century, under whose aegis there was a great revival of Biblical scholarship in Spain. See *Complutensian Polyglot*.

Ysengrimus: Famous beast-epic by Nivard of Ghent. An allegorical satire on the evils of monasticism. Ysengrimus, the wolf, represents the monk.

Zanchi, Basilio: 1501-1558. Italian scholar and poet. Compiled a dictionary of Latin epithets, wrote Latin poetry (*De Horto Sophiae*, etc.).

Zander: Reconstructed some of the Phaedrus' fables in iambic senarii.

Zasius, Ulrich: 1461-1535. Swiss scholar. An excellent Latin stylist.

Zbylitowski, Andrzej: 16th century Polish-Latin poet, writer of occasional verse.

Zerbold van Zutphen, Gerard: 1367-1398. Dutch theologian, scholar of the *Devotio Moderna* (q.v.).

Zevecote, Jacob van: 1590-1642. Dutch poet and rhetorician. Wrote Latin plays in the classical form (with choruses, etc.).

Zielinski, Th.: Scholar who did much research on prose-rhythm, q.v., especially the sentence cadences, or *clausulae*, of Cicero.

Zimorowicz, Bartlomiej: 1597-1677. Polish-Latin writer of miscellaneous poetry.

Zmyrna: Lost epyllion by Cinna (q.v.).

Zosimus, Pope: Author of letters, tractoria. Fifth century.

REFERENCES

The Oxford Classical Dictionary [OCD] (Oxford, 1949)

Literary History of Rome from the Origins to the Close of the Golden Age, J. Wight Duff (Revised Ed., Barnes & Noble, New York, 1953)

Literary History of Rome in the Silver Age, J. Wight Duff (London, 1927)

Histoire de la Littérature latine chrétienne, Labriolle (Paris, 1947)

Founders of the Middle Ages, Rand (Harvard, 1928)

The Wandering Scholars, Waddell (London, 1949)

Gateway to the Middle Ages, Duckett (New York, 1938)

European Literature and the Latin Middle Ages, Curtius (Bollingen Series, 1952)

Geschichte der lateinischen Literatur des Mittelalters, Manitius (Munich, 1911, 1923, 1931)

History of Christian Latin Poetry from the Beginnings to the Close of the Middle Ages [CLP], Raby (Oxford, 1927)

History of Secular Latin Poetry in the Middle Ages [SLP], Raby (Oxford, 1934)

Where a name (i.e., Waddell, Rand, etc.) appears after one of the articles, it should be taken to refer to one of the above works. The Oxford Classical Dictionary (OCD) contains the most definitive treatments of classical authors, and in such fields as law, religion, history, mythology, philology, textual criticism, etc., as well as in literature, it is excellent.